White-Collar Crime

White-Collar Crime

The Abuse of
Corporate and
Government Power

Ronald J. Berger

LYNNE
RIENNER
PUBLISHERS

BOULDER
LONDON

Published in the United States of America in 2011 by
Lynne Rienner Publishers, Inc.
1800 30th Street, Boulder, Colorado 80301
www.rienner.com

and in the United Kingdom by
Lynne Rienner Publishers, Inc.
3 Henrietta Street, Covent Garden, London WC2E 8LU

Library of Congress Cataloging-in-Publication Data
Berger, Ronald J.
  White-collar crime : the abuse of corporate and government power / Ronald J. Berger.
      p. cm.
  Includes bibliographical references and index.
  ISBN 978-1-58826-790-0 (hardcover : alk. paper)
  ISBN 978-1-58826-765-8 (pbk. : alk. paper)
  1. White collar crime—United States. 2. Corporations—Corrupt practices—
United States. 3. Abuse of administrative power—United States. 4. Political crimes
and offenses—United States. I. Title.
  HV6769.B468 2011
  364.16'80973—dc22

                                                                    2010039670

British Cataloguing in Publication Data
A Cataloguing in Publication record for this book
is available from the British Library.

Printed and bound in the United States of America

∞   The paper used in this publication meets the requirements
    of the American National Standard for Permanence of
    Paper for Printed Library Materials Z39.48-1992.

    5   4   3   2   1

*If we don't change the direction we're headed,
we will end up where we are going.*
—Chinese proverb

Contents

Preface

IN HIS 1939 PRESIDENTIAL ADDRESS TO THE AMERICAN
Sociological Society, Edwin Sutherland first introduced the concept of
"white-collar crime" into the vernacular of social science and the general
public. Sutherland defined white-collar crime as a "crime committed
by a person of respectability and high social status in the course of his
occupation" and urged others to focus more attention on such hitherto
neglected acts of wrongdoing. In this book, I focus on two broad categories of crime that fit Sutherland's formulation, *corporate crime* and
government crime, which dovetail with what others have called "elite
deviance" or "corporate and governmental deviance." My emphasis is
not on individual acts of occupational criminality but on the *organizational* varieties of white-collar crime—that is, those crimes committed
in the pursuit of corporate profits and government policies or involving
a network of co-conspirators acting in concert. In adopting this
approach, I present a framework through which students can engage in a
critique of economic and political power in the United States. The book
is designed for use as a main text for courses on white-collar crime, as
well as a supplemental text for courses on general criminology,
deviance, and social problems.

Chapter 1 delineates in broad terms the nature of the subject matter
that constitutes the field of white-collar crime and identifies some of the
controversies entailed in expanding this subject matter beyond what is
statutorily defined as crime by existing criminal law. It also provides
background on the emergence of the corporation as the driving economic force of contemporary society and on the attempts by the US government to rein in through regulatory reform the harmful conduct that is a
consequence of unchecked corporate power.

Chapter 2 also takes a broad look at the phenomenon of white-collar crime, examining the key microsociological and macrosociological perspectives that help explain it. Chapters 3 and 4 then turn to a consideration of two general categories of corporate crime—financial crime and physically harmful crime against workers, consumers, and the environment, respectively. Chapters 5 and 6 examine two general categories of government crime—political corruption and state crimes of foreign policy, respectively. Chapter 7 concludes the book by offering remedial solutions for the prevention and control of white-collar crime.

*   *   *

This book evolved out of many years of teaching a course on white-collar crime, and I thank the many students who were in those classes for their responses to the material. I also thank Andrew Berzanskis and Lynne Rienner for their support and guidance on this project, as well as the anonymous reviewers who offered valuable feedback. Lastly, I appreciate the fine work of Lesli Brooks Athanasoulis, Jason Cook, and the rest of the staff at Lynne Rienner Publishers in bringing the manuscript to publication.

White-Collar Crime

1

The Problem of White-Collar Crime

ONE OF THE OPENING ACTS OF THE TWENTY-FIRST CENTURY
was the fall of the mega-corporation, Enron. Under the leadership of
Kenneth Lay, Enron was transformed from a relatively small gas
pipeline operation into a powerful energy-trading business that was at
one time "nominally" the eighth largest corporation in the United States
(Kuttner 2003). Enron capitalized on its dominant market position to
create an artificial energy shortage that enabled it to raise prices, most
notably in California. As that state was experiencing energy blackouts
and escalating prices, Enron's stock price soared. But Enron was not
really making as much money as it appeared—it was "cooking the
books." It did this by creating a myriad of corporate subsidiaries and
using these subsidiaries and other accounting gimmicks to disguise debt
and financial losses, aided and abetted by the onetime prestigious
accounting firm Arthur Andersen (Toffler 2003). When the bubble finally burst in the latter part of 2001, Enron investors lost about $60 billion,
which included the pensions and retirement savings of thousands of people, among them Enron employees who were prohibited by the company
from selling their stock. In the meantime, just before the stock price collapsed, Enron executives collectively unloaded nearly $1 billion worth
of stock for themselves (McLean and Elkind 2004; Reiman 2007;
Rosoff, Pontell, and Tillman 2007; see Chapter 3).

Around the time the Enron scandal was in the news, there were also
the September 11, 2001, terrorist attacks on the World Trade Center and
Pentagon, and the subsequent US military invasion of Afghanistan, followed by the invasion of Iraq, the latter justified on the basis of misleading and partly fraudulent evidence. The surveillance capacity of the federal government was expanded, and a regime of warrantless electronic

surveillance was unleashed that was arguably in violation of the Foreign Surveillance Intelligence Act, passed in 1978, which requires surveillance requests to be reviewed by a panel of judges. There also was the torture of Muslims by US personnel, famously revealed to the world in the spring of 2004 through Internet dissemination of photos from Abu Ghraib prison in Iraq, but this torture also took place elsewhere, and in violation of US and international antitorture laws (Bamford 2008; Cole and Lobel 2007; Mayer 2009; McCoy 2006; see Chapter 6).

These types of corporate and government actions, which fall under the broad category of "white-collar crime," constitute the focus of this book. My emphasis is not on individual acts of occupational criminality but on the *organizational* varieties of white-collar crime—that is, those that are committed in the pursuit of corporate profits and government policies or involving a network of co-conspirators acting in concert. This focus dovetails with what others have called "elite deviance" or "corporate and governmental deviance" (Ermann and Lundman [1978] 2002; Simon [1982] 2006). In adopting this approach, we will also be engaging in a critique of economic and political power in the United States.

The costs of the crimes of the "higher circles," as C. Wright Mills (1957) called them, are arguably greater than the costs of conventional crimes of theft and violence. But because of the privileged status of the perpetrators, they remain relatively unchecked. Stephen Rosoff, Henry Pontell, and Robert Tillman note, for example, that the cost of the taxpayer bailout of a single corrupt, federally insured savings and loan in the late 1980s "surpassed the total losses of all the bank robberies" in US history (2007:201; see Chapter 3). Jeffrey Reiman (2007) estimates that the financial costs of white-collar crime now exceed $400 billion annually, to say nothing of the physical consequences of unsafe working conditions, defective consumer products, and environmental pollution (see Chapter 4).[1] He notes as well that far more people are now seriously harmed each year from occupational hazards than from ordinary street crime. After reviewing available data on deaths and injuries due to occupation-related diseases and other workplace hazards, he concludes that about 55,000 workers die and another 2.3 million get sick or are injured each year as a result of dangerous occupational conditions. This toll greatly exceeds the approximately 16,000 homicides and 860,000 aggravated assaults that are annually reported to law enforcement authorities (Berger, Free, and Searles 2009). Moreover, the ongoing corruption and criminal malfeasance of political officials who abuse their power has a corrosive impact on democracy in the United States, contributing to a growing cynicism and mistrust that Americans feel toward their government. Nowadays few would deny that the ties that once bound US citizens to their government have been "broken," though hopefully not beyond repair (Dean 2007; Nye, Zelikow, and King 1997; see Chapters 5 and 6).

We begin our inquiry into the problem of white-collar crime with a review of the history of the concept, especially the groundbreaking work of Edwin H. Sutherland (1883–1950), who coined the term and introduced it into the vernacular of social science and the general public. My primary objective here is to delineate in broad terms the nature of the subject matter that constitutes the field of white-collar crime and to identify some of the controversies entailed in expanding that subject matter beyond what is statutorily defined as crime by the existing criminal law. The second part of the chapter provides additional introductory background on the emergence of the corporation as the driving economic force of contemporary society and on the attempts by the US government to rein in through regulatory reform the harmful conduct that is a consequence of unchecked corporate power. The chapter also considers the deregulatory movement that emerged in the last quarter of the twentieth century and the corrupting influence of corporate power on regulatory agencies, which illustrates the adage about "the fox guarding the hen house." Nevertheless, it remains fair to say that a social movement has been under way to change this disconcerting state of affairs and put the prevention and control of white-collar crime more squarely on the agenda of the American public (Cullen et al. 2006; Katz 1980).

Delineating the Subject Matter

The Legacy of Edwin Sutherland

In his 1939 presidential address to the American Sociological Society, at a conference held jointly with the American Economic Association, Edwin Sutherland gave a talk titled "The White Collar Criminal." He disparaged theories of crime that "blamed such factors as poverty, broken homes, and Freudian fixations for illegal behavior, noting that healthy upbringing and intact psyches had not served to deter monstrous amounts of lawbreaking by persons in positions of power" (Geis and Goff 1983:ix).[2] Sutherland defined **white-collar crime*** as a "crime committed by a person of respectability and high social status in the course of his occupation," and he urged his colleagues to focus more attention on such hitherto neglected acts ([1949] 1983:7).

---

*Key terms are indicated in **boldface** the first time they appear in the book.

The son of a Baptist minister and educator, Sutherland was undoubtedly driven by a sense of moral outrage against those whose selfishness, greed, and cutthroat predatory behavior belied, in his view, Christian principles. During World War II, in a letter to the secretary-manager of the Hoosier Motor Club in Indianapolis, Sutherland expressed a degree of anger not found in his professional work. The secretary-manager had been encouraging Indiana residents to petition their congressional representatives to postpone implementation of gas rationing, which some deemed necessary to the war effort. Sutherland accused the man of putting "financial interest in promoting the driving of automobiles . . . ahead of the national interest." In a fiery tone, Sutherland went on to say: "This is an effort to interfere with the successful prosecution of the war and is subversive. I feel that the government is entirely justified in sending the FBI to investigate you. They may find that your action is directed from Berlin, or they may find that it is merely selfish interest in your own welfare; the effects are the same" (cited in Geis and Goff 1983:xv).

The secretary-manager replied by sending Sutherland a packet of literature defending his position and demanding an apology for "probably the most insulting . . . letter I have ever received." Sutherland forthrightly apologized for "the personal reference in my former letter," saying that he knew nothing about the secretary-manager "as a person and had no justification in making personal statements" about him. But he went on to "recant nothing . . . regarding the organized effort to delay the rationing program" and insisted that if rationing came to fruition, "all of the literature you are distributing will encourage the blackmarkets and crookedness which you so freely predict" (cited in Geis and Goff 1983:xvi).

Sutherland, of course, was not the first academician to consider the criminality of the privileged classes. Nineteenth-century French jurist and sociologist Gabriel Tarde, for instance, noted that the common people were moved to their transgressions through imitation of their social superiors. According to Tarde, as Piers Beirne and James Messerschmidt note: "Drunkenness, smoking, moral offenses, political assassination, arson, and even vagabondage are . . . crimes that originated with the feudal nobility. . . . Criminal propensities . . . typically travel downward and outward—from the powerful to the powerless" (1995:367). In the early twentieth century, Charles Henderson, a Baptist minister turned sociologist, also indicted the privileged classes:

> The social classes of the highest culture furnish few convicts, yet there are educated criminals. Advanced culture modifies the form of crime; tends to make it less coarse and violent, but more cunning; restricts it to quasi-legal forms. But education also opens up the way to new and

colossal kinds of crime, as debauching of conventions, councils, legis-
latures, and bribery of the press and public officials. The egoistic
impulses are masked and disguised in this way, the devil wearing the
livery of heavenly charity for a cloak of wrong. (1901:250)

FURTHER EXPLORATION

Box 1.1 The Criminaloid

Sociologist Edward Alsworth Ross, who published an article called "The
Criminaloid" in the *Atlantic Monthly* in 1907, was a noteworthy influence on Sutherland. In fact, prior to Sutherland's coinage of the term
"white-collar crime," Sutherland used the term "white-collar criminaloid" in the 1934 edition of his *Criminology* textbook. Ross described
the **criminaloid** as follows:

> The key to the criminaloid is not evil impulse, but moral insen-
> sibility. They are not degenerates tormented by monstrous crav-
> ings. They want nothing more than what we all want—money,
> power, consideration—in a word, success; but they are in a
> hurry and they are not particular as to the means. . . . The crimi-
> naloid prefers to prey on the anonymous public. . . . Too . . .
> prudent to practice treachery, brutality, and violence himself, he
> takes care to work through middlemen. Conscious of the antipo-
> dal difference between doing wrong and getting it done, he
> places out his dirty work. ([1907] 1977:31)

Ross also noted that "[t]he criminaloid practices the protective mimicry
of the good. . . . [H]e is often to be found in the assemblies of the faithful.
. . . Full well he knows that giving a fountain or a park or establishing a
college chair . . . will more than outweigh the dodging of taxes . . . and
the corrupting of city councils" (p. 34). Finally, Ross concluded:

> The criminaloid flourishes until the growth of morality overtakes
> the growth of opportunities to prey. . . . Fresh opportunities for
> illicit gain are continually appearing, and these are eagerly
> seized by the unscrupulous. The years between the advent of
> these new sins and the general recognition of their heinousness
> are few or many according to the alertness of the social mind. . . .
> The narrowing of this gap depends chiefly on the faithfulness of
> the vedettes that guard the march of humanity. If the editor,
> writer, educator, clergyman, or public man is zealous to recon-
> noiter and instant to cry aloud the dangers that present them-
> selves, . . . our regulative opinion quickly forms and the new sins
> soon become odious. (pp. 36–37)

And in the 1930s, criminologist Albert Morris wrote about the "criminals of the upperworld . . . whose social position, intelligence, and criminal technique permit them to move among their fellow citizens virtually immune to recognition and prosecution as criminals" (1935:153).

Be that as it may, there is little doubt that Sutherland considered the corporate variety of white-collar crime to be the most consequential, agreeing with John Farley, who wrote: "The average politician is the merest amateur in the gentle art of graft compared with his brother in the field of business" (quoted in Sutherland [1940] 1977:41). Indeed, Sutherland's main contribution to empirical research on white-collar crime was devoted to documenting the extensive law violations of the largest corporations in the first four decades of the twentieth century.

In this research, Sutherland ([1949] 1983) reviewed 980 documented cases of law violation committed by the 70 largest US corporations of the time (the corporations had an average life-span of about 45 years). It is noteworthy that Dryden Press, the publisher of the original edition of Sutherland's book, forced him to omit the actual names of the corporations for fear of lawsuits. It was not until 1983, three decades after Sutherland's death, that a new, uncut version was published that included the names of the companies.

Overall, Sutherland found that each of the 70 corporations had been cited for at least one violation. Two companies had been cited for as many as 50 (Armour & Company, Swift & Company), one for 40 (General Motors), and two for 39 (Montgomery Ward, Sears Roebuck). Over 90 percent of the corporations had four or more violations, perhaps qualifying them for prosecution as habitual or repeat offenders. The largest proportion of violations was for restraint of trade such as non-competitive price-fixing (31 percent), infringement on patents, copyrights, and trademarks (23 percent), unfair labor practices (16 percent), and misrepresentation in advertising (10 percent). Other violations included commercial and political bribery, tax fraud, manipulation of the stock exchange, short weights and measures, misrepresentation of financial statements, and fraudulent bankruptcies. Importantly, Sutherland found that about half of the companies had engaged in law violations at their origin or in their early years of operation, making crime an essential part of their initial period of capital accumulation.

While collecting his data, Sutherland did not limit his research to violations of *criminal* law, but included violations of *civil* and *regulatory* law as well. All three systems of law—criminal, civil, and regulatory—are concerned with the social control of what has been deemed harmful or injurious conduct by a legislative body. These systems of law all involve procedures set up to adjudicate competing claims and to ascertain responsibility for such conduct. Technically speaking, **criminal law** defines harmful conduct as a public matter and mandates the intervention of law enforcement authorities such as police and prosecutors. **Civil law** defines harm as a private matter to be settled by individuals (and their attorneys) as private parties in the courts. **Regulatory law** is concerned with the imposition of rules and standards for business-related activity, and at the federal level involves agencies like the Environmental Protection Agency (EPA), the Occupational Safety and Health Administration (OSHA), and the Securities and Exchange Commission (SEC). While the lines of demarcation between these three systems of law are not always clear, only criminal law allows for the imposition of jail or prison sanctions instead of or in addition to financial penalties, although failure to comply with civil or regulatory rulings may lead to such sanctions. Violation of criminal law carries the greatest moral condemnation, because of the stigma associated with crime (Friedrichs 2007).

Only 16 percent of the cases examined by Sutherland were, technically speaking, violations of criminal law, although about 60 percent of the corporations did have at least one criminal conviction, and among these the average was four apiece. Regardless, Sutherland believed it was appropriate to include the full range of offenses in his study, because corporate law violations, even if not enforced as "crime," were *potentially* punishable by criminal law, contained the essential elements of criminal intent, and caused considerable harm to society.

Paul Tappan (1947), a lawyer and sociologist, was arguably the most prominent critic of Sutherland's inclusive approach to white-collar crime. Tappan argued for a narrower, **legalistic approach** to crime, defining it as "an intentional action in violation of criminal law . . . committed without defense or justification, and sanctioned by the state as a felony or misdemeanor" (p. 100). Tappan believed that criminologists should confine their subject matter to behaviors that met this definition and not equate civil and regulatory violations with criminal violations (see also Caldwell 1958).

Sutherland, on the other hand, noted that corporations that engaged in harmful conduct were able to avoid the application of criminal law, and the consequent stigma associated with such application, because of their economic and political clout. He was unwilling to also allow corporations to exert such influence on criminological research.

Years later, Raymond Michalowski (1985) would advance an expansive definition of criminology's subject matter that was consistent with

FURTHER EXPLORATION

Box 1.2 The Clinard-Yeager Study

Since the 1930s the Federal Bureau of Investigation has published an annual tabulation of crime data from across the United States in the *Uniform Crime Reports.* White-collar crime is strikingly absent from these reports, with the exception of cases of embezzlement, fraud, and forgery, which generally are committed by less affluent offenders rather than high-status businesspeople or corporations. Researchers interested in documenting the overall prevalence of white-collar crime, therefore, cannot rely on conventional sources of crime data such as the *Uniform Crime Reports,* and few have taken on the daunting task of culling through the documents of disparate government agencies (Berger, Free, and Searles 2009).

In addition to Sutherland's study, Marshall Clinard and Peter Yeager's (1980) research on corporate law violations in the mid-1970s stands out as a seminal work of this nature. Clinard and Yeager collected data on legal actions initiated against the 477 largest US manufacturing corporations during 1975 and 1976. The researchers found that about 60 percent of the companies had at least one action against them, 50 percent had two or more, and 18 percent had five or more. Over 75 percent of the cases involved what Clinard and Yeager classified as manufacturing violations (consumer health and safety), labor violations (worker health and safety, wage and hour violations, employment discrimination), and environmental violations (pollution). The largest corporations were the chief offenders, with just 8 percent of the companies accounting for over half of all violations. The most frequent offenders were in the motor vehicle, oil refinery, and pharmaceutical industries. Less than 3 percent of the imposed legal sanctions were for criminal offenses, however, and less than 1 percent involved nonmonetary criminal penalties against an officer of the corporation.

this sentiment. Emphasizing social harm as the key element of crime, Michalowski argued that criminology's subject matter should include **analogous social injuries**—that is, "legally permissible acts or sets of conditions whose consequences are similar to those of illegal acts" (p. 317). In a more recent book with Ronald Kramer, Michalowski added: "Comparing the nature and origins of analogous social injuries with those of prohibited acts . . . [allows us] to examine the political and cultural forces that result in some harms being labeled crimes, others regulatory violations, others noncriminal deviance, and still others praiseworthy acts" (Michalowski and Kramer 2006:13). Michalowski and

Kramer also noted the importance of considering international law and standards of human rights as criteria in determining the illegality of white-collar crime, whether regarding the disposal of toxic hazardous waste around the globe or the invasion and occupation of foreign countries.[3] This is a perspective that informs this book.

Alternative Formulations

During Sutherland's lifetime, as James Coleman observes, the idea that "many of the fabled captains of industry should be considered criminals had a very un-American sound to it" (2006:2). Additionally, the rise of McCarthyism (named after Wisconsin senator Joseph McCarthy) at the height of the Cold War in the 1950s—which created a "witch hunt" atmosphere that overzealously charged too many reputable citizens with "Communist" sympathies—had a chilling effect on white-collar crime research (Brightman 2009). In its stead, for reasons not entirely political but conceptual as well, Sutherland's focus on corporate criminality gave way to alternative formulations of the subject matter.

Recall that Sutherland's definition of white-collar crime included two components: crime committed (1) in the course of an occupation and (2) by persons of respectability and high social status. Several sociologists and criminologists writing from the late 1950s to the early 1970s pointed out that there were a variety of crimes that met the first part of the definition but not necessarily the second—such as those committed by farmers, repairmen, and other non-white-collar workers (Bloch and Geis 1962; Newman 1958). In this vein, Marshall Clinard and Richard Quinney delineated an area of inquiry called **occupational crime**, noting that corporate crime was but one form of occupational crime and defining occupational crime as a violation of law "in the course of activity in a legitimate occupation" (1967:31). Years later, Gary Green similarly defined occupational crime as "any act punishable by law which is committed through opportunity created in the course of an occupation that is legal" (1990:12–13).

This occupational crime perspective is an example of an *offense-based* definition, as opposed to Sutherland's *offender-based* definition, which focused on the social status of the actor. In 1970, Herbert Edelhertz, a former head of the Fraud Section in the US Department of Justice, advanced an influential offense-based definition in a pamphlet of 70-plus pages published by the National Institute of Law Enforcement and Criminal Justice. Edelhertz adopted the term *white-collar crime*, but defined it as "an illegal act or series of illegal acts committed by nonphysical means and by concealment or guile to obtain money or property, to avoid the payment or loss of money or property, or to obtain business or personal advantage" (p. 3). He eschewed the term *occupational crime* because of the fact that many white-collar crimes occur outside of one's occupation, such as "personal and nonbusiness false income tax returns, fraudulent claims for social security benefits, concealing assets in a personal bankruptcy, and use of large-scale buying on credit with no intention or capability to ever pay for purchases" (p. 3).[4] At the same time, he argued, Sutherland's focus on crimes of the "upper class" was too narrow. Rather, the definition and enforcement of white-collar crime should be more "democratic," given that "it can be committed by a bank teller or the head of his institution" (p. 4).

As a former investigator himself, Edelhertz helped put white-collar crime on the law enforcement agenda of the US government, and his definition became the one favored by government investigators and applied criminal justice practitioners (Brightman 2009; Poveda 1994). His so-called democratic approach, however, eschewed important questions of economic and political power, leaving the "very people that Sutherland originally sought to bring to the attention of criminologists ignored" (Benson and Simpson 2009:12). Moreover, his emphasis on the *nonphysical* nature of white-collar crime diverted attention from physically harmful conduct. It is arguably true that the modus operandi of white-collar crime is most often nonphysical, but the consequences of such conduct can most assuredly be *physical*—as in the case of workplace hazards, defective consumer products, and environmental pollution, or if we turn our attention to government crime, in the case of torture and other state-sanctioned violence (Friedrichs 2007; Kramer and Michalowski 2005; Rosoff, Pontell, and Tillman 2007).

In response to issues such as these, analysts in the late 1970s and 1980s began delineating a criminological subject matter concerned with the *organizational* elements of white-collar crime, which they termed **organizational crime**. From this perspective, individual actors are of interest mainly insofar as they act in the pursuance of organizational goals that are advanced through law violation (Ermann and Lundman [1978] 2002; Gross 1978; Schrager and Short 1978; Vaughan 1983). Although organizations are composed of individuals, the collectivity is, in fact, a legal entity that can be held accountable for its "behavior under the law, without any of the individuals who took actions on behalf of the organization" being held legally liable (Reiss and Tonry 2001:32).

Within the organizational approach, **corporate crime** and **government crime** constitute the two main typologies of white-collar crime, each with subcategories of its own. Corporate crime may be subdivided according to characteristics such as the nature of the harm (e.g., financial, physical), victim (e.g., workers, consumers, general public), or industry (e.g., automobile, pharmaceutical, banking). Government crime may be divided according to whether it is "carried out by the state or on behalf of some state agency" or by public officials and politicians for direct personal gain (Friedrichs 2007:116). The former may be called **state crime** and the latter **political corruption**; and Michalowski and Kramer (2006) also identify a hybrid category—**state-corporate crime**, which occurs in the nexus between the state and corporate institutions (Friedrichs 2007).[5]

The Deviance Frame

One way that sociologists have eluded the controversy surrounding an expansive extralegal definition of "crime" is by invoking the concept of **deviance**. Deviance as a sociological concept can be traced to Robert Merton's seminal work "Social Structure and Anomie" (1938), in which he discussed criminality, drug addiction, and political radicalism as antisocial, aberrant, or deviant behaviors that arose as a consequence of social dislocations in society. By the 1950s the deviance concept had taken shape as an identifiable sociological construct delineating social phenomena that were, statistically speaking, deviations from the norm (or deviations from assumptions about the norm). In general, sociologists studying deviance focused on four areas of inquiry: crime and delinquency, mental illness and medical/psychological problems, drug use and addiction, and homosexuality and other sexual behaviors (Best 2004).

In the 1960s, a conceptual shift in the sociology of deviance took place with the emergence of **labeling theory**, whereby deviance was viewed not as an objective condition but as a matter of social definition and the societal reaction to apparent rule-violating behavior. According to Howard Becker, a chief proponent of this view, "deviance is *not* a quality of the act the person commits, but rather a consequence of the application by others of rules and sanctions to an 'offender'" (1963:9). Sociologists working in the labeling tradition view crime as "a label attached to behavior and events by those who create and administer the criminal law," and they are concerned with the process of **criminalization**—that is, the process by which the criminal law is selectively applied to social behavior, making some individuals and groups more or less vulnerable or immune from legal control (Barlow 1996:10; Hartjen 1974; Quinney 1970).

By the early 1970s, however, labeling theory and the entire school of deviance were being criticized for a class bias that focused on powerless "nuts, sluts, and perverts," to the neglect of people in positions of economic and political power (Liazos 1972; Spitzer 1975; Thio 1973). The social turmoil of the 1960s, particularly over civil rights and the Vietnam War, facilitated the emergence of **conflict theory**, which views society as an arena of struggle between competing groups who attempt to use the law to advance their interests. Richard Quinney, one notable proponent of this view, defined crime as "human conduct that is created by authorized agents in a politically organized society. . . . Criminal definitions describe behaviors that conflict with the interests of the segments of society that have power to shape public policy. . . [and] the enforcement and administration of criminal law" (1970:15–16, 18; see also Best 2004; Chambliss and Seidman 1971; Quinney 1974, 1977).

The 1960s was also the period in which Rachel Carson (1962) published *Silent Spring,* an exposé of the harmful effects of synthetic chemicals that spawned the contemporary environmental movement; and Ralph Nader ([1965] 1972) published *Unsafe at Any Speed,* a critique of the automobile industry that spawned the consumer movement. Moreover, the Watergate scandal of the early 1970s, which led to the resignation of President Richard Nixon and the criminal conviction of numerous White House officials, brought the deviance of government officials to public attention. The Watergate scandal takes its name from the burglary of the Democratic National Committee's headquarters at the Watergate hotel and office complex by a group of men under the employ of President Nixon's Committee for the Reelection of the President. It has come to refer not just to a single burglary but to a larger cluster of crimes and abuses of government power, including (but not limited to) other burglaries, illegal wiretappings, and obstruction of justice (Rosoff, Pontell, and Tillman 2007; see Chapter 6).

Additionally, in the aftermath of Watergate, the US Congress undertook investigations of the abuse of power by the Federal Bureau of Investigation (FBI) and the Central Intelligence Agency (CIA). These abuses included the FBI's spying on political protesters, including Martin Luther King Jr., for the purpose of discrediting oppositional political movements, as well as the CIA's involvement in the violent overthrow of foreign governments and the assassination of foreign leaders (deHaven-Smith 2010; Kinser 2006; Mayer 2009; Rosoff, Pontell, and Tillman 2007). It was in this wider sociopolitical context that conflict theorists called for a sociology of deviance that examined the malfeasance of the economic and politically powerful, what M. David Ermann and Richard Lundman ([1978] 2002) called "corporate and governmental deviance" and David Simon ([1982] 2006) called "elite deviance" (see also Douglas and Johnson 1977; Johnson and Douglas 1978).

One problem with the deviance construct, as David Friedrichs (2007) has observed, is that many actions that constitute white-collar crime do not, unfortunately, deviate from typical, institutionalized patterns of behavior in the United States. Nevertheless, the construct does offer a framework for addressing the question posed earlier about the difference between social injuries that are statutorily designated as crimes, and other noncriminal harms. Consideration of social factors that account for the disparate legal treatment of officially labeled crimes and other analogous social injuries should be part of the subject matter of white-collar crime. The field of inquiry must, by necessity, entail an expansive definition of the subject matter.

FURTHER EXPLORATION

Box 1.3 The Marketing of Infant Formula

The controversy over the marketing of infant formula (milk powder) by multinational corporations in underdeveloped countries is an example of the type of behavior that would fall within a broadened definition of white-collar crime or analogous social injury. Problems associated with the use of infant formula in the poverty-stricken and rural areas of these countries had been reported since the late 1950s. Corporations aggressively marketed the product as a modern alternative to breastfeeding, but illiteracy, lack of clean water, and inadequate refrigeration made infant formula more dangerous than mother's milk.

Moreover, the cost of infant formula unnecessarily consumed a large portion of a family's income, and parents often diluted the mixture to make it last longer. Thus, bottle-fed babies in these countries were more likely than breastfed babies to experience malnutrition, disease, brain damage, and even death. In the late 1970s, public attention to this issue focused on the Swiss-based Nestlé corporation, one of the largest food processors in the world. By the early 1980s, a worldwide protest and boycott finally forced Nestlé to abandon its aggressive marketing techniques, which had included the oversupplying of hospitals with free samples and the bribing of hospital staff to encourage pregnant women to purchase the product (Ermann and Clements 1984; Gerber and Short 1986).

The Corporate-Government Nexus

The second goal of this chapter is to provide background on the emergence of the corporation as a dominant mode of social organization in contemporary society and on the efforts of the US government to regulate the adverse effects of unchecked corporate power. This overview also considers the relationship between corporate and political elites, who all too often thwart the regulatory process in ways that many believe are antithetical to the interests of the American public.

The Origins of Business Concentration

The **industrial revolution**, which began in Great Britain and took hold in the United States in the nineteenth century, introduced both power-driven machinery and factory organization into the production process. In the post–Civil War United States, industrialization dovetailed with westward expansion to fuel unprecedented economic growth. The business **corporation** emerged as the capitalist economic unit most capable of coordinating and rationalizing large-scale economic activity and of providing a vehicle for the concentration of investment capital. Through the legal chartering of corporations, the government (mostly at the state level) granted these enterprises the right to own property, manufacture and buy and sell products, and bring lawsuits as if they were individual persons (Cullen et al. 2006; Inverarity, Lauderdale, and Feld 1983).

In the latter part of the nineteenth century, the railroads played a key role in the early expansion of corporations by providing a system of transportation that integrated the nation into a single marketplace. Thus companies like Montgomery Ward and Sears Roebuck were able to sell their products directly to consumers through mail-order catalogs. Similarly, national "chain" stores were able to integrate wholesaling, distributing, and retailing functions; guarantee sufficient supply and uniform products; and extend credit to subsidiaries.

The corporate mode of organization proved highly suitable to the national marketplace. Its militarylike, top-down organizational structure was capable of administering hundreds of subunits across a wide geographic territory. An expanded cadre of professional executives, middle-level managers, and functional and technical specialists worked together "to mobilize capital, equipment, technological talent, and labor over the extended periods associated with modern industrial production" (Inverarity, Lauderdale, and Feld 1983:223).

One of the problems facing corporations, however, was their inability to rationalize or achieve predictability in the marketplace. Competition among firms threatened their profitability, even their survival. Businesspeople came to realize that cooperation might serve them better than competition. Railroads, for example, entered into pools or trade associations that fixed rates of profit and allocated business among competing lines. Some corporations entered into cooperative trusts or holding companies whereby a board of trustees would "coordinate the economic activities of the various member corporations, who voluntarily surrendered their individual autonomy to a centralized authority" (Inverarity, Lauderdale, and Feld 1983:225).

At the same time, corporations remained unaccountable to the public, despite the fact that their concentrated wealth and cooperative arrangements seemed antithetical to many Americans' belief in a "free market" competitive economy. Small farmers in particular blamed the exploitative profit-making of railroad and grain elevator operators for a

---

FURTHER EXPLORATION

Box 1.4 The Credit Mobilier Scandal

The **Credit Mobilier scandal**, which came to light in 1872, is a classic historical case of the corruption that can occur at the nexus of corporate and political power. Credit Mobilier was a construction and finance company, and a subsidiary of the Union Pacific Railroad. Both Credit Mobilier and Union Pacific Railroad were essentially owned by the same individuals, and when Union Pacific Railroad was awarded a multimillion-dollar federal government contract to build a transcontinental railroad to the western United States, Credit Mobilier was given the job. It submitted inflated bills to Union Pacific Railroad, and Credit Mobilier officials pocketed millions of dollars.

All this was made possible, in part, because of Oak Ames, who was not only the director of Union Pacific Railroad but also a Republican member of the US House of Representatives. Ames had secured the compliance of a number of key congressmen by selling them Credit Mobilier stock at far below market value and allowing them to finance their investment with expected future dividends they had not yet earned. A congressional investigation of the scandal resulted in little more than censure (official condemnation) of the participants, including Republican congressman James Garfield, who later became president, and two Republicans who served as vice president under President Ulysses Grant, Congressman Schuyler Colfax and Senator Henry Wilson (Dickenson 1977).

series of agricultural depressions that occurred in the latter third of the nineteenth century. They attributed "falling prices, rising costs, increased debts, and massive foreclosures [to] the monopolistic control of corporations and trusts," and they organized opposition political groups and parties to press for regulatory reform (McCormick 1977:31).

Antitrust Law and the Decline of Moral Indignation

As state laws proved inadequate to regulate corporations that were national in scope, the US Supreme Court gave the federal government the exclusive right to regulate interstate commerce. In 1890 the US Congress also passed the landmark **Sherman Antitrust Act** (SAA), which contained both criminal and civil provisions. For the first time in history, business combinations that resulted in a *restraint of trade* (including cooperative agreements to fix prices) or the *monopolization* of an industry could be prosecuted as federal criminal offenses, with maximum penalties initially set at one year in prison and a $5,000 fine (currently set at three years in prison and a $350,000 fine for individuals and $10 million for corporations). In addition, any private person who claimed to be adversely affected was now allowed to initiate a civil lawsuit and try to recover treble damages for any injuries suffered (Inverarity, Lauderdale, and Feld 1983; McCormick 1977).

The SAA defined as crimes business activities that were previously legitimate. The moral stigma associated with these new crimes, however, was relatively weak, for although the large corporation was perceived as a threat to the traditional American way of life, it was also viewed as a source of economic efficiency, employment, and improved living standards. Some regulation of corporations was deemed necessary, but not regulation "so stringent as to curtail seriously the desirable" benefits of corporate capitalism (Inverarity, Lauderdale, and Feld 1983:227).

Albert McCormick (1977) argued that the most critical period for establishing a new law as an effective mechanism of social control occurs immediately following the law's enactment. Failure to enforce the SAA was thus a key factor in the neutralization of the moral stigma associated with antitrust violations. McCormick noted that no extra funds were allocated by Congress for antitrust enforcement, and a separate antitrust division in the Department of Justice (DOJ) was not created for another 13 years. Up until then the DOJ had initiated just six criminal cases and sixteen civil cases. Among these, only one criminal case and three civil cases were successfully prosecuted, and no one was incarcerated.

Although the US Supreme Court upheld the constitutionality of the

SAA, laying the groundwork for future expansion of regulatory law, the Court narrowed the scope of the SAA's authority. In an 1895 case the Court ruled that the law did not apply to companies that manufactured their products within a single state. Thus the American Sugar Refining Company, for instance, which accounted for 98 percent of the country's sugar manufacturing, was not considered an illegal monopoly. And in a 1911 case involving the Standard Oil and American Tobacco corporations, the Court ruled that the SAA applied only to "unreasonable" and not "reasonable" business combinations. The SAA, therefore, had relatively little impact on the growth and consolidation of corporations in the United States throughout the twentieth century (Cullen et al. 2006; Inverarity, Lauderdale, and Feld 1983; Neuman 1998).

McCormick (1977) examined data on the 1,551 antitrust cases that were brought by the DOJ between 1890 and 1969. Less than half of these cases (45 percent) were brought as criminal violations, and only a third (35 percent) resulted in conviction. Moreover, nearly three-quarters of the criminal cases (73 percent) were brought between 1940 and 1944, during a time when monopolistic practices were deemed threatening to the US war effort. It was not until 1961, in an electrical equipment price-fixing case that netted the industry millions of dollars in illegal profits, that any corporate officials were actually imprisoned, and these men served just 25 days in jail (Geis 1967; see Chapter 2). In fact, the first 11 individuals to be imprisoned for antitrust violations were *labor* and *union* defendants.

James Inverarity, Pat Lauderdale, and Barry Feld conclude that the SAA "symbolically affirmed a legal commitment to free competition while institutionalizing consolidation and regulation" (1983:231). For the most part, successful corporations could "have their cake and eat it too." Some federal involvement would help stabilize the economy and achieve greater market predictability. And a centralized regulatory authority made it easier for corporations to lobby the government on their behalf. At the same time, failure to establish an identifiable group of corporate offenders (and victims) neutralized the already tenuous moral stigma associated with antitrust violations and gave rise to a dual or contradictory economic value system. As McCormick observed, American society "officially recognizes and pays lip service to the ideals of free competition but practices private . . . collectivism" (1977:36)—what Sutherland ([1949] 1983) described as **corporate socialism**, or what others have called **corporatism**: the fusion of big business and big government to serve the interest of private profit-making (Hayes 2010; Klein 2007).[6]

Regulatory Law and the Deregulation Movement

Federal regulatory agencies have the primary responsibility for dealing with corporate law violations in the United States. For the most part these agencies evolved during three periods of regulatory enactment (Friedrichs 2007). The first wave of regulation came in the early twentieth century in the wake of the social movement that had led to antitrust reform. Upton Sinclair's *The Jungle* (1906), an exposé of the horribly unsanitary conditions in the meatpacking industry, was especially instrumental in generating public support for passage of the Pure Food and Drug Act and the Meat Inspection Act in 1906. And as Sinclair's book triggered a dramatic drop in sales due to the loss of public confidence in meat products, the larger corporations also supported this legislation, for government inspection of meat served to restore public confidence. Smaller companies, however, were unable to absorb the additional cost of regulatory compliance. Hence some regulatory reform actually helped large corporations consolidate their control of the market.

A second wave of regulatory initiatives was associated with President Franklin Roosevelt's New Deal policies of the 1930s. This period of reform was motivated in large part by the 1929 stock market crash and the ensuing economic depression. Many people lost their life savings to failed banks. The government hoped that public confidence could be restored through greater regulatory protection afforded by newly established agencies such as the Federal Deposit Insurance Corporation, the Securities and Exchange Commission, and the National Labor Relations Board.

A third wave of regulatory reform occurred during the period of social protest and liberal reform in the 1960s and early 1970s. The Consumer Protection Agency, the Environmental Protection Agency, and the Occupational Safety and Health Administration are among the regulatory bodies that were created during this era. The Food and Drug Administration (FDA), established by the Pure Food and Drug Act in 1906, was also given expanded regulatory powers at this time. At the outset, FDA regulatory activity had been limited to spot-checks designed to detect adulterated or mislabeled food and drugs. But over the years, well-publicized scandals involving harmful products prompted legislation to broaden its role in consumer protection (Clinard and Yeager 1980).

Friedrichs notes that the relatively "high level of consensus on the desirability of government regulation" began to erode in the late 1970s, especially among Republicans (2007:256). An economic downturn coupled with high inflation was crippling the economy. Corporate officials and their political supporters blamed federal government regulation (and high taxes) for much of the nation's economic woes. They felt that regulation had been carried too far, that there were too many rules, and that the rules were too costly, complex, and unfair. They thus called for the **deregulation** of the economy.

The movement toward deregulation emerged full blown with the 1980 election of President Ronald Reagan. James Coleman (2006) believes that the Reagan administration would have liked to dismantle the federal regulatory structure almost entirely, but the public did not support such a radical approach. Instead the administration began a three-pronged effort to debilitate regulatory agencies: (1) the Office of Management and Budget, a federal agency that assists the president in preparing the federal budget and evaluating government agencies and programs, was authorized to review all new regulatory proposals, subject them to cost-benefit analysis, and reject them if deemed appropriate; (2) the budgets and staff of regulatory agencies were dramatically cut; and (3) new administrators sympathetic to deregulation were appointed to head the regulatory agencies.

Kitty Calavita (1983) observed that curtailment of the Occupational Safety and Health Administration was an especially high priority of the Reagan administration, which was hoping to undermine the influence of the trade union movement. OSHA had been established in 1970, Calavita argued, as a symbolic concession to organized labor, whose support President Nixon had sought for his reelection campaign. At that time it was estimated that harmful workplace conditions in the United States resulted in the death of at least 100,000 workers and the disablement of 390,000 others annually. From the very beginning, however, OSHA was underfunded and understaffed. Although it was supposed to promulgate new standards, in its first four years of operation it adopted only one, a maximum legal level of asbestos exposure. In the meantime, workers at that time were exposed to nearly 600 new toxic substances generated by corporate industrial production each year.

As OSHA is housed in the Department of Labor, it came under the supervision of Raymond Donovan, Reagan's first secretary of labor. Prior to his appointment, Donovan was one of two principal owners of Shiavone Construction, a New Jersey firm that had been accused several times of making illegal payoffs and bribes to union officials and local politicians. Shiavone also had a lengthy history of OSHA violations. In the six years prior to Donovan's appointment, Shiavone had been cited for 135 violations, 57 of which were for workplace conditions involving "a substantial probability that death or physical harm could result." In addition, the National Labor Relations Board had filed six charges against Shiavone for unfair labor practices (violating federal wage standards), and the Department of Labor's Employment Standards Administration had investigated a dozen complaints of race and sex discrimination. In 1985 Donovan became the first cabinet officer in US history to be criminally indicted while in office. Charged with criminal fraud associated with the operation of Shiavone, he was forced to resign, even though a jury eventually found him not guilty. Such was the record of the man President Reagan appointed to protect the workers of the United States (Brownstein and Easton 1982).

Anne Gorsuch, an antiregulatory state legislator from Colorado, was Reagan's choice to head the Environmental Protection Agency.[7] Gorsuch's appointment was sponsored by Joseph Coors, the archconservative Coors brewery mogul, who had founded the Mountain States Legal Foundation, a group dedicated to eviscerating environmental regulations. During Gorsuch's term in office, she increasingly staffed the EPA with people who had once worked for the very corporations they were supposed to be regulating. In 1982 the so-called **Sewergate scandal** erupted, involving the EPA's rather cozy relationship with regulated firms, which included assurances of nonenforcement of environmental laws, "sweetheart" deals allowing polluting companies to avoid full payment of environmental cleanup costs, and delays in waste-site cleanup timetables. The scandal forced Gorsuch to resign. And Rita Lavelle, who had been appointed to head the EPA's Superfund environmental cleanup program, was convicted on criminal charges of perjury for lying under oath about her antiregulatory activities. The negative publicity associated with Sewergate forced Reagan to appoint a more moderate EPA director (Kennedy 2004; Szasz 1986b).

Another Coors protégé, James Watt, was appointed by Reagan to head the Department of Interior, which houses the Bureau of Mines. Watt was an advocate of **dominion theology**, which Robert Kennedy Jr. describes as "an authoritarian Christian heresy that advocates man's duty to 'subdue' nature" (2004:24). During a Senate hearing, "Watt tried to explain why he was selling off protected public lands and water and mineral rights at what the General Accounting Office called 'fire-sale prices' . . . rather than preserving them for future generations," asserting, in his words, "I do not know how many future generations we can count on before the Lord returns" (p. 25). Like Gorsuch, Watt was forced to resign because of public backlash and Democratic opposition to his radical deregulatory agenda.

President Bill Clinton was considerably more favorable toward environmental regulation than were his predecessors, but when President George W. Bush took office in 2001, the deregulatory movement returned full throttle. Gale Norton, for example, was appointed to head the Department of Interior. Previously, Norton had been a member of an antiregulatory group deceptively called "Wise Use," whose founder, Ron Arnold, once said, "Our goal is to destroy, to eradicate the environmental movement. We want . . . to be able to exploit the environment for private gain, absolutely" (quoted in Kennedy 2004:27). Additionally, J. Steven Griles, a lobbyist for the mining industry, was appointed to head the Bureau of Mines. Government scientists and inspectors responsible for evaluating risks and enforcing law violations reported being thwarted in their efforts to protect the public from corporate practices that savaged and polluted the environment. Former interior secretary James Watt happily remarked that the Bush administration was "saying exactly what we were saying 20 years ago, precisely. Twenty years later, it sounds like they've just dusted off the old work" (quoted in Kennedy 2004:44).[8]

Regardless of the regulatory policies of particular administrations, larger corporations are always better able than smaller firms to withstand the constraints of regulatory controls. Their greater financial resources and market share enable them to absorb costs or pass them on to customers, and they are more likely to have the technical and legal expertise to challenge regulations effectively and negotiate favorable terms with regulators (Coleman 2006; Yeager 1987). Typically, the regulatory response of first resort is for a federal agency to enter into negotiations with the corporation and/or issue an official warning that further action will be forthcoming unless the company takes measures to remedy the activity in question. Successful negotiations between regulators and corporations may involve a consensual agreement to "cease and desist" from further violations and/or recall the product, make necessary repairs, or take other ameliorative action. In doing so, the company admits to no legal culpability that can be used against it in subsequent civil or criminal cases. If a settlement cannot be reached, then the regulatory agency may decide to pursue further regulatory, civil, or even criminal actions that carry heavier sanctions. Marshall Clinard and Peter Yeager (1980), however, found that no penalties were issued in over three-quarters of the cases they documented in their study (see Box 1.2).

Summary

In this opening chapter of the book, we have begun our investigation of white-collar crime with a review of the history of the concept, including the groundbreaking work of Edwin Sutherland. We delineated the nature of the subject matter that constitutes the field and identified some of the issues involved in expanding our notions of corporate and government crime beyond what is statutorily defined as crime by existing criminal law, to include not only civil and regulatory law violations, but also analogous social injuries—that is, "legally permissible acts or sets of conditions whose consequences are similar to those of illegal acts" (Michalowski 1985:317). As noted, this book will focus on the organizational elements of corporate and government crime—that is, those crimes that are committed in the pursuit of corporate profits and government policies or that involve a network of co-conspirators acting in concert.

The chapter also provided background on the corporate-government nexus, including the emergence of the corporation as a dominant force in society and the government policies that aim to regulate the adverse effects of unchecked corporate power. We considered the emergence and failed promise of antitrust law, and reviewed three stages of regulatory reform (the 1900s, the 1930s, and the 1960s to early 1970s), which were followed in the last quarter of the twentieth century with the rise of the deregulation movement, most notably during the administration of Ronald Reagan in the 1980s. Finally, we considered the interrelationship between corporate and political elites and the corrupting influence of corporate power on regulatory agencies, an influence that can negate efforts to prevent and control white-collar crime.

Notes

1. Reiman extrapolates this estimate, adjusting for inflation and population growth, from an earlier study published by the Chamber of Commerce of the United States in 1974.

2. Sutherland is also noteworthy for his development of differential association theory, which, he noted, is a general sociological explanation that applies to the criminality that occurs in all social classes. We will consider this theory in more detail in Chapter 2.

3. Similarly, Herman Schwendinger and Julia Schwendinger advanced an alternative definition of crime as a violation of "human rights," arguing that egalitarian principles of social justice mandate that all individuals should be entitled to certain inalienable rights that are "the fundamental prerequisites of well-being" (1970:145). From this perspective, economic or political systems of injustice that deny these rights or that promote racism, sexism, economic exploitation, or environmental degradation are proper topics of criminological investigation.

4. David Friedrichs (2007) calls these "avocational crimes."

5. Friedrichs (2007) also identifies other categories of white-collar crime: "enterprise crime," more commonly associated with "organized crime" syndi-

cates; "contrepreneurial crime," more commonly associated with "professional" or "career" criminals; and "technocrime," more commonly associated with "computer" criminals.

6. In terms of numbers, small businesses dominate the US economy; in terms of scope, influence, and financial assets, corporations dominate (Inverarity, Lauderdale, and Feld 1983).

7. Gorsuch later married and became Anne Gorsuch Burford.

8. In 2008, federal investigators uncovered a scandal involving over a dozen Department of Interior officials who engaged in illicit sex and drug use with representatives of oil companies who contract with the government to drill offshore and on government land (Savage 2008). And in 2009, the Justice Department opened a criminal investigation into whether Norton had abused her position as secretary of interior to benefit Royal Dutch Shell, a company she went to work for after she left government. The investigation centers on whether Norton misused her office "to award three lucrative oil shale leases on federal land in Colorado to a Shell subsidiary, . . . [a] deal that could net the company hundreds of billions of dollars" (Tankersley and Meyer 2009:1).

2

Explaining White-Collar Crime

BARBARA LEY TOFFLER (2003) HAD BEEN ON THE FACULTY AT THE Harvard Business School and had owned her own management consulting business when she accepted a position in 1995 with the consulting division of the prestigious auditing firm Arthur Andersen. The firm wanted Toffler to provide ethics consulting services for companies interested in protecting themselves from federal prosecution. In 1991, as Toffler explains, the US Sentencing Commission had "issued guidelines for sentencing corporations convicted of federal offenses," guidelines that levied "extremely high fines for companies whose employees committed misdeeds while doing their jobs." If, however, the company had put in place an "effective ethics program . . . [with] an ethics officer, policies and procedures, and a reporting mechanism such as a hot line or ombudsperson," it would be relieved of any responsibility for the transgressions of its employees (p. 22).

Once employed by Arthur Andersen, Toffler soon learned of a range of unethical practices that the company was itself engaged in, including systematic overbilling of clients and complicity in the fraudulent bookkeeping of major corporations such as Enron, WorldCom, Sunbeam, and Waste Management (see Chapter 3). She also observed that the socialization practices within the organization appeared to induce otherwise well-intending employees to participate in unethical behaviors and even crimes, which eventually led to the prosecution, conviction, and ruin of the auditing firm. Toffler came to the conclusion that the malfeasance that was prevalent at Arthur Andersen was not the result of a few "rotten apples." Rather, the top management of the organization was very much responsible for creating an environment in which wrongdoing was tolerated and in fact expected.

25

John Dean (1976) had a similar experience when he went to work at the White House in 1970 as chief legal counsel to President Richard Nixon after serving as an attorney in the US Justice Department. It was a job he held for a thousand days before the unraveling of the Watergate scandal. It was not long into his White House tenure that Dean learned that in order to make his "way upward, into a position of confidence and influence, . . . [he] had to travel downward through factional power plays, corruption, and finally outright crimes." As he said, "Although I would be awarded for diligence, true advancement would come from doing those things which built a common trust—or guilt—between me and my superiors" (p. 21). The opening salvo in this process was an assignment to look into the feasibility of initiating a federal investigation and lawsuit against "a new muckraking magazine called *Scanlan's Monthly* that had published a bogus memo linking Vice-President [Spiro] Agnew with a top-secret plan to cancel the 1972 election and to repeal the entire Bill of Rights" (p. 22). Dean was also asked to look into initiating an Internal Revenue Service (IRS) investigation on the tax front, a request that he considered particularly "dangerous, unnecessary, and wrong" (p. 23). But, he was told by a colleague:

> [I]f Richard Nixon thinks it's necessary you'd better think it's necessary. If you don't, he'll find someone who does. . . . [T]he President is the head of the executive branch of the damn government. If he wants his tax collectors to check into the affairs of anyone, it's his prerogative. . . . It's the way the game is played. Do you think for a second that [President] Lyndon Johnson was above using the IRS to harass those guys who were giving him a hard time about the [Vietnam] war? No sir. Nor was Lyndon above using the IRS against some good Republicans like Richard Nixon. (p. 24)

Dean decided that if he "was going to play ball in Richard Nixon's league, [he] would have to get over [his] squeamishness" (p. 24). He recommended an IRS investigation against not only the magazine but also its "principal organizers and promoters" (p. 25). Dean admitted that at this point he "had crossed an ethical line," but at the time he thought he "had no choice" (p. 26). Months later he would find himself embroiled in one of the biggest political scandals in US history (see Chapter 5).

C. Wright Mills (1959) famously called for the cultivation of a **sociological imagination** that would enable us to understand the ways in which *personal* troubles—such as those experienced by Toffler and Dean—are related to *public* issues. This chapter pursues this quest by focusing on social explanations and theories that help us understand white-collar crime, particularly as it occurs in complex corporate and government organizations. Whereas an **explanation** may be viewed as an interpretive account of a particular phenomenon or event, a **theory** is a more formal scheme that consists of "a system of interconnected abstractions or ideas that condense and organize knowledge" (Neuman 2003:42; see also Friedrichs 2007; Vold, Bernard, and Snipes 2002).

This chapter is not intended to catalogue every theory or explanation imaginable, but rather to focus on those that are most important to understanding the organizational varieties of white-collar crime. We will consider factors associated with the *internal* environment of organizations, which may be described as **microsociological**, as well as factors associated with the *external* environment of an organization, which may be described as **macrosociological**. Microsociological theories and explanations focus on the link between individual actors and their immediate organizational circumstances, whereas macrosociological theories and explanations focus on the broader historical, economic, and political factors that impact organizations themselves.

It is of course difficult to make generalizations about varying forms of crime, even if we restrict our focus to white-collar crime. Nonetheless, consideration of our subject matter in terms of generalizations is a useful prelude to a subsequent examination of particular types of corporate and government crime. We begin with some analytical observations about the difference between individualistic and sociological approaches and then turn to microsociological and macrosociological approaches.

The Individual in Social Context

Individualistic explanations of criminal behavior focus on the causes of crime that are located within the individual rather than the social environment. Although this chapter focuses on sociological perspectives, it is worth asking whether some individuals are more *predisposed* than others to be influenced by crime-inducing social contexts. Most researchers agree that white-collar offenders are, psychologically speaking, clinically normal, but that some offenders are somewhat more likely than nonoffenders to display personality attributes that may be variously described as ambitious, reckless, risky, egocentric, arrogant, and power-driven.[1] Other analysts have characterized white-collar offenders as lacking self-control or as having a pronounced fear of failure, while others have noted offenders' desire *for* control (for reviews see Benson and Simpson 2009; Coleman 2006; Friedrichs 2007).[2]

James Coleman observes that some of the psychological traits attributed to white-collar offenders are often the very ones that are encouraged by the more general **culture of competition** that undergirds capitalist economies, in which "the competitive struggle for personal gain" is defined as a "positive, rather than a negative or selfish, activity" (2006:200). Moreover, competition is viewed not only as character-building for individuals but also as producing "maximum economic value for society as a whole" (p. 200). Coleman notes that in this culture of competition, especially in the United States, winners are admired and losers are disparaged. As eminent historian R. W. Tawney wrote of the "secret" of capitalism's triumph:

> It concentrates attention upon the right of those who possess or can acquire power to make the fullest use of it for their own self-advancement. By fixing men's minds, not upon the discharge of social obligations, which restricts their energy . . . but upon the exercise of the right to pursue their own self-interest, it offers unlimited scope for the acquisition of riches. . . . To the strong it promises unfettered freedom for the exercise of their strength; to the weak the hope that they too one day may be strong. Before the eyes of both it suspends a golden prize, which not all can attain, but for which each may strive, the enchanting vision of infinite expansion. It assures men that there are no ends other than their own ends, no law other than their desires, no limit other than that which they think advisable. . . . It relieves communities of the necessity of discriminating . . . between enterprise and avarice, energy and unscrupulous greed, property which is legitimate and property which is theft. (1920:30–31)[3]

In a culture of competition like this, personal financial problems, not surprisingly, are among the individual attributes that motivate many white-collar offenders. In his classic study of embezzlement, for example, Donald Cressey (1953) found that embezzlers typically had a "non-shareable" financial problem that made them more likely to violate a position of trust and steal money from their employer. These problems stemmed from matters such as gambling losses, the demands of a mistress, or simply living beyond their means. Studies of women embezzlers also implicate financial problems, although women are more likely than men to mention family need or pressure to comply with their husband's or boyfriend's wishes (Daly 1989; Dodge 2009; Zietz 1981; see also Box 2.1).

W. Steven Albrecht, Keith Howe, and Marshall Romney (1984), on

Box 2.1 Gender and White-Collar Crime

Although women have made great strides over the past few decades, American society remains stratified by gender. The high-status cohort of women notwithstanding, women, on average, continue to earn less than men, exercise less authority in the workplace, and have less economic and political power. Women are less likely than men to be socialized to value risk-taking, competitiveness, and behavioral aggression, and they are comparatively less likely to engage in criminal offending (Berger, Free, and Searles 2009; Messerschmidt 1993, 1997).

Uniform Crime Report data indicate that women are much less likely than men to be arrested for conventional crimes of theft and violence such as burglary, robbery, assault, and homicide, with women comprising only about 10 to 25 percent of arrests. Women approach parity with men (about 40–50 percent of arrests) only for shoplifting and lower-level white-collar crimes like forgery and counterfeiting (which includes check forgery), fraud (which includes passing bad checks, credit card fraud, and welfare fraud), and embezzlement (Berger, Free, and Searles 2009).

Research indicates that women who embezzle from their employers tend to steal smaller amounts than men do. One early study found that 70 percent of those who embezzled over $1,000 were men, while over 80 percent of those who embezzled less than $150 were women (Franklin 1979). A study of bank embezzlers found that 60 percent of convicted women were bank tellers, compared to 14 percent of convicted men (Daly 1989). These women were more likely to steal cash from the till, while men were more likely to manipulate financial documents and to work in conjunction with others.

Women are also less likely to engage in corporate law violations not recorded in the *Uniform Crime Reports*. One study found that men committed 98 percent of Securities and Exchange Commission violations, 99.5 percent of antitrust violations, and 95 percent of bribery violations (Daly 1989). At the same time, more recent research based on a survey conducted by the Association of Certified Fraud Examiners using 1997–2002 data found that women had achieved near parity with men in "theft or misuse of an organization's assets" (48 percent) and "wrongfully using their influence in business transactions to obtain benefits for themselves that were contrary to duties to their employer" (45 percent), although women accounted for under a third of "falsification of an organization's records or documents" (31 percent) (Holtfreter 2005:357–358). In a study of the Enron and post-Enron financial scandals, however, women constituted just 7 percent of the 355 defendants (Brickey [2008] 2009).

the other hand, found that individual "perpetrator characteristics"—such as financial problems, inclination toward risk-taking, or an overweening desire for personal gain—were, overall, comparatively less important than features of the organizational environment. These researchers interviewed the internal auditors of companies that had been victimized by employee theft. Although the auditors did believe that individual attributes were factors in the crimes that had been committed in their companies, they also thought that the opportunity to put such motivations into action depended on organizational factors. For instance, crimes were more likely to occur in companies that lacked proper procedures for financial authorization, where there were no independent checks on employee performance, and where there was no separation of transaction authority from asset custody or accounting.

Michael Benson and Sally Simpson (2009) advance an **opportunity theory** of white-collar crime that can be used to interpret these findings. Drawing on an approach first developed by Lawrence Cohen and Marcus Felson (1979), they note that the probability of crime increases—whether it is conventional street crime or white-collar crime—when there is a convergence of three basic elements: *motivated offenders, suitable targets,* and *absence of capable guardians.*[4] From the perspective of opportunity theory, the latter two elements are especially important, because different organizational environments offer different levels of opportunity for offenders to translate their criminal inclinations into successful action. Moreover, as other criminologists have observed, access to organizational resources is "for white-collar criminals what the gun or knife is for the common criminal—a tool to obtain money from victims" (Hagan 1992:9), often enabling "individuals operating through formally organized associations and businesses [to] perpetrate larger-scale crimes than individuals acting alone" (Wheeler and Rothman 1982:1406).

The question of opportunity to commit white-collar crime also raises the issue of **deterrence**—that is, manipulation of the *costs* and *benefits* associated with criminal opportunities in order to dissuade or prevent potential offenders from engaging in crime. The expectation of deterrence is based on the assumptions of **rational-choice theory**, which assumes that individuals "are self-interested and make decisions about whether to engage in criminal or conventional behavior according to [a rational] assessment of costs and benefits" (Benson and Simpson 2009:66). Rational-choice theory assumes that individuals are not averse to breaking the law and will do so if they think the potential benefits of crime (e.g., financial or political gain) are greater than the potential costs (e.g., shame, financial penalties, or incarceration).

Unfortunately, as we have seen, the legal system can be rather forgiving of white-collar crime, especially when committed by privileged individuals in positions of power. Even when prosecuted and convicted, white-collar offenders are more likely than conventional offenders to be fined or put on probation rather than sent to prison, more likely to receive shorter terms when they are sent to prison, and more likely to obtain reversals of their convictions on appeal. The average fines imposed on corporations tend to be less than the amount of financial harm they cause; and companies responsible for the greatest amount of harm tend to pay much lower fines, as a percentage of harm caused, than companies responsible for more modest harm. Bank embezzlers and those who commit mail fraud or who defraud the government are among the white-collar offenders who receive the most serious penalties (Cohen 1989; Friedrichs 2007; Reiman 2007).

Richard Quinney (1963) suggested that a person's **occupational role orientation** also plays a part in deterring or facilitating white-collar crime.[5] Occupational role orientation refers to the differential proscriptions for action that are embedded in occupational cultures. In his research, Quinney distinguished between *financial* and *professional* occupational roles: the former entailing a primary commitment to making money, and the latter a commitment to ethical conduct and serving the public. In a study of pharmacists, Quinney found that those who were financially oriented committed more prescription law violations than did those who were professionally oriented. Quinney noted that many occupations contain inherent conflicts, what he called **occupational role strain**, which symbolically orient occupants to alternative and sometimes contradictory courses of action.

Retired middle-level managers of Fortune 500 corporations interviewed by Marshall Clinard (1983) similarly distinguished between financial-oriented managers, who were primarily concerned with company profits and their personal ambition and financial gain, and professional-oriented managers, who were concerned with a corporation's responsibility to consumers, the community, and the society at large. These managers admitted that corporate personnel are often financially driven, to the exclusion of professional concerns, with about a third of them saying that they disapproved of the ethical standards (or lack thereof) that were practiced in their respective industries.

The arrogance or hubris of some white-collar offenders also mitigates any potential deterrent effect of adverse consequences for wrongdoing. As Benson and Simpson note, some individuals at the upper echelons of corporate power "are accustomed to being in charge and doing things their own way. Convinced of their own superiority, they assume that whatever they want to do must be right. They do not have to be bothered with minor technicalities of the law, because in their view their personal integrity is beyond question. . . . [T]hey seem to believe that their personal success in reaching the top . . . indicates that they have been chosen by a higher power" (2009:49; see also Shover and Hochstetler 2006). Such hubris is indicative of the financial managers and executives whose reckless investments contributed so much to the economic crisis that hit the United States in 2008, requiring a massive bailout of major financial institutions in order to avert further economic calamity (see Chapter 3). But after receiving billions of dollars in taxpayer money, these corporate officials continued to spend lavishly, giving themselves obscene bonuses as if the American public wouldn't notice or, even if they did notice, wouldn't take action to stop this behavior (Leopold 2009a, 2009b).

Benson and Simpson add that the exercise of power and superiority over others can be psychologically rewarding to some people and may even "become a source of motivation for continued offending" (2009:48). Alfred McCoy draws this conclusion in his study of torture, noting that whenever the government authorizes brutality, there are inevitably some interrogators who "suffer a dangerous expansion of ego, leading to escalating cruelty. . . . Though any ordinary man or woman can be trained to torture, every gulag has a few masters who take to the task with sadistic flair" (2006:9; see Chapter 6). Such disconcerting behavior was apparent at Abu Ghraib prison during the height of the Iraq War. After receiving authorization from superiors to "take the gloves off" and escalate "enhanced interrogation" techniques, some US prison personnel embraced their work with relish, even posing for photos (some of which were disseminated through the Internet) that showed themselves smiling alongside the suffering prisoners they were abusing (McCoy 2006; Zimbardo 2007). US interrogators at the facility in Guantánamo, Cuba, were similarly enthusiastic about the prospect of implementing increasingly aggressive interrogation techniques. Diane Beaver, a high-ranking military lawyer at Guantánamo who attended a meeting of interrogators, described the men as "glassy eyed" about what they were planning to do. "You could almost see their dicks getting hard as they got new ideas," she said (Mayer 2009:198).

Internal Organizational Processes

Individual action, as we have seen, cannot be understood in a social vacuum. In this section we consider the microsociological context of white-

Box 2.2 Computer Crime

Computer technology has created opportunities for crimes that were not available in less high-tech times, and in the world of computer crime, it is not necessary for motivated offenders and suitable targets to meet in the same physical space and time. A knowledgeable computer programmer, for example, can access payroll or bank accounts from afar and program the computer for a crime that will take place at some future date. In one case, an employee of a big-city welfare department stole $2.75 million "by entering fraudulent data into the computerized payroll system and . . . creating a phantom workforce complete with fake social security numbers" (Rosoff, Pontell, and Tillman 2007:508–509). In a practice known as **salami slicing**, or **shaving**, programmers siphon off small amounts of money from a large number of accounts to yield huge ill-gotten gains. In one case, an employee of an investment firm stole $200,000 by creating fraudulent computer accounts and then filling them "by diverting three tenths of a cent interest [earned] from actual accounts" (p. 509). Some computer thieves are fairly adept at covering their crimes. "We only read about the failed computer criminals. The really successful ones are never detected in the first place" (Schuyten 1979:D2).

Computer hackers—individuals who gain access to an individual's or organization's computer system without authorization—have caused abundant damage. Hackers are primarily intelligent young men who are often "motivated by the challenge of figuring out how to beat a security system" and who exhibit a "high level of skill, knowledge, commitment, and creativity" (Barlow and Kauzlarich 2002:109). Hackers have spawned their own subculture, in which they exchange information on the Internet, communicate through a common argot, and develop a sense of camaraderie (Carter and Bannister 2002; McCaghy, Capron, and Jamison 2003).

Most hackers do not commit crimes but simply enjoy exploring a system to learn about its capabilities and vulnerabilities. Some, however, implant malicious **computer viruses** into other systems. Viruses are sets of instructions that cause a computer to perform unauthorized operations and that spread from one computer system to another as "the 'infected' program is copied or transmitted. . . . Viruses may be relatively benign, such as . . . [one] that merely displays an innocuous message on a computer screen," or they can create serious damage by erasing files, changing data, or forcing the system to crash (Barlow 1996:208). Hackers have forced businesses to shut down and caused millions of dollars in damage. They have broken into military computers and stolen sensitive information about weapon systems and battle simulations. Copyright infringement, through the illegal downloading of software, music, and business information, abounds. Computerized power-grid systems and electronic voting machines

continues

Box 2.2 continued

are also susceptible to hacking (see Box 5.3). Indeed, the entire digital infrastructure of the United States is becoming increasingly vulnerable to cyber attacks. And this threat comes not just from conventional hackers but also from terrorists and agents working for foreign governments (Brightman 2009; Clarke and Knake 2010; Goldsmith 2010; Miller 2008).

Two types of cyberfraud—**identity theft** and **phishing**—have become growing concerns, and some observers think that the conventional hacking subculture is being transformed by a professional class of **organized online criminals** who operate a cyperspace underground economy that reaps tens of billions of dollars each year (Blitstein 2007; Micci-Barreca 2004). Identity theft involves cybercriminals who access databases that contain information on individuals (e.g., social security numbers, credit reports, automated teller machine and charge accounts) and then use this information for fraud and theft. Corporations that sell private customer information to other companies make the public even more vulnerable to this type of crime (Carter and Bannister 2002; Court 2003; Rosoff, Pontell, and Tillman 2007).

Phishing refers to cybercriminals who send unsolicited e-mails to Internet users to try to lure unsuspecting "fish" into providing them with passwords and financial data (the "ph" is probably a tribute of sorts to the first generation of hackers, known as "phone freaks," who hacked into telephone company systems). The unsolicited e-mails give the appearance of originating from a legitimate business, typically a business that the "fish" has used, such as a bank, a credit card company, eBay, PayPal, or Amazon.com. The e-mail instructs the recipient to "update" or "validate" their account information in order to keep their account active. If the user accepts the bait, a link directs them to a website that imitates the legitimate site, complete with matching logos, colors, and design. If the user submits the information, the phisher can use the data to commit identity theft. These phishing e-mails are sent out in mass (spam), so even if only a small proportion of recipients respond, large amounts of money can be stolen (Rosoff, Pontell, and Tillman 2007).

In addition, financial securities fraud has migrated from the "boiler rooms" of the past—where con artists phoned volumes of unsuspecting investors—to the Internet. Phony financial advisers and brokers, sometimes using Internet bulletin boards and chat rooms, try to lure the gullible into making fraudulent investments. Some operate "pump and dump" schemes, whereby they post fabricated messages about a major development in a small company, hoping to drive up the value of a stock. Then they sell their shares at the peak of the price spike, leaving "other stockholders with near-worthless paper when the stock inevitably plummets" (Rosoff, Pontell, and Tillman 2007:283).

collar crime to illuminate the link between individual actors and their immediate organizational environment.

Differential Association Theory

In addition to his work on white-collar crime, Edwin Sutherland is known for developing **differential association theory**, which seeks to account for the criminality of people in all social strata. According to this theory, "criminal behavior is learned in interaction with others in a process of communication . . . within [an] intimate interpersonal group." The learning of crime includes not only "the techniques of committing the crime, which are sometimes very complicated and sometimes very simple," but also "the specific direction of motives, drives, rationalizations, and attitudes" underlying the illegal behavior. A person becomes criminal when he or she is exposed to "an excess of definitions favorable to violation of law over definitions unfavorable to violation of law" (1947, cited in Akers and Sellers 2009:86).[6]

In *White Collar Crime,* Sutherland presented several personal accounts to illustrate this theory, accounts that resonate with the experiences of Barbara Toffler and John Dean described at the beginning of this chapter. One was by a young man who underwent a redefinition of self upon entering the labor force after college:

> While I was a student in the school of business I learned the principles of accounting. After I had worked for a time for an accounting firm I found that I had failed to learn many important things. . . . An accounting firm gets its work from business firms and, within limits, must make the reports which those business firms desire. On my first assignment I discovered some irregularities in the books of the firm and these would lead anyone to question the financial policies of that firm. When I showed my report to the manager . . . he said that was not a part of my assignment and I should leave it out. Although I was confident that the business firm was dishonest, I had to conceal this information. Again and again I have been compelled to do the same thing in other assignments. I get so disgusted with things of this sort that I wish I could leave the profession . . . [but] it is the only occupation for which I have training. ([1949] 1983:239)

Another man described his trouble maintaining employment in retail sales after he graduated from college because he did not like to deceive his customers about price and quality, as his bosses expected him to do. After resigning from jobs selling typewriters and then sewing machines, he was in difficult financial straits:

I occasionally met some of my classmates and they related experiences similar to mine. They said they would starve if they were rigidly honest. . . . My own feelings became less determined than they had been when I . . . got a job in the used-car business. I learned that this business had more tricks for fleecing customers than either of those I had previously tried. Cars with cracked cylinders, with half the teeth missing from the fly wheel, with everything wrong, were sold as "guaranteed." When the customer returned and demanded his guarantee, he had to sue to get it and very few went to the trouble. . . . If hot cars could be taken in and sold safely, the boss did not hesitate. . . .

I did not quit as I had previously. I sometimes felt disgusted . . . but I [told myself] that I did not have much chance to find a legitimate firm. I knew that the game was rotten but it had to be played. I knew I was dishonest and to that extent felt that I was more honest than my fellows. The thing that struck me . . . was that all these people were proud of their ability to fleece customers. They boasted of their crookedness and were admired . . . [for] their ability to get away with a crooked deal. . . . Another thing was that these people were unanimous in their denunciation of gangsters, robbers, burglars, and petty thieves. They never regarded themselves as in that class and were bitterly indignant if accused of dishonesty: it was just good business. ([1949] 1983:241–242)

The men whom Sutherland interviewed justified or rationalized their eventual acquiescence to unethical (if not illegal) behavior by noting their financial dilemmas and suggesting that "everybody does it." Studies of embezzlers also note these rationalizations, as well as claims by offenders that they only intended to "borrow" the money and would eventually pay it back or that they somehow deserved the money because their pay was not commensurate with their work (Benson 1985; Cressey 1953; Green 1990; Shover and Hochstetler 2006).

Techniques of Neutralization

The rationalizations used by offenders to account for their actions are often described in terms of Gresham Sykes and David Matza's (1957) **techniques of neutralization theory** (or neutralization theory), which they first developed through their research on delinquent youths. Sykes and Matza argued that most law violators have some appreciation or respect for conventional values and must therefore diminish the hold these values have on them through various self-rationalizations or justifications that neutralize their commitment or feeling of obligation to follow the law. As applied to white-collar crime, techniques of neutralization allow offenders to symbolically construct or interpret the meaning of theirs actions in "non-criminal terms" (Benson and Simpson

2009:141). It is important to reiterate, as Sutherland suggested, that offenders do not invent or conceive of these rationalizations out of whole cloth—they are culturally available and learned from others in their social milieus (Benson and Simpson 2009; Coleman 2006; Shover and Hochstetler 2006).

In their research, Sykes and Matza identified five general techniques of neutralization: denial of responsibility, denial of injury, denial of the victim, condemnation of the condemners, and appeal to higher loyalties. *Denial of responsibility* entails the offender's assertion that his or her behavior is due to external factors such as financial problems or pressure from superiors, coworkers, or investors. In a well-documented price-fixing case that came to light in the early 1960s, for instance, corporate personnel from General Electric, Westinghouse, and other electrical equipment manufacturers conspired for a period of years to avoid the competition that would have kept industry prices down, netting the industry millions of dollars in illegal profits (Geis 1967). The offenders claimed that they were only stabilizing prices in order to correct, as one executive said, "a horrible price level situation. . . . Corporate statements can evidence the fact that there have been poor profits during all those years." Another added, "I thought we were more or less working on a survival basis in order to try to make enough to keep our plant and our employees." Another said that the price-fixing conspiracy "had become so common and gone on for so many years that I think we lost sight of the fact that it was illegal." Still others said that if they "didn't do it . . . [they] would be removed and somebody else would do it," or simply that it was a "dog-eat-dog" business (Geis 1967:144–145, 147).

Denial of injury entails the offender's claim that no harm has been caused by his or her actions. One executive in the electrical equipment case claimed: "The prices which . . . purchasers . . . have paid during the past years were appropriate to value received and reasonable as compared with the general trends of prices in the economy." Another said, when asked in a Senate subcommittee hearing whether he was aware that his meetings with competitors were illegal: "Illegal? Yes, but not criminal. . . . I assumed that criminal action meant damaging someone, and we did not do that" (Geis 1967:142, 144).

Denial of the victim is used as a way to distinguish people who are deserving targets of crime from those who are not. Embezzlers, for example, may claim that their employer deserves to be targeted because he or she underpays their workers, makes too much money, or won't miss what is stolen (Green 1990; Shover and Hochstetler 2006). But white-collar offenders usually don't have to "look into the eyes" of their victims, who as individuals remain anonymous to them. In some cases, as Benson and Simpson note, "the 'victim' may not be an individual at all but rather a vast governmental agency, such as Medicare in the case of health care fraud" (2009:144). In cases of price-fixing, "there may be millions of victims, each of whom loses only a trivial amount of money . . . [so] that it may be difficult to identify victims in the traditional sense at all" (2009:144). Moreover, it is generally not a white-collar offender's explicit intention to do harm. As Jeffrey Reiman suggests, in describing a mine disaster:

> What keeps a mine disaster from being [viewed as] a mass murder . . . is that it is not a one-on-one harm. What is important in one-on-one harm is . . . the *desire of someone (or ones) to harm someone (or ones) else*. An attack by a gang on one or more persons or an attack by one individual on several fits the model of one-on-one harm; that is, for each person harmed there is at least one individual who wanted to harm that person. Once he selects his victim, the rapist, the mugger, the murderer all want this person they have selected to suffer. A mine executive, on the other hand, does not want his employees to be harmed. He would truly prefer that there be no accident, no injured or dead miners. What he does want is something legitimate. It is what he has been hired to get: maximum profits at minimum costs. . . . If ten men die because he cut corners on safety, . . . [the] men are dead as an unwanted consequence of his (perhaps overzealous or undercautious) pursuit of a legitimate goal. (2007:72–73, original emphasis)

A fourth technique of neutralization, *condemnation of the condemners,* shifts attention away from the offender and toward disapproving others, such as an overbearing "big government" that is marred by too much red tape, inept bureaucrats, unnecessary and confusing regulations that restrict the "free market," or overzealous prosecutors. Moreover, offenders may reject the legitimacy of the law altogether, allowing themselves to view their actions as wholly untainted by moral stigma; their law violation, they believe, is a mere technicality, not a real crime, for by restricting the pursuit of profits, the government is undermining the economy and harming the general social welfare (Benson and Simpson 2009; Coleman 2006; Conklin 1977).

Finally, *appeal to higher loyalties* involves the imperative to circumvent the law in order to obtain a higher value. One often finds this rationalization in cases of government crime involving purported "national security." During the early years of the Cold War, for instance, when the Soviet Union was viewed as the most dangerous adversary of the United States, a secret report, prepared for the White House in 1954 by a group of distinguished citizens and headed by former president Herbert Hoover, asserted:

> It is now clear that we are facing an implacable enemy whose avowed objective is world domination. . . . There are no rules in such a game. Hitherto accepted norms of human conduct do not apply. . . . If the United States is to survive, long-standing American concepts of fair play must be reconsidered. . . . We must learn to subvert, sabotage and destroy our enemies by more clever, more sophisticated, more effective methods than those used against us. (cited in Moyers 1988:42)

Or take the case of torture, where law violation is justified in order to obtain vital information to protect the public, although there is, in fact, little evidence that torture is as effective as less coercive interrogation techniques (Mayer 2009; McCoy 2006; see Chapter 6).

Critics have faulted Sykes and Matza for failing to establish that techniques of neutralization actually *precede* rather than *follow* criminal acts, arguing that techniques of neutralization are mechanisms that facilitate the "hardening" of offenders who are already involved in crime or that are used by offenders to mitigate culpability after they get caught or to persuade coworkers to participate in wrongdoing (Hamlin 1988; Minor 1984; Schwendinger and Schwendinger 1985). These criticisms notwithstanding, the concept of neutralization techniques sensitizes us to some of the ways in which white-collar offenders use culturally available rationalizations to interpret or account for their actions.

Corporate Culture and the (Mis)management of Power

Earlier we explored Marshall Clinard's (1983) research based on interviews with retired middle-level managers from Fortune 500 corporations, which found that about a third of these managers disapproved of the ethical standards practiced in their respective industries. When explaining corporate crime they tended to downplay *external* factors such as "corporate financial problems, unfair practices of competitors, or the type of industry" and instead attribute the wrongdoing to the *internal* cultural environment of the organization (p. 70). These middle managers said that in many cases the ethical history or tradition of the corporation had been established long ago by the company founder and had been passed on to subsequent generations of managers. Over 90 percent of the middle managers felt that *top managers* were responsible for setting the ethical (or unethical) tone of corporations. Over 70 percent thought that top management was generally aware of *all* the violations that were occurring in their companies, and an additional 22 percent thought that top management knew about *some* of the violations. The middle managers believed that top managements' knowledge was especially likely in cases of product-safety design defects, illegal kickbacks and foreign bribery, and antitrust (including price-fixing), as well as in cases of labor, environmental, and tax violations. One manager noted, "Corporations with many violations are being run primarily for the top and bottom line in order to make a buck." Another said, "Violations are likely if top management is seeking to advance their personal reputations and be 'hot shots'" (p. 57).

Other research indicates that top managers are more likely than middle managers to attribute law violations to financial strains facing the company. According to one top-management official, "Business executives . . . have no right to wrap themselves in the mantle of moral philosophers and judges—especially to the detriment of the interests of their shareholders whose money they are using" (Silk and Vogel 1976:229). Top management, however, "tends to 'signal' its expectations [to subordinates] rather than [issue] specific orders to break the law" (Friedrichs 2007:207). As Christopher Stone observed, top management prefers "not to know" everything their organization is doing and "they arrange patterns of reporting so they cannot find out (or . . . if they do find out, . . . only in such a way that it can never be proved)" (1975:53).

Take the case of the Ford Pinto, for example. Between 1971 and 1976, Ford Motor Company manufactured Pinto automobiles that suffered substantial fuel-tank leaks during rear-end collisions at low to moderate speeds (about 30 miles per hour). These leaks stemmed from a design problem involving the placement of the gas tank only six inches from the rear bumper. This placement was intended to reduce trunk space to make the car smaller, lighter, and cheaper in order to compete with Japanese and German automakers who had cornered the market on small-car sales. Upon impact, however, large quantities of gasoline could spill out of the Pinto if the tube leading from the tank to the gas cap was severed or if the bolts on the differential housing (the bulge in the middle of the rear axle) punctured the tank. "At that point, all that was needed to ignite the fuel and . . . create an inferno was a spark—from steel against steel or from steel against pavement" (Cullen et al. 2006:147).

At one time it was estimated that burning Pintos had caused the deaths of at least 500 burn victims who otherwise would not have been seriously injured, to say nothing of the countless others who suffered serious burn injuries (Cullen et al. 2006; Dowie 1977). This death estimate is probably exaggerated, but a report published by the National Highway Traffic Safety Administration (NHTSA) in 1978 did verify 38 Pinto fires involving 27 fatalities (26 due to burns and 1 due to impact injuries) and 24 nonfatal burn injuries (Birsch and Fielder 1994). As these figures are based on police accident reports that often fail to report fires or distinguish between deaths due to fires and deaths due to impact, some fire deaths were probably not recorded as such. Douglas Birsch and John Fielder concluded, "It is likely that the number of unnecessary deaths exceeded [the NHTSA estimates] . . . but it is impossible to determine accurately how many deaths there were" (1994:10).

Especially controversial was the fact that the design problem was known to Ford managers and engineers *before* the Pinto was put on the market. Ford had considered alterations that could have prevented the gas leakage (e.g., lining the gas tank with a rubber bladder or covering the bolts on the housing with a polyethylene shield). Ford officials, however, did not think these safety measures were worth the cost. A high-ranking Ford Motor Company engineer recalled, "Whenever a problem was raised that meant a delay on the Pinto," Lee Iacocca, the chief executive at Ford, "would chomp on his cigar, look out the window and say, 'Read the product objectives and get back to work.'" Another said, "Safety wasn't a popular subject around Ford in those days. With Lee it was taboo" (Dowie 1977:21).

Most corporate employees will do what they're told, in part because all organizations tend to "selectively recruit new members who in many respects match those already there" (Vaughan 1982:1389). New managers are led "through an initiation period designed to weaken their ties with external groups, including their own families, and encourage a feeling of dependence on and attachment" to the company (Clinard and Yeager 1980:63). Employees quickly learn not to question standard operating procedures.

Toffler (2003) describes a two-week training program that all new employees of Arthur Andersen were required to attend before formally beginning their jobs. The hiring process had already aimed to screen out people who would not fit into the institutional culture; and the training program was designed to mold new employees, "like raw clay," into an "Arthur Andersen man," what Toffler calls an "android" (p. 25). Later, at an ethics workshop that Toffler conducted for Arthur Andersen employees, she asked the attendees what they would do if a superior in the company wanted them to do something they thought was wrong. "No one dared to breathe," until one timid man spoke up: "I guess I might ask a question. But if he insisted I do it, yes, I would." Toffler asked him if he would tell anyone else. He replied, "No. It could hurt my career" (p. 193).

Similarly, in the electrical equipment price-fixing conspiracy mentioned earlier, executives testified that price-fixing had been an ongoing practice before they joined their respective companies and that they were expected to conform (Geis 1967). In another case involving the marketing of an anticholesterol drug that was known by company officials to have harmful side effects, "no one involved expressed any strong repugnance or even opposition to selling the unsafe drug. Rather they all seemed to drift into the activity without thinking a great deal about it" (Carey 1978:384).

Dennis Gioia, who worked as Ford Motor Company's field recall coordinator in 1973 during the Pinto controversy, remembers that at the time he felt "no strong obligation to recall" the vehicle and saw "no strong ethical overtones to the case whatsoever" ([1992] 1996:54). The crashworthiness of the Pinto was consistent with federal standards for subcompacts and, from the viewpoint of company personnel, within the range of "acceptable risk." Matthew Lee and M. David Ermann suggest that the Pinto tragedy should not be understood as an outcome of management's explicit intention to do harm, but rather as a case of "institutionally embedded unreflective action" (1999:43), what Diane Vaughan (2005) calls the **normalization of deviance**.[7]

Even when managers have ethical reservations about what they are doing, the pressure from superiors to meet production quotas and target dates can be immense. As one of Clinard's subjects related, "You get the pressure so strong from top management that you will make judgmental efforts to make things come out right even if you use unethical practices such as lying about production or marketing progress . . . [or] cutting corners . . . on quality" (1983:142). Another middle-level manager said, "When we didn't meet our growth targets the top brass really came down on us. And everybody knew that if you missed the targets enough, you were out on your ear" (p. 143).

James Messerschmidt (1997) added that corporate managers often conflate profit-making with masculinity. "Real man(agers)" take risks and are willing to "go to the limit" to bring the company success and prove themselves worthy combatants in the competitive struggle for corporate profits (p. 101). **Man(agerial) masculinity** requires one to set aside personal or emotional concerns and make decisions without regard to the effects on people. In this context a cost-benefit approach is the perfect vehicle for corporate decisionmaking. In the midst of the Pinto controversy, Mark Dowie (1977) published a chart from a Ford Motor Company memorandum that contained calculations regarding the costs and benefits of installing a special valve in all cars and light trucks to prevent carburetor and other fuel leakages during a rollover accident (see Figure 2.1). Ford reasoned that the costs ($137 million) of installing this valve far outweighed the benefits ($49.5 million). Notice that in this estimate the potential benefits ignored by Ford included saving human injuries and lives!

The External Environment

Whereas microsociological approaches attempt to specify the link between individual actors and their organizational milieu, macrosociological approaches focus on the broader historical, economic, and political factors that impact organizations themselves.

Anomie-Strain Theory

Arguably the most oft-cited macrosocial theory cited by criminologists is Robert Merton's anomie theory (1938, 1968), also referred to as strain theory (which we will call anomie-strain theory). Merton drew insights from the early work of the French sociologist Émile Durkheim ([1893] 1964, [1897] 1952), who introduced the term **anomie** into the lexicon of sociology. In Durkheim's formulation, anomie refers to a state of normlessness whereby individuals are isolated, cut adrift, and lacking in a

Figure 2.1   Ford Motor Company Cost-Benefit Memorandum

Costs
Sales: 11 million cars, 1.5 million light trucks
Unit cost: $11 per car and truck
Total cost: 11,000,000 x ($11) + 1,500,000 x ($11) = $137 million

Benefits
Savings: 180 burn deaths, 180 burn injuries, 2,100 burned vehicles
Unit cost: $200,000 per death,[a] $67,000 per injury, $700 per vehicle
Total benefits: 180 x ($200,000) + 180 x ($67,000) + 2,100 x ($700) = $49.5 million

Source: Adapted from Dowie 1977.
Note: a. Ford obtained the $200,000 figure from the NHTSA, which had given in to auto industry pressure to institutionalize cost-benefit analysis in regulatory decisionmaking. The memorandum was intended to persuade regulators to not adopt a new safety standard (Lee and Ermann 1999).

44

Box 2.3 The *Challenger* Disaster

Shortly after liftoff on January 28, 1986, the space shuttle *Challenger* exploded in midair, killing six astronauts and schoolteacher Christa McAuliffe. An investigation after the tragedy revealed that officials at the US National Aeronautics and Space Administration (NASA) had been forewarned about a problem with the rubber O-ring seal in the joint of the solid rocket booster that was used to launch the *Challenger* into space. They were told that cold weather at the time of the launch could stiffen and shrink the O-ring and make it vulnerable to hot gas leakage, which could lead to an explosion (Boisjoly, Curtis, and Mellican [1989] 1992; Kramer 2006; Vaughan 2005).

The rocket booster had been manufactured by the Morton Thiokol corporation. Engineers at Morton Thiokol, concerned about the cold weather, believed that the launch was too risky. But NASA managers overrode the recommendations and authorized the launch anyway. Morton Thiokol and NASA engineers had apparently been aware of this problem years earlier, in the research and development stage, but the information was not passed on to higher-level NASA officials who would have been in a position to delay production, had they been inclined to do so. Thus Diane Vaughan attributes the *Challenger* debacle, in part, to the problem of **structural secrecy**: an organization's "division of labor, hierarchy, complexity, [and] geographic dispersion of parts [that] systematically undermines the ability of people situated in one part of an organization to fully understand what happens in other parts" (2005:152; see also Kramer 2006).

In the years leading up to the launch, NASA was also under pressure from the federal government to move forward with the shuttle program quickly. In 1982, President Ronald Reagan proclaimed that the "fully operational" shuttle program was "the primary launch system for both national security and civil government missions" (Presidential Commission 1986:164). NASA, under budget constraints as well, was under pressure to partially recoup expenditures by becoming a cargo hauler for commercial communication satellites. The House Committee on Science and Technology concluded:

> NASA's drive to achieve a launch schedule of 24 flights per year created pressure . . . that directly contributed to unsafe operations. . . . [A] reliable flight schedule with internationally competitive flight costs was a near-term objective. Pressures within NASA to attempt to evolve from a R&D [research and development] agency into a quasi competitive business operation caused a realignment of priorities in the direction of productivity at the cost of safety. (US House of Representatives 1986:22)

continues

FURTHER EXPLORATION

Box 2.3 continued

Just prior to the launch, managers at both NASA and Morton Thiokol were informed by engineers about their concerns. Under the aforementioned pressure, and in a context where risk-taking had become routine—there is no such thing as a completely safe launch—they made the decision to proceed (Kramer 2006).

Vaughan (2005) thinks that the risk-taking milieu at NASA created an environment in which deviance had become normalized, that the officials who authorized the launch followed all proper decisionmaking procedures, and that they did not have guilty intentions. In other words, she thinks the *Challenger* disaster was a "mistake" but not a crime (but see Kramer 2006). On the other hand, Russell Boisjoly, a senior scientist at Morton Thiokol and acknowledged rocket-seal expert, believes that managers' judgment was clouded by **groupthink**, whereby "members' strivings for unanimity over[rode] their motivation to realistically appraise alternative courses of action" (Janis 1972:9). Boisjoly asserts that the *Challenger* disaster is indicative of the tendency within organizations to deny individual responsibility for organizational actions: "One of the most pernicious problems of modern times is the almost universally held belief that the individual is powerless, especially within the context of large organizations. . . . The end result can be a cancerous attitude that so permeates an organization or management system that it metastasizes into decisions and acts of life-threatening irresponsibility" (Boisjoly, Curtis, and Mellican [1989] 1992: 130–131).

common bond that brings them into sympathetic relationships with other people in society.[8]

Merton, however, gave Durkheim's formulation a new twist, arguing that the social condition of anomie was constituted not by normlessness per se but by a disjuncture or lack of integration between *cultural goals* (or values) and *institutionalized means* (or opportunities). Merton believed that the predominant cultural goal of American society was the dream of financial success and bountiful material consumption. People who lacked access to the legitimate means to turn this dream into reality were structured into a relationship of *strain* with society and experienced a sense of frustration, anger, and injustice about their lot in life. In this sense, crime is endemic to a social system that dangles the enticements of materialism before everyone without being able to deliver the goods to all.

Anomie-strain theory, most often applied to lower-class criminali-

ty, views crime as a response to blocked opportunities for the achieve-
ment of culturally valued goals of financial success.[9] As such, it is a theory that is applicable to white-collar crime as well, as Merton himself
observed. Goals of financial success are especially acute in business
organizations, and an organization's prestige and status—as well as the
prestige and status of its members—are dependent upon its ability to
maintain and expand profits. Indeed, in a capitalist society profit maxi-
mization is the *primary* goal of corporations. Corporate actors respond
to competitive pressures, unpredictable economic markets, and government regulatory controls by adapting illegal means to meet the "bottom
line," achieve a competitive edge, or quite simply to make as much
money as possible (Friedrichs 2007; Passas 1990; Vaughan 1983).[10]
Moreover, as Benson and Simpson point out: "There is no obvious stop-
ping point at which enough is enough. Weak competitors may fall by the
wayside, but new ones emerge to take their place. . . . [E]ven companies
that are leaders in their industries must always worry about potential
competition. Hence, because of the competitive structure of capitalist
economies, corporations are continually under pressure to do better"
(2009:59).

Anomie-strain theory also suggests that crime occurs not only when
legitimate opportunities are blocked but also when illegitimate opportunities are available (see Cloward and Ohlin 1960). In this regard, as
noted earlier, organizations provide members with greater resources for
committing crime on a large scale, and getting away with it, than individuals acting alone would have. The division of labor within the organization allows for the diffusion of tasks and responsibility, making it difficult to pinpoint the person (or persons) who actually committed the
act. Importantly, individuals higher up in the organization are able to
delegate tasks and responsibility to others in order to insulate themselves from legal liability. Moreover, weak regulatory controls undermine deterrence and enhance opportunities for corporate malfeasance by
freeing companies from external surveillance and accountability
(Prechel and Morris 2010; Vaughan 1983).

Criminogenic Market Structures

As noted in Chapter 1, Sutherland (1949) found that nearly half of the
70 largest US corporations had engaged in law violations at their origin
or in their early years of operation, making crime an essential part of
their initial period of capital accumulation. He also observed that corporations within the same industry tended to have comparable rates of law

violation, with companies in the meatpacking and mail-order businesses leading the way. Similarly, Marshall Clinard and Peter Yeager's study (1980) of the largest manufacturing corporations in the mid-1970s found that the most frequent offenders were concentrated in three areas: the motor vehicle, oil refinery, and pharmaceutical industries (see Box 1.2). While a majority of corporations had a record of law violation, 40 percent did not, and just 8 percent accounted for over half of the violations in the Clinard-Yeager study. What makes some corporations more prone to law violation than others? Are there conditions within particular industries or economic markets that are more or less conducive to law violation?

William Leonard and Marvin Weber (1970) introduced the term **criminogenic market structure** to identify elements of the external social environment that produce the strain that generates crime. According to Leonard and Weber, criminogenic market structures consist of industries characterized by (1) a limited number of manufacturers who can easily collaborate to avoid unprofitable competition, and (2) products that retain an inelastic demand—that is, products that remain in demand and continue to be purchased even if prices are increased.

The automobile industry, for example, has relatively few domestic manufacturers due to the formidable entry barriers inherent in a market that requires a high volume of sales in order to maintain a profitable business. Between the early 1900s and the late 1920s, the number of US automakers declined from 181 to 44. Currently, there are only 3 US-owned companies (General Motors, Ford, and Chrysler). There has not been a successful new domestic entrant into the US market since Chrysler began in 1925, and in 1980 that company needed the federal government to guarantee a $1.5 billion loan to prop up its sagging profits (Simon [1982] 2006).[11]

Historically, the automobile industry had a well-deserved reputation for emphasizing style over safety (Nader [1965] 1972). But Leonard and Weber (1970) focused on a less acknowledged problem: the pressure manufacturers exert that constrains dealers' ability to operate ethically or within the law. The franchise agreements that manufacturers offer dealers typically require dealers to sell a high volume of vehicles at a low per-unit cost. If dealers fail to comply, they may lose their franchise or receive unfavorable treatment from the manufacturer (e.g., slow delivery or insufficient supply of popular models), thus forcing dealers to recoup profits elsewhere. For instance, dealers may order new cars with accessories that customers have not ordered and require them to pay for these if they want to receive the car. Dealers also mark up used-car prices excessively and fail to disclose the mechanical problems with these vehicles.

In addition, dealers enjoy an excessively high profit margin in their service departments. An industry-wide flat rate is generally charged for particular repairs, allowing dealers to charge customers for more time than is actually spent fixing the vehicle. Dealers also have a monopoly on new parts, which enables them to charge exorbitant prices for these products; and they may charge for unnecessary repairs and unnecessary replacement of parts, as well as for repairs that are not made and parts that are not used.[12] Other industry-wide practices include dealers turning back odometers on used cars—even on "executive" cars that have been used by the dealers themselves. Dealers also cut corners by not inspecting vehicles before they are delivered to customers, and they may fail to honor warranties, claiming that repairs that should be covered are not. But again, according to some criminologists, it is the criminogenic market structure in the automobile industry that pressures dealers to engage in such practices. As Harvey Farberman noted, a small number of "manufacturers who sit at the pinnacle of an economically concentrated industry" have established an economic policy that "causes lower level dependent industry participants to engage in patterns" of unethical and illegal activities (1975:456; Leonard and Weber 1970).[13]

James Coleman (2006), however, finds the evidence regarding the effect of market structures on corporate crime more difficult to evaluate. Much corporate crime research, he observes, is based on official records and thus suffers from some of the same flaws as official rates of ordinary crimes (e.g., they do not include large numbers of unreported crimes). Coleman suggests, for example, that the high rates of law violation in the motor vehicle, oil refinery, and pharmaceutical industries studied by Clinard and Yeager (1980) may be due, in part, to the fact that large "industries whose products cause serious and clearly identifiable harm to the public or the environment tend to be subject to more stringent regulation than those that do not" (Coleman 2006:218).

Coleman also notes the inconsistent results of quantitative research in the United States on the association between market structure and official rates of antitrust violations by corporations. Some studies have found higher rates of antitrust violations among firms in highly concentrated industries (industries with few firms), some have found higher rates in moderately concentrated industries, and some have found no relationship at all between antitrust violations and degree of industry concentration. Coleman reasons that antitrust practices like price-fixing would appear easier in markets dominated by a few large firms, but that more competitive markets, on the other hand, might exacerbate the economic strains that encourage crime. In addition, Coleman notes that these studies are methodologically flawed in that they tend not to consider the effect of international competition.

Inconsistent findings in studies of corporate bribery of government officials also suggest an ambiguous relationship between market structure and crime. Coleman concludes that in noncompetitive industries dominated by a few firms, "*political* bribery aimed at influencing government policies and programs" may be more common, but intense competition in less concentrated industries "appears more likely to be associated with *commercial* bribery [of sales or purchasing agents] to promote the sale of a firm's products" (2006:216, emphasis added). In either case, it is clear that one cannot understand the behavior of corporate organizations without examining the broader market structure in which they do business.

The State

Political sociologists refer to the **state** as the apparatus of government that includes its various branches, divisions, and agencies, including the military, legal system, and criminal justice system (Neuman 2005). The **pluralist theory** of the state views it as a neutral institutional mechanism for responding to public demands and arbitrating competing interests in society. In contrast, the **elite theory** of the state views it as a mechanism by which more powerful ruling groups exercise hegemonic control.[14] C. Wright Mills (1956) is noteworthy for advancing a view of the **power elite** as composed of the largest corporations, the federal government, and the military, and to a lesser extent the mass media. These elites circulate between the most influential corporations and the state, ensuring that the interests of the elite are represented in government deliberations and policies. Representation of their interests is also facilitated through large campaign contributions, political lobbying, policy advisory boards, and corporate-sponsored think tanks (Domhoff 1990; Neuman 2005; Simon [1982] 2006).

In Chapter 1, we explored the phenomenon of corporatism, the fusion of big business and big government to serve the interest of private profit-making, which too often contributes to what Raymond Michalowski and Ronald Kramer (2006) call "state-corporate crime." A center point of this fusion of interests is the billions of tax dollars that are funneled into the private sector through federal contracting work in areas such as weapons manufacturing, privatization of military func-

tions, homeland security, disaster relief, and various energy and construction projects. Naomi Klein (2007) calls this amalgam of interests
the **disaster-capitalism complex**, which, as we shall see, is marked by
the exploitation of war and catastrophic events as opportunities to profit
from the public largesse, often in corrupt ways (see Chapters 3 and 5).

Other analysts point out that the power elite is not a homogeneous
group and that different factions of elites may circulate in and out of
power along with "shifts in technology, new ideas, or differences in their
willingness to use force" to suppress dissent (Neuman 2005:96; Pareto
[1901] 1991). Still others note the "relative autonomy" of the state in
capitalist societies, whereby the state may deviate from elite interests,
but only insofar as the long-term interests of the dominant capitalist
class is secured—that is, the state (in conjunction with other nonmarket
mechanisms) helps maintain the preconditions for the further private
accumulation of capital (Jessop 2002). As Fred Block (1977) argued,
there are certain historical periods in which state actors have some freedom to advance interests and policies that are resisted by economic
elites, but only if the state secures the long-term stability of the capitalist
system. Regulatory reforms, for instance, may be opposed by some corporations but are nonetheless necessary to correct instabilities in the system caused by unregulated markets and criminal behavior. According to
this view, the "state operates to keep capitalism running . . . but to do
this, the state must [at times] constrain the freedom of specific capital-
ists" (Neuman 2005:103).[15]

In Chapter 1 we also noted the corrupting influence of corporate
power on regulatory agencies. Some political sociologists would explain
this phenomenon in terms of **capture theory**. According to this theory,
"regulatory agencies begin by actively enforcing rules in the public
interest, but as the political conditions that give rise to . . . regulation
change, agencies slowly align with the business interests they are supposed to regulate and business influence grows until agencies defend the
regulated business's interests instead of the public interest" (Neuman
2005:472–473).[16] This process of capture is facilitated by a circulation
of personnel in and out of the private and public sectors, which Mills
(1956) described as a "revolving door." Corporations also ensure that
the administrative appointments they desire are selected by making
financial contributions to politicians who support their interests.

Andrew Szasz (1986a) described regulatory contexts that facilitate
crime or analogous social injuries through conflicts of interest, laxity of
enforcement, or political corruption as **criminogenic regulatory structures**, a concept that is similar to Leonard and Weber's (1970) crimino-

genic market structures.[17] At the same time, different administrations may be more or less favorable to regulation, and politicians who receive support (financial or electoral) from proregulatory advocacy groups will at times enact and enforce policies that heed their wishes.

Of course, political officials themselves also engage in criminality, not only through financially remunerative corruption and the abuse of power for political gain (see Chapter 5), but also through state crimes of political repression, which may be defined as the illegal use of state-sanctioned *violence* and *nonviolence* to maintain social order or foment disorder, as the case may be, through various police, military, security, and intelligence apparatuses. When the US government, for example, takes actions to overthrow a foreign government—in violation of US law, international law, or the law of the affected nation—a state crime of violent repression has been committed (see Chapter 6). Or when it attempts to repress domestic dissent through illegal surveillance of the citizenry, a state crime of nonviolent repression has been committed (Barak 1991; Friedrichs 2007; Green and Ward 2004; Rothe 2009).

Take the case of the Federal Bureau of Investigation's **COINTEL-PRO** (counterintelligence program) of the 1960s, which, in the FBI's words, aimed to "disrupt" and "neutralize" dissident individuals and groups through illegal surveillance and the spreading of disinformation (Senate Select Committee on Intelligence [1976] 1978:160). One notable target of this operation was Martin Luther King Jr. According to a 1976 report of the Senate Select Committee on Intelligence, headed by Senator Frank Church, from late 1963 until his death in 1968: "[King] was the target of an intensive [FBI] campaign . . . to 'neutralize' him as an effective civil rights leader. . . . The FBI gathered information about Dr. King's activities through an extensive surveillance program in order to obtain information about the 'private activities of Dr. King and his advisors' to use to 'completely discredit them' . . . [and] the civil rights movement" ([1976] 1978:161–162). As part of this operation, microphones hidden in King's hotel rooms picked up information about his extramarital sexual affairs. The FBI mailed a tape recording of these conversations to King with an unsigned note that read: "King, there is only one thing left for you to do. You know what it is. . . . There is but one way out. . . . You better take it before your filthy fraudulent self is bared to the nation" (cited in Harris 1977:40). According to the Church Committee, King and his advisers interpreted this note as a threat to publicly release the tape "unless Dr. King committed suicide" (Senate Select Committee on Intelligence [1976] 1978:162; see also Wise 1973).

Indeed, the FBI, under the leadership of J. Edgar Hoover from 1924 to 1972, engaged in illegal wiretapping, burglaries, illegal opening of citizens' mail, character assassination, and dissemination of misinformation against members of the Southern Christian Leadership Conference (King's organization), the American Civil Liberties Union, the Socialist Workers Party, and numerous other *nonviolent* groups and individuals, including some notable justices of the US Supreme Court.[18] The FBI also engaged in the practice of **agent provocateuring**, deploying undercover operatives to infiltrate organizations and encourage members to adopt violent tactics, which in turn were used to justify law enforcement against them (Marx 1981; Roebuck and Weeber 1978). The Church Committee concluded that Hoover's FBI investigated too many people and collected too much information for too long to justify any legitimate law enforcement objective. Its actions were not only deviant but in violation of the law (Charns 1992; Halperin et al. 1977; Poveda 1990; Rosoff, Pontell, and Tillman 2007).

More recently, as mentioned in Chapter 1, after the September 11, 2001, terrorist attacks, the US government unleashed a regime of warrantless electronic surveillance. In an exposé of the National Security Agency (NSA), "the largest, most costly, and most technologically sophisticated spy organization the world has ever known," James Bamford documents the warrantless eavesdropping program that has been illegally monitoring millions of e-mails and phone calls an hour, both domestic and international, including the monitoring of confidential personal and business matters unrelated to national security (2008:1; see also Cole and Lobel 2007; Hersh 2004; Mayer 2009).[19]

Summary

In this chapter we reviewed sociological explanations of white-collar crime, noting how individual actions cannot be understood without illuminating the social context in which such actions are embedded. In doing so, we examined microsociological factors internal to corporate and government organizations that highlight the link between individuals and their immediate organizational environment. Here we introduced concepts derived from differential association theory and techniques of neutralization theory, and considered elements of corporate culture that lead to the abuse of managerial power.

Additionally, we examined macrosociological factors external to organizations that focus on broader conditions that structure the actions of organizations themselves. Here we reviewed anomie-strain theory and considered the impact of criminogenic market structures. We also examined theories of the state, noting the fusion of corporate and government power, as epitomized by the disaster-capitalism complex, which profits from the exploitation of war and catastrophic events, all too often at the expense of the societal good. Finally, we discussed capture theory, criminogenic regulatory structures, and state crimes of political repression to round out our explanatory overview of white-collar crime.

Notes

1. Another individualistic approach to explaining criminality focuses on biological factors. However, the "pervasiveness of white-collar crime would seem to offer a powerful refutation of the proposition that criminality can be generally explained" by offenders' biogenic makeup (Friedrichs 2007:201; see also Berger, Free, and Searles 2009).

2. The question of the social context of control is also a focus of Travis Hirschi's (1969) "social control" theory of crime, initially developed to explain juvenile delinquency, which views criminal action as stemming from a lack of social bonds between individuals and society. Following Émile Durkheim, Hirschi argued that "the more weakened the groups to which [one] belongs, the less he depends on them, the more he consequently depends only on himself and recognizes no other rules of conduct than what are founded in his private interests" (Durkheim [1897] 1952:209). In a survey of corporate executives, James Lasley (1988) tested social control theory and found that those executives who were strongly attached to other managers, coworkers, and the formal rules of the company were less likely to engage in white-collar crime. This finding, however, is contraindicated by other research and evidence that indicates that conformity to the informal norms of an organization can also be the raison d'être for white-collar crime.

3. In a survey about cynicism in American society, Donald Kanter and Philip Mirvis found that about 46 percent agreed with the statement: "Most people are just out for themselves"; and 60 percent agreed with the statement: "People claim to have ethical standards regarding honesty and morality, but few stick to them when money is at stake" (1989:9). They also identified a management type, which they called "command cynics," who were prepared to do whatever it took to survive in an organization and not "agonize over the people they hurt to advance themselves" (p. 30).

4. Cohen and Felson call this the "routine activities" approach, arguing that the confluence of motivated offenders, suitable targets, and absence of capable guardians can be found in the patterns of everyday life.

5. Quinney actually uses the term "organization" in reference to occupational roles. However, I think the term "orientation" better captures the way such roles impact the perceptions and social actions of the individuals who occupy them.

6. Differential association theory has been described as both symbolic interactionist and behaviorist in orientation (Berger, Free, and Searles 2009).

The former focuses on the subjective meaning of action and the ways in which a person's sense of self or personal identity is acquired through social interaction with others. The latter assumes that criminal behavior is learned or conditioned through the particular mix of rewards and punishments that are attached to a person's behavior.

Since individuals are typically exposed to both crime-inducing and crime-inhibiting associations, what matters is the relative *frequency* (how often they spend time with particular others), *duration* (how much time they spend with them on each occasion), *priority* (how early in life they began associating with them), and *intensity* (how much importance they attach to them) of each.

7. More generally, as initially used in the sociology of deviance, normalization refers to a process by which individuals attempt to disavow deviant status and reduce or avoid the societal stigma associated with their actions (Schur 1979).

8. Durkheim argued that anomie was most likely to occur during periods of social upheaval, such as the transition from traditional agrarian to modern industrial societies. During these times, individuals were forced into unfamiliar surroundings or circumstances (i.e., cities) where old rules governing social interaction no longer applied and new ones had yet to develop. Such conditions could lead to various forms of deviant behavior (see also note 2 in this chapter).

9. Merton argued that individuals adapt to anomie-strain in a variety of ways, of which "innovation" is the most relevant to our subject matter. Innovation refers to actions that embrace goals of financial success but pursue them through illegitimate means.

10. A survey of corporate executives by the KPMG accounting firm found that 70 percent thought that illegal conduct in corporations stemmed from pressure to meet production schedules, 65 percent from unrealistic earnings goals, and 65 percent from a desire to succeed or advance careers. Another 50 percent thought that illegal conduct stemmed from inadequate training, and only 22 percent thought it stemmed from a desire to steal from or hurt the company (cited in Laufer 2006:141).

11. In 2009, both Chrysler and General Motors required a multibillion-dollar taxpayer bailout to avoid bankruptcy.

12. Of course, dealers are not the only establishments that make unnecessary or fraudulent auto repairs. Overall, an estimated one-third of the money consumers spend on auto repairs involves unnecessary or fraudulent work. One study found that as many as two-thirds of repair shops did unnecessary work. An investigation of Sears auto repair centers found that at one time about 90 percent of the work done was unnecessary (Blumberg 1989; Coleman 2006; Friedrichs 2007).

13. Because of competition from Japanese and European manufacturers, the entire motor vehicle industry has become more competitive. But Barry Lynn (2009) points out a neglected aspect of the current industry: the consolidation of the component supply sector. Historically "most manufacturers were vertically integrated and built most of the components in their own factories" (p. 21). In the late 1980s and early 1990s, however, manufacturers began outsourcing this production, enabling them "to sell off in-house operations and offload costly liabilities like union pensions" (p. 22). Since then, the supply sector has consolidated, in part due to the deregulation of antitrust law (see Chapter 3). Such con-

solidation has raised prices on component parts, and manufacturers pass on this increased cost to consumers.

14. For a more complete review of the range and nuances of social theories of the state, see Neuman 2005.

15. James O'Conner (1973) argues that the state performs two essential but sometimes contradictory functions: maintaining the conditions for capitalist profit-making and expansion, and maintaining its legitimacy in the eyes of the citizenry as an institution that represents their values and interests.

16. The origin of capture theory is typically credited to the work of political scientists (Bernstein, 1955; Lowi 1979; Wilson 1980).

17. In a study of 69 manufacturing corporations between 1995 and 2000, Brian Wolf (2009) found that the number of corporate violations of environmental law, as well as the severity of those violations, was positively associated with the amount of money spent on political campaign contributions. Similarly, in a study of the 500 largest publicly traded companies between 1994 and 2004, Harland Prechel and Theresa Morris (2010) found that the number of financial restatements, which was indicative of corporate malfeasance, was related to the amount of corporate contributions to political action committees.

18. The Central Intelligence Agency has also engaged in *domestic* surveillance, in violation of its legal mandate (Commission on CIA Activities Within the United States 1975; Halperin et al. 1977; Rosoff, Pontell, and Tillman 2007).

19. In addition, the USA PATRIOT Act authorized the FBI to conduct residential searches of individuals deemed a risk to national security; search phone, medical, financial, library, and other records; trace Internet communications; and detain noncitizens without charge for up to six months prior to deportation (Anderson 2003; Cole and Lobel 2007; McCaffey 2003; Williams 2003). Anthony Romero, executive director of the American Civil Liberties Union, believes that the FBI has been "dangerously targeting Americans who are engaged in nothing more than lawful protest and disobedience" (quoted in Lichtblau 2003:A3). But John Ashcroft, the first attorney general in the George W. Bush administration, thought that "those who scare peace-loving people with phantoms of lost liberty . . . only aid terrorists—for they erode our national unity and diminish our resolve. They give ammunition to America's enemies, and pause to America's friends" (quoted in Kappeler and Potter 2005:364). For an analysis of the "politics of fear" and the PATRIOT Act as a "state crime against democracy," see Thorne and Kouzmin 2010.

3

Corporate Financial Crime

CHARLES PONZI, A YOUNG IMMIGRANT FROM ITALY, OPENED the Financial Exchange Company of Boston in 1919, guaranteeing investors a 50 percent rate of return within 45 days. Ostensibly, Ponzi's plan "was to purchase international postage coupons in countries where the exchange rate was low and then re-sell them in countries with higher rates. Within six months, Ponzi had persuaded 20,000 investors to give him nearly $10 million." The secret of Ponzi's success was to pay "early investors with new investors' money, thereby attracting more and more investors. At its height, his company had a *daily* cash flow of $250,000" (Rosoff, Pontell, and Tillman 2007:6). A **Ponzi scheme**, as this type of fraud became known, is dependent upon an ever increasing supply of investors; but at some point the offender's greed outstrips their luck and the "house of cards" inevitably collapses. After an exposé in the *Boston Globe* revealed Ponzi's fraud in 1920, he was arrested, convicted, and sentenced to four years in prison (and later deported). 4 yrs !

More recently, in 2008, a modern-day Ponzi scheme hit the news. Amid the multibillion-dollar taxpayer bailout approved by the US government to help prop up failing financial institutions, the FBI initiated a fraud investigation of several major financial and insurance firms (CNNMoney.com 2008). One notable case involved Bernard Madoff, former chairman of the NASDAQ Stock Market and founder of Bernard L. Madoff Investment Securities. Since the early 1990s, Madoff had been perpetrating a fraud that bilked investors out of some $18 billion, with fabricated gains totaling $65 billion, the largest Ponzi scheme in the history of the country (Foley 2009).[1]

Regulatory authorities had been suspicious of Madoff's investments for some time, because the gains Madoff claimed to be delivering were

57

unrealistic. Investors, however, did not complain, feeling they were privy to a "sweet deal," which included no fees on investments. No one bothered to ask or find out how Madoff raked up his incredible returns or to request statements from a reputable accounting firm. Investors who knew him through common membership in the exclusive Palm Beach Country Club thought they had an inside track to making a lot of money (Frank et al. 2009; Gross 2009).

Madoff said that when he first began the fraud, he felt "compelled" to give investors high returns despite the weak stock market at the time. "When I began the Ponzi scheme," he said, "I believed it would end shortly and I would be able to extricate myself and my clients from [it]. However, this proved difficult and ultimately impossible" (quoted in Frank et al. 2009:2). David Shapiro, an economics professor and former FBI agent, observed that Madoff, like other white-collar offenders, was able to divorce himself from the human impact of his actions. "When you're making all this money and you realize nobody's really checking on you," said Shapiro, "the temptations become too great" (quoted in Frank et al. 2009:2).

Madoff pled guilty to multiple charges and was sentenced to 150 years in prison. In the long run, Madoff's story may prove the adage: crime does *not* pay. But much white-collar crime does pay indeed; the cases we hear of are just the ones about offenders who get caught. And as we have seen, even white-collar offenders who get caught don't generally receive the punishments they deserve, Madoff's sentence notwithstanding. In this chapter, we will consider several types of corporate financial crimes—antitrust violations, crimes of high finance and banking, and corporate fraud—that demonstrate that Madoff's criminality was not an isolated case.

Antitrust Violations

In Chapter 1 we considered the landmark Sherman Antitrust Act of 1890, which aimed to curtail the consolidation of corporate economic power that was undermining competition in the US economy. This legislation contained both criminal and civil provisions for regulating business combinations that resulted in a restraint of trade (including cooperative agreements to fix prices) or the monopolization of an industry. We also noted, however, that the Supreme Court interpreted the SAA as allowing for "reasonable" business combinations, that the lack of enforcement neutralized the moral stigma originally associated with such violations, and that antitrust law has had relatively little impact on the growth and consolidation of corporations in the United States.

Moreover, in the early 1980s, as the social and political consensus regarding the desirability of regulation began to erode, President Ronald Reagan overhauled existing antitrust law by establishing new criteria by which the law would be applied. Rather than seeking "to ensure competition for the sake of competition, the aim now was to clear the way for any [cost] efficiencies that might benefit the consumer, no matter how much consolidation this entailed" (Lynn 2009:22). Even during the administration of President Bill Clinton, which was more favorable to regulation (see Chapter 1), corporate mega-mergers that would have been unthinkable a few years earlier were permitted, although the benefits to consumers were not usually forthcoming.[2]

Price-Fixing

Price-fixing is arguably the quintessential antitrust violation and, in many respects, the "perfect" corporate crime. In price-fixing, the higher cost of a product is distributed across millions of customers so that each person only pays a small price. Moreover, at the time of the purchase, consumers do not realize they are being victimized by crime. They may think they are being ripped off by greedy companies perhaps, but they don't consider themselves crime victims. Yet corporations make millions of dollars in illegal profits each year from price-fixing activities.[3]

In Chapter 2 we explored the infamous electrical equipment price-fixing conspiracy that came to light in the 1960s, marking the first time in the United States that corporate officials were jailed for antitrust violations. Some of the most notable cases since then have occurred in the oil, airline, computer, dairy, vitamin, and insurance industries (Coleman 2006; Friedrichs 2007; Rosoff, Pontell, and Tillman 2007; Simon 2006).

Two of the most frequent targets of antitrust litigation have been oil and airline companies. During a period of oil shortages in the 1970s, for example, seven major oil corporations (ARCO, Chevron, Exxon, Mobil, Shell, Texaco, Unocal) drove up oil prices in what plaintiffs in a civil lawsuit described as an unlawful price-fixing conspiracy. In cases that lingered in the courts for 17 years, the companies eventually settled the lawsuits for a combined $150 million, an amount that was far less than the plaintiffs had asked for (Coleman 2006; Rosoff, Pontell, and Tillman 2007).

Between 1988 and 1992 the leading US airlines (American, Continental, Delta, Northwest, PanAm, TWA, United, USAIR) used a shared electronic-fare database to artificially inflate prices, sending coded signals to each other to announce future rate hikes that each would match. In an out-of-court settlement totaling $458 million, the companies agreed to provide some 10 million customers with coupons as compensation for their malfeasance. However, the coupons could only be used for a portion of each full-fare ticket and expired in three years. Some analysts estimated that individual customers would have had to buy as many as 60 round-trip tickets before receiving full compensation, which of course they never recouped. The major beneficiaries of the lawsuit were other large corporations. IBM alone received $3.3 million in discounts (Rosoff, Pontell, and Tillman 2007).

Although the Clinton administration, as noted earlier, allowed for considerable corporation consolidation, it did issue the largest criminal fines ever given to individual companies for price-fixing. In 1996, Archer Daniels Midland (ADM), a grain and soybean–processing conglomerate whose products are used in a wide range of goods, led the way with a record-breaking $100 million criminal fine. ADM's price-fixing violation involved the lysine used in animal feed and the citric acid used in food and beverages. According to an FBI wiretap of a meeting between ADM and a foreign competitor, an ADM executive said, "We have a saying here in this company that penetrates the whole company. Our competitors are our friends. Our customers are the enemy" (quoted in Rosoff, Pontell, and Tillman 2007:72).

ADM agreed to the $100 million fine in order to avoid an even more costly penalty (which the government agreed to waive) for antitrust activity involving its corn syrup. As ADM had $2 billion in cash on hand, it was easily able to absorb the fine. In 1998 and 1999, however, three ADM executives were found guilty and sentenced to two to three years in prison. Later, in 2004, the firm negotiated a $400 million settlement of civil lawsuits associated with its illegal actions (Coleman 2006; Eichenwald 1999; Rosoff, Pontell, and Tillman 2007; Simon 2006).

The ADM record for price-fixing fines did not stand long, however. It fell in 1998 and 1999 with penalties of $110 to $135 million levied against companies in the graphite electrode industry, which provides the source of heat for steelmaking. In 1999, Mylan Laboratories, the second largest maker of generic drugs in the United States, was also fined $135 million. In this case Mylan conspired to raise the price for ingredients of two drugs by as much as 3,000 percent! Still, Mylan chairman Milan Puskar said, "We continue to believe we acted properly" (quoted in Rosoff, Pontell, and Tillman 2007:73).

Criminal prosecution for price-fixing requires the government "to prove conscious and covert collusion on the part of the firms involved"

(Clinard and Yeager 1980:136). However, such covert collusion is not necessary to subvert competition when the economy is dominated by **oligopolies**, industries characterized by the domination of a few firms. Under these conditions, prices are inflated throughout the industry using the practices of **price-leadership** and **price-signaling**. Price-leadership involves actions by which the leading firm in an industry is the first to raise prices, but with the tacit understanding that other companies will soon follow. Similarly, price-signaling involves announcing price increases or publishing price lists in the media or industry publications, enabling companies to share pricing information without explicit collusion (Clinard and Yeager 1980; Simon 2006). "The effect on consumers," as Elliott Currie and Jerome Skolnick point out, "is that prices in such industries . . . rarely go down and almost always go up . . . even during recessions" (1988:86). Like more blatant price-fixing criminality, price-leadership and price-signaling enhance corporate profits while undermining competition in the economy.

The Microsoft Case

In the 1990s the Clinton administration pursued a controversial antitrust case against Bill Gates's Microsoft Corporation, and in 1999 a federal judge ruled that the company had abused the virtual monopoly it had on its Windows operating system to gain an unfair advantage over competitors on the sale of other products. The most egregious practice involved Microsoft exerting pressure on retailers who sold Windows to also sell Microsoft's Internet Explorer browser rather than the Netscape Navigator browser. At one time, Netscape had controlled a larger share of the Internet browser market, but Microsoft quickly came to dominate this area. Microsoft also denied competitors technical information about Windows, which caused problems for consumers who used other companies' products. The vice president of Apple testified at trial, for instance, that Microsoft "demanded that Apple stop making its QuickTime multimedia software for Windows-based computers" or else Microsoft would withdraw its support for Microsoft Office, which was critical to Apple's operations (Rosoff, Pontell, and Tillman 2007:77).

Bill Gates, who gave a 20-hour deposition on videotape that was introduced at trial, appeared aloof and unrepentant. He could not recall, for example, an e-mail he had written that expressed his intention to undermine archrival Sun Microsystems. "Time and time again, Gates claimed to have been out of the loop during discussions and key meetings. And time and again, his taped testimony was contradicted by memos and e-mails" he had written (Rosoff, Pontell, and Tillman 2007:76).

The judge in the federal case suggested that severe sanctions might be in order, including breaking Microsoft into two or more companies and increasing governmental monitoring of its contracts with retailers and its future acquisitions. Microsoft appealed the ruling, and when the George W. Bush administration took office a more modest settlement was reached. This settlement essentially limited sanctions to a requirement that Microsoft provide competitors with technical information that would allow them to run their software more seamlessly with Windows.

By 2003, however, rival companies were again leveling charges against Microsoft for returning to its familiar tactics in an effort to corner the $40 billion yearly market for servers that run office network systems. Server software developers like Sun Microsystems and IBM require access to Windows codes in order to run their products. Although the terms of the settlement require Microsoft to grant other developers access to these codes under "reasonable terms," it has been reluctant to do so (Rosoff, Pontell, and Tillman 2007).

High Finance and Banking

Some observers believe that capitalism in the United States today has evolved into a **casino economy**. "In contrast to **industrial capitalism**, where profits are dependent on the production and sale of goods and services," profits in the casino economy of "**finance capitalism** increasingly come . . . from speculative ventures designed to bring windfall profits for having placed a clever bet. . . . Nothing is . . . produced but capital gains" (Calavita and Pontell 1990:335–336; Leopold 2009a; Phillips 2006).

The shift from industrial to finance capitalism—from an economy based on the circulation of goods to an economy based on the circulation of money—has been under way for some time. Whereas in 1940 there were 7.1 manufacturing jobs for every financial services job, by 2008 there were only 1.6. In 2008, up until the market crash that year, the financial sector of the US economy generated about 20 percent of the country's gross domestic product and 27.4 percent of all corporate profits (Leopold 2009a; Phillips 2006). But, we must ask, who benefits from this type of system, and is it fair?

There is little doubt that the wealthiest Americans have been benefiting. The earnings (adjusted for inflation) of the wealthiest *1 percent* of

Box 3.1 Wal-Mart: The High Cost of Low Price

Another corporation that has been singled out by critics for abusing its economic power is Wal-Mart, a company that "does more business than Target, Sears, Kmart, J.C. Penney, Safeway, and Kroger combined" (Rosoff, Pontell, and Tillman 2007:80). Consumers are attracted to Wal-Mart's low prices, but this is not without cost. Wal-Mart ruthlessly pressures suppliers to lower their costs, which Wal-Mart then passes on to consumers. But in order to meet this demand, suppliers are increasingly forced to outsource their production to low-wage and weakly regulated countries like China, hence contributing to the decline of the US economy overall (Lichtenstein 2009).

It is not so much harm to the economy, however, that has brought Wal-Mart into conflict with the law. Rather, it is charges of race and gender discrimination, firing workers for union activity, and other acts of exploitation, such as not paying workers entitled to overtime, forcing them to work "off the clock," and locking doors to prevent them from leaving. These practices have resulted in scores of civil lawsuits and complaints to the Equal Employment Opportunity Commission and the National Labor Relations Board. Moreover, wages are often so low at Wal-Mart that its employees must "apply for food stamps, Medicaid, and other public assistance" to make ends meet (Rosoff, Pontell, and Tillman 2007:83). Wal-Mart has also been cited multiple times for environmental violations related to pollution of the nation's waterways from stormwater runoff and garden chemicals at its store sites (Featherstone 2005; Lichtenstein 2009).

One of Wal-Mart's most incendiary practices is its purchase of life insurance policies on low-level employees. When these employees die, Wal-Mart collects the money. The families of the deceased get nothing, while Wal-Mart takes a tax deduction on the premiums, and the profits from the cashed-in policies are purportedly used to fund Wal-Mart's executive retirement plan (Rosoff, Pontell, and Tillman 2007).

Americans rose from 8 percent of gross national income in 1973 to 23 percent in 2006, the highest share since 1929, while the average worker's wages remained flat. By the early 2000s, the top-paid executives in the largest US firms made about 370 times the pay of an average full-time worker, up from about 40 times the average worker's pay in the 1970s; and the second- and third-highest-paid groups of executives made about 170 times the average worker's pay, up from about 30 times over the same period. Moreover, these executives often made their high

salaries and bonuses even when their companies were laying off workers and losing money (Krugman 2007; Leopold 2009a).

The financial assets of the wealthiest Americans also increased
because of new tax policies enacted by the Reagan administration during the 1980s. Often referred to as "supply side" or "trickle down" economics, **Reaganomics** favored tax cuts to the most affluent members of
society in order to encourage more investment, to in turn spur economic
growth. This transfer of wealth to the richest Americans was financed in
large part by increasing the federal debt, which rose by $1.49 trillion
from 1983 to 1989 (Leopold 2009a; Phillips 2006).

But the wealthy did not necessarily invest this newfound money in
ways that benefited average Americans. Rather, they invested it into a
growing array of exotic financial instruments (explained later) that the
financial services industry created to attract their business, thus channel-
ing enormous amounts of cash into speculative financial ventures rather
than the industrial economy, with devastating consequences for the
entire country, as the calamity of the late 2000s attests (Krugman 2007;
Leopold 2009a, 2009b; Stiglitz 2010).

Insider Trading

A particular problem with the US system of finance capitalism is that
many investors do not play by the rules. In 1934 the Securities
Exchange Act criminalized **insider trading** to try to ensure fairness in
the system. Insider trading occurs when "stockholders, directors, officers, or any recipients of information not publicly available . . . take
advantage of such limited disclosure for their own benefit" (Rosoff,
Pontell, and Tillman 2007:247). The logic behind the prohibition of
insider trading is that the legitimacy of capitalism depends upon the
expectation of a positive association between the economic risk taken by
an investor and the potential return. But "the insider trader collects the
highest returns with little risk at all, while the ordinary investor, who
assumes most of the risk, is exploited like some naive bumpkin lured
into a rigged game of chance" (p. 262).

Between 1934 and 1979, the Securities and Exchange Commission
took just 53 actions against insider trading. Between 1980 and 1987
alone, it took 177 actions (Friedrichs 2007). Indeed, the 1980s was a
period in which the crimes of high-flying insider traders like Ivan
Boesky and Michael Milken were in the news. These men made millions
of dollars based on insider knowledge of pending corporate mergers and
other financial transactions. They also raised money from others by

promising high rates of return on high-risk investments aimed at acquiring companies, then "downsizing" the companies by firing workers to save costs and selling off company assets. These investment strategies made millions for insiders while devastating the lives of ordinary workers who lost their jobs. As historian Kenneth Starr observed, it used to be that businessmen got rich by putting people to work; now they get rich by putting people out of work (cited in Martz 1986).

Boesky and Milken, among others, were eventually prosecuted for their crimes. In 1987, Boesky was fined $100 million and sentenced to three years in prison. It is estimated, however, that he made about $200 million in illegal trades alone. In 1989, Milken was fined a record-breaking $600 million and sentenced to two years in prison; his financial dealings had earned him over $1 billion (Friedrichs 2007; Rosoff, Pontell, and Tillman 2007; Stewart 1991).

George W. Bush is another high-profile businessman who appears to have profited from insider trading in the 1980s, although Bush did not make as much money as did professional investors like Boesky and Milken, and he was not prosecuted for his alleged misdeeds. During the time his father, George H. W. Bush, was vice president, the younger Bush's failing Spectrum 7 Oil Company, which was $5 million in debt, was purchased by Harken Energy Corporation. Harken paid Bush with generous stock options and benefits and put him on the corporate board that was responsible for auditing the company's financial assets. By the time George H. W. Bush became president, Harken was in dire financial straits and under investigation by the SEC for using a subsidiary to hide company debt (as did Enron). In 1990, Harken insiders sold their stock, eight days *before* the audit committee publicly disclosed that Harken had suffered huge financial losses, which led to a precipitous drop in the value of its stock. Bush made $848,560 on his sales, but denied that he had profited from insider information, even though he was, in fact, on the audit committee (Corn 2003; Ivins and Dobose 2003; Rosoff, Pontell, and Tillman 2007).

Insider trading continues to be profitable, and perhaps this is why the practice has by no means been curbed. The widely publicized case of homemaking diva and corporate entrepreneur Martha Stewart reminds us of this truism. In 2003 Stewart was charged with receiving and acting on privileged information from her stockbroker, Peter Banovic. She sold about 4,000 shares of ImClone Systems Inc. the day *before* "a negative government report on the ImClone cancer drug Erbitux sent its share price falling" (McClam 2003:D10). Stewart avoided losses of about $50,000 from the deal.

Stewart claimed that she had a "stop-loss" agreement with her broker to sell her stock if the price went below a certain amount. No evidence of this agreement was found, however, and Stewart was charged and convicted—but not for insider trading per se. Rather, she was convicted of obstruction of justice and lying to investigators about the transaction, for which she served five months in prison. At Stewart's trial, Banovic, who was also indicted, testified that he had been told by his boss at Merrill Lynch to pass on the information about ImClone to Stewart. Her personal assistant also reluctantly testified that Stewart had told her that she had known about the situation and had altered a computer log of a message from Banovic. Upon her release from prison, Stewart remained unrepentant, telling Barbara Walters in an interview: "I didn't cheat anybody out of anything" (quoted in Rosoff, Pontell, and Tillman 2007:270). Of course, as we have noted, the reason that insider trading is illegal in the first place is that it allows a privileged few to make money at the expense of others who are not privy to the inside information.

Insider trading is not the only way naive investors are disadvantaged in the stock market. They are also duped through intentional manipulation of stock values, such as **pump-and-dump schemes**, whereby con artists or corrupt stock brokers recommend stocks or issue fraudulent information about these stocks to drive up their value, and then sell their own shares before the stock price collapses (Rosoff, Pontell, and Tillman 2007; Simon [1982] 2006; see also Box 2.2). Even the formerly venerated mutual fund industry, in which some 100 million Americans are invested through various bundles of financial securities[4] that are managed by others, was rocked with scandal in the 2000s. In practices known as **late trading** and **market timing**, a few favored, big-money shareholders were allowed to profit at the expense of small investors.[5] Financial adviser Humberto Cruz explains the problems associated with these practices:

> Late trading, which is illegal, involves the placing of buy or sell orders for mutual fund shares after the stock market has closed for the day at 4 P.M., but using that day's closing price. By law, those orders should receive the next day's price. Shareholders allowed to engage in late trading profit illegally from knowledge of events that occur after the market has closed when those events can be expected to affect the next day's share price in a certain way. These illegal profits in turn dilute the returns that shareholders like you and I would get. Market timing, which is the rapid-fire trading of fund shares to profit from short-term market swings, is not in itself illegal. But most funds have policies against it because it drives up fund transaction costs and can disrupt the management of the portfolio. (2003:C1, C4)

Furthermore, the mutual fund companies charged investors excessive and hidden fees, and made direct payoffs to brokers to steer customers their way (Friedrichs 2007).

The Savings and Loan Scandal

One of the most devastating financial debacles in the history of the United States involved the savings and loan (S&L) scandal of the 1980s. By the time the borrowed money for the entire taxpayer bailout is paid back some 20 years into the twenty-first century, the estimated bill may exceed $1 trillion. Moreover, it is no small matter that criminal activity was a major factor in 70 to 80 percent of the failed S&Ls and that as much as 25 percent of the losses were due to crime. The story of what happened to this industry should have been a forewarning about the pitfalls of deregulating financial markets, but regrettably the lesson was not learned (Leopold 2009a; Rosoff, Pontell, and Tillman 2007).

What was this scandal all about? The federally insured S&L system was established in the early 1930s as a depression-era measure designed to ensure the availability of home loans, promote the construction of new homes, and protect depositors from the types of financial devastation (massive investment losses and withdrawal of bank funds) that followed the 1929 stock market crash. Federal regulations prohibited S&Ls from making risky investments, essentially confining them "to the issuance of home loans within 50 miles of their home office" (Calavita and Pontell 1990:331). By the 1970s, however, S&Ls could no longer compete with other financial institutions such as mortgage companies (for home loans) and mutual funds and money markets (for savings investments). They were locked into long-term, low-interest loans they had previously made and were prohibited by law from offering adjustable-rate mortgages or from paying more than 5.5 percent interest on deposits (even during a period of double-digit inflation).

During the 1970s, the S&L industry's net worth declined dramatically, and by 1980, 85 percent of S&Ls were losing money. At that time, a complete bailout of the industry utilizing taxpayer dollars might have cost about $15 billion. But instead of cutting losses at this level, President Reagan and the Democratic-controlled Congress opted for a strategy of deregulation. Federal legislation passed in the early 1980s— the **Depository Institutions Deregulation and Monetary Control Act** of 1980 and the **Garn–St. Germain Depository Institutions Act** of 1982—phased out restrictions on interest rates and opened up new areas of investment for S&Ls, which were now authorized to "make consumer loans up to 30 percent of their total assets; make commercial, corporate or business loans; and invest in nonresidential real estate worth up to 40 percent of their assets" (Calavita and Pontell 1993:530; Jackson 1990; Pizzo, Fricker, and Muolo 1989).

The new (de)regulations also gave the S&Ls unprecedented access to funds by removing the 5 percent limit on brokered deposits (brokered deposits are "jumbo" or aggregated deposits placed by middlemen that yield high interest rates for investors and exorbitant commissions for brokers). These funds were used to finance risky speculative investments that had the potential for either high payoffs or financial calamity. In addition, S&Ls were allowed to provide 100 percent financing to borrowers, essentially giving them risk-free loans. And the government dropped the requirement that S&Ls "have at least 400 stockholders with no one owning more than 25 percent of stock," thereby allowing a single entrepreneur to own and operate a federally insured S&L (Calavita and Pontell 1993:530). At the same time, the amount of federal depository insurance was raised from $40,000 to $100,000 per account.

Deregulation was "the cure that killed" (Calavita and Pontell 1990:312). S&Ls lost billions of dollars through legal investments that were previously illegal, and the deregulated climate, or criminogenic regulatory structure (see Chapter 2), opened the industry to insider abuse and criminality. Kitty Calavita and Henry Pontell (1990, 1993) identify three general categories of deviant activities that occurred: *unlawful risk-taking, collective embezzlement,* and *illegal cover-ups.*

Unlawful risk-taking involved S&Ls that extended their investment activities beyond the levels allowed by law—for example, by exceeding the 40 percent limit on commercial real estate loans. In addition, S&Ls compounded the risk they undertook by failing to conduct adequate marketability studies to ensure the feasibility of their investments, as they were required by law to do.

Unlike ordinary instances of embezzlement, which typically entail lone, relatively subordinate employees stealing from the company in which they work, **collective embezzlement** involved the misuse and theft of funds by the S&L's top management. During the 1980s, some S&L owners and managers treated their institutions as personal slush funds, throwing elaborate parties and purchasing expensive luxury goods like artwork, antiques, yachts, airplanes, and vacation homes. They also violated the law by giving themselves and their associates excessive "salaries as well as bonuses, dividend payments, and perquisites" beyond what was "reasonable and commensurate with their duties and responsibilities" (Government Accounting Office, cited in Calavita and Pontell 1990:323). In addition, S&L operators engaged in a number of fraudulent loan schemes. For instance, "straw borrowers" outside of the S&L were used to obtain loans on behalf of individuals within the S&L, thus circumventing the legal limit on the proportion of an institution's loans that could be made to insiders. Another scheme entailed insiders from one S&L authorizing loans to insiders of another S&L in return for a similar loan.

Illegal cover-ups entailed the manipulation and misrepresentation of S&Ls' financial books and records to conceal fraudulent practices from government regulators, hence preventing regulators from learning about an S&L's impending financial insolvency and delaying the closure of the institution. Regulators were not always adversaries of S&Ls, however. Some, wooed by lucrative "job offers at salaries several times . . . their modest government wages," even collaborated with S&L operators to protect themselves from scrutiny and criminal prosecution (Calavita and Pontell 1993:535).

S&Ls also poured millions of dollars into the campaign coffers of influential members of Congress, who shielded them from regulatory oversight. California congressman Tony Coelho, who also served as chair of the Democratic Congressional Campaign Committee in the mid-1980s, is particularly noteworthy for having regularly solicited S&L industry money, which he used to fund the campaign committee. Coelho admitted that "doing official favors for donors was permitted. The unforgivable sin was to make the connection explicit" (quoted in Jackson 1988:104).

Texas Democratic congressman Jim Wright, who served as Speaker of the House from 1987 to 1989, was another beneficiary of S&L industry campaign contributions. Wright intervened on the S&L industry's behalf and threatened to withhold much needed funding for federal S&L regulators if they did not back off from their investigation of his particular S&L associates. In 1989, Wright was forced to resign from Congress when it was learned that he had accepted about $145,000 worth of gifts from a Texas real estate developer who stood to benefit from legislation over which Wright had control (Calavita and Pontell 1993).

In perhaps the most well-known case involving collusion of elected officials and the S&L industry, antipornography crusader and S&L magnate Charles Keating received the support of the **Keating Five**—Senators Alan Cranston (D, California), Dennis DeConcini (D, Arizona), John Glenn (D, Ohio), John McCain (R, Arizona), and Don Riegle (D, Michigan)—in his effort to thwart regulators from investigating his California-based Lincoln S&L. Keating contributed a total of $1.4 million to these senators' campaigns (Cranston's especially). When Keating's S&L was finally closed in 1989, taxpayers were left with a bailout bill of over $3.4 billion (Friedrichs 2007; Jackson 1990; Rosoff, Pontell, and Tillman 2007).

By 1990, over 300 S&L executives, accountants, and lawyers had been convicted of criminal law violations related to the scandal.[6] The average prison term they received was just over two years; the average sentence for ordinary bank robbery at the time was nearly eight years (Simon 2002). In 1992, Keating was convicted in a California state court on multiple counts of fraud for a scheme involving the sale of millions of dollars of soon-to-be worthless bonds to thousands of customers, most of them elderly or poor, who were told that the bonds were government-insured when, in fact, they were not; some of the victims lost their entire life savings. The next year, he was convicted in federal court on multiple counts of fraud, criminal conspiracy, and **racketeering** (federal racketeering law, which was originally developed to deal with organized crime, refers to a pattern of criminal activity associated with a financial enterprise that occurs over a period of time). In 1996, however, his convictions were overturned due to various legal technicalities (Rosoff, Pontell, and Tillman 2007).[7]

Calavita and Pontell observe that there were elements of the S&L scandal that "more closely approximate organized crime than corporate crime" (1993:519). **Organized crime** may be conceptualized as a business that is organized for the explicit purpose of making money through illegal activity, whether or not the organization also appears to be involved in a legitimate business enterprise. Calavita and Pontell cite a Government Accounting Office study of 26 failed S&Ls, which found that 62 percent had undergone a change of ownership in the period just preceding their financial insolvency. Typically the new owners were individuals who had never been in banking before but who were attracted to the opportunities afforded by the deregulated environment. These cases indicate that the *primary* purpose of the S&L, like organized crime, was to serve as a vehicle for illegal transactions. Unlike corporate crime, which is "driven by the desire to maximize corporate profits," these S&L crimes were "perpetrated by insiders and affiliated outsiders for the purpose of personal gain without regard for the impact on the institutions" (p. 533). Like the Mafia "bust-outs" characteristic of conventional organized crime, these S&L operators "often got into the business precisely to loot their institutions" (p. 533).

Fantasy Finance

Some of the most pernicious economic effects of the US banking system have come from the recent consolidation of the financial industry,

Box 3.2 Money Laundering

An additional way in which banks are implicated in criminality is through **money laundering**, the process by which illegal "dirty" money is made "clean" and recycled into the legitimate economy. Under US law, money laundering entails a financial transaction that the person knows to involve illegal proceeds, as well as attempting to conceal or disguise information about those proceeds or failing to comply with transaction-reporting requirements (Abadinsky 2007; Richards 1999).

Much of the money earned by large-scale drug dealers and other criminal organizations is taken in as cash, most often in bills no larger than $20. When somebody shows up at a bank with a suitcase of small bills, tellers are surely aware that something is awry. Banks may even charge a percentage for accepting such deposits or for electronically transferring funds from one bank to another. In the United States, banks are required to report currency transactions of $10,000 or more. But this is not the case in many places abroad. Countries such as Austria, Panama, Switzerland, and the Cayman Islands, among others, allow bank accounts to be numbered without identifying the depositor by name. Moreover, the sheer volume and speed of bank-to-bank electronic transfers make it "extremely difficult to trace . . . funds or document their illegal nature" (Webster and McCampbell 1992:5). And complicit bank officials often accommodate criminal organizations by wiring the money between their bank's own account (rather than their customer's account) and the account of another bank, making the laundering of illegal funds nearly indistinguishable from legal banking transactions (Adler, Mueller, and Laufer 2007; Richards 1999).

The Bank of Credit and Commerce International (BCCI) illustrates a case in which a bank's *primary* function was to provide financial services (including money laundering) to an assortment of drug and arms traffickers, smugglers, tax evaders, political dictators, and intelligence agencies around the globe. Established in 1972 by a Pakistani financier, the BCCI became one of the largest financial institutions in the world, with over 400 branches operating in 75 countries, including the United States. The BCCI's most infamous clients were a motley crew: the Colombian Medellín cocaine cartel, dictators Saddam Hussein (Iraq) and Manuel Noriega (Panama), the Abu Nidal terrorist organization, and the US Central Intelligence Agency. Between 1988 and 1992, the BCCI twice pled guilty to money laundering and once to racketeering, and was forced to pay several million dollars in fines. Some bank officials were sentenced to prison after the bank was closed and its assets were frozen (Passas 1995; Richards 1999; Simon 2006).

beginning in 1999 with the repeal of major components of the **Glass-Steagall Act** of 1933, also known as the Banking Act. Glass-Steagall was a depression-era reform designed to create a wall of separation between traditional *commercial banks*, which receive deposits that are insured by the federal government and lend money to borrowers, and *investment banks*, which raise uninsured capital for risky high-stakes investments, trade in stocks and other financial securities, and manage corporate mergers and acquisitions. Glass-Steagall aimed to prevent the conflict of interest that is endemic to a financial institution that loans money to the same company in which it invests, and also to prevent financial institutions from funneling deposits from the federally insured commercial sector into the noninsured investment sector (Cohan 2009; Greider 2009; Leopold 2009a; Prins 2004).

Like the deregulation of the S&L industry, the repeal of Glass-Steagall protections by the **Gramm-Leech-Bliley Act** of 1999 was a bipartisan effort, only this time it was enabled by a Republican-controlled Congress and Bill Clinton, a Democratic president, and his secretary of treasury and chief financial adviser, Robert Rubin. Rubin had been an executive at the highly influential investment firm Goldman Sachs, and after leaving public office he accepted a top position at Citigroup, one of the largest financial conglomerates in the world, where Rubin would earn over $100 million during the following decade (Drum 2010).[8]

The repeal of Glass-Steagall allowed for the consolidation of commercial and investment banks, brokerage houses, and insurance companies, creating a new industry of huge financial "supermarkets." It also put taxpayer money at risk, because if these "too big to fail" institutions became insolvent, the government would have little choice but to bail them out in order to prevent the entire economy from sliding into a depression, as witnessed in the late 2000s. To make matters worse, the **Commodities Future Modernization Act** of 2000 also was passed, which exempted many of the financial instruments known as **derivatives** from regulatory oversight (Greenberger 2010; Johnson and Kwak 2010; Leopold 2009a; Prechel and Morris 2010).[9]

Derivatives are the product of a financial industry looking to attract investors seeking high rates of return. The most commonly known financial securities are traditional stocks and bonds. A *stock* represents a share of ownership in a company, while a *bond* represents a loan for which the investor is owed interest. A derivative, on the other hand, is a "financial instrument whose value is derived from something else, called the underlying or referenced stock, bond, or other financial instrument" (Leopold 2009a:193; see also Greenberger 2010; Stiglitz 2010; Tett 2009).

One type of derivative is a **collateralized debt obligation**, which bundles pools of similar loans like home mortgages or car loans into securities that can be sliced and diced and bought and sold at various degrees of risk. Another type of derivative is a **credit default swap**, which functions like an insurance policy by shifting "risk from a party that doesn't want the risk to a party that is willing to accept it . . . for a price" (Leopold 2009a:192). In other ways, however, a credit default swap is nothing like an insurance policy as we know it, because neither party to the agreement needs to own the item they are insuring. The investment simply involves a bet on the future value of a particular asset. As noted by Lynn Stout, professor of corporate and securities law at the University of California–Los Angeles: "The most important thing to understand about derivatives is that they are bets. That's not a figure of speech—they are literally bets. You can make a million dollar bet on a $1,000 horse" (quoted in Puzzanghera 2010:1). According to economist Les Leopold, the derivatives market is similar to fantasy baseball:

> [F]antasy baseball . . . [is] a derivative game of betting based on statistics based on the behavior of real major league players. You don't own the real players, or even a piece of them. . . . When you own a fantasy baseball team, you don't own anything except your derivative statistics compiled for you by a service. Yet your bet has value because other players and their derivative teams are willing to bet with you. There can be tens of thousands of fantasy baseball leagues based on only the two major leagues. Similarly, there are tens of thousands of derivative securities based on combinations of the same underlying real securities. (2009a:193–194)

One problem with the derivatives market is that the investments are based on speculative assumptions and are so complicated that investors (and regulators) have difficulty estimating the actual value of the assets; and in the lead-up to the financial crisis of the late 2000s, some bankers and investors got greedy and began taking on too much risk. As Charles Prince, the former chief executive officer (CEO) of Citigroup, told the *Financial Times,* "As long as the music is still playing, we are still dancing—and the music is still playing" (quoted in Tett 2009:148).

Another problem with the derivatives market is not simply that it goes unregulated but that it multiplies the risk of the original asset many times, spreading the consequences of failed investments throughout the entire economy.[10] If the home mortgage market goes bust, for instance, as it did in the late 2000s, not only are the original lenders and borrowers in trouble, but so are thousands of other nonprincipals who are invested in securitized mortgages (including those who rely on invested pension funds). Moreover, the interlocking nature of financial institutions that are "too big to fail" means that a problem in one large firm portends problems in other firms as well. When insurance giant American International Group (AIG) faced bankruptcy, for example, its collapse would have undermined major investment banks like Goldman Sachs that had a stake in AIG's derivatives contracts (Cohan 2009; Greider 2009; Leopold 2009a; Stiglitz 2010).[11]

In all fairness, the practices of the derivatives market, despite their role in the financial calamity of the late 2000s, do not constitute criminality per se. However, many American taxpayers justifiably feel that they have been robbed by a system that privatizes profit but collectivizes risk and that is riddled with conflicts of interest and outright fraud. Take the case of Jack Grubman, an investment adviser for the brokerage firm Salomon Smith Barney, which is part of the Citigroup conglomerate, who at one time was among the country's "star" stock analysts. In his advice to clients, Grubman touted stocks in which Citigroup had a vested financial interest, most notably fraud-ridden WorldCom and Global Crossing, in an attempt to drive up stock prices. For his transgressions, Grubman was investigated by New York State's attorney general, fined $15 million, and barred from further working in the industry. To help soften the blow, Citigroup agreed to forgive a $15 million loan it had made to Grubman and also pay his legal fees (Guyon 2005; Prins 2004; Smith 2003).[12]

No criminal charges were brought against Grubman, but Robert Citron of Orange County, California, did not escape the arms of the criminal law. Citron, the lone Democrat on the Republican-dominated county board of supervisors, was at the center of the largest governmental bankruptcy in US history. Citron was the money manager for Orange County's investment pool, which he funded with investments from various public and private sources, including the Orange County school district. He invested heavily in the derivatives market, even borrowing $12 billion in public money to maximize profits for a conservative political district "hungry for revenues in an antitax environment" (Will, Pontell, and Cheung 1998:368).

For a while, Citron was the darling of Orange County, dubbed a "financial guru" for creating a financial portfolio that outperformed other investments in the state and nation. One of Citron's colleagues on the supervisory board described him as "a person who has gotten us millions of dollars. I don't know how the hell he does it, but it makes us all look good" (quoted in Will, Pontell, and Cheung 1998:368). But when the investments went bust in 1994, the supervisory board declared losses

Box 3.3 Who Is to Blame for the Home Mortgage Crisis?

Some conservative politicians and pundits have blamed federal government programs Fannie Mae and Freddie Mac for much of the crisis in the **subprime home mortgage market** that emerged in the late 2000s. Subprime mortgages are "loan products intended for borrowers with poor-to-average credit worthiness and characterized by higher interest rates, higher fees, [and] higher risk of default" (Nguyen and Pontell 2010:593). Fannie Mae, or the Federal National Mortgage Association, is a hybrid public-private institution that was created in 1934. Its function is to buy up bank home loans, freeing the bank to use that capital to make additional loans, while at the same time allowing the originating bank to collect the mortgage payments on behalf of Fannie Mae. Freddie Mac, or the Federal Home Loan Mortgage Corporation, was created in 1970 to help expand the secondary market for mortgages. It buys mortgages, pools them, and resells them to investors. Like Fannie Mae, its purpose is to increase the supply of money available for home loans.

Conservatives have been especially critical of the **Community Reinvestment Act** of 1977, which, they say, "forced banks to give mortgages to low-income minorities, and then pressured Freddie Mac and Fannie Mae to buy up these risky mortgages" (Leopold 2009a:74). According to Les Leopold, however, there is little evidence that the 1977 act "had a substantial impact on the housing bubble and bust, let alone the broader economy" (2009a:75). The act did request banks to make more loans to low-income residents, but was designed to stop the discriminatory practice of "redlining," which entails denying loans to residents of particular (primarily minority) neighborhoods, even when these residents are as qualified as buyers in other neighborhoods. One study even concluded that banks operating under the Community Reinvestment Act "were substantially less likely than other lenders to make the kinds of risky home purchase loans that helped fuel the foreclosure crisis" (cited in Leopold 2009a:76). Joseph Stiglitz adds, "The banks jumped into subprime mortgages . . . without any incentives from the government" (2010:10).

On the other hand, it is certainly true that the **predatory lending** practices of some firms did cause mortgage borrowers to default on their loans and lose their homes. Predatory lending entails the practice of deceiving borrowers into accepting unfavorable terms, such as charging them excessive payment fees, convincing them to accept variable rates that "balloon" into exorbitant payments, and steering them away from loans with better terms they may have been qualified to receive (Center for Responsible Lending 2008; Oliver and Shapiro 2008; Stiglitz 2010; Warren 2010). Moreover, much of the recent mortgage crisis was due to the high volume of loans issued on the basis of fraudulent information

continues

FURTHER EXPLORATION

Box 3.3 continued

about the borrowers' financial status and credit ratings and the value of the properties in question. The perpetrators of these frauds were not simply borrowers but the lending institutions themselves. According to the federal Financial Crimes Enforcement Network, activities involving suspicious loans increased 1,411 percent between 1997 and 2005 (Nguyen and Pontell 2010).

of between $1.5 and $2 billion. Citron blamed Merrill Lynch, the prestigious brokerage firm he used, for giving him bad advice. Merrill Lynch officials, in turn, claimed that they had advised Citron about the risks he was incurring, although they continued to sell him the very derivatives they said they had warned him about. Susan Will, Henry Pontell, and Richard Cheung suggest that "Orange County acted like a gambling addict, while Merrill Lynch and other brokerage houses behaved like dealers offering a revenue-starved community new chances to win" (1998:375). Moreover, "the Board of Supervisors, county staff and officials, and the public were as unlikely to challenge Citron's magic as the members of the kingdom were ready to tell the emperor that he was not wearing clothes," instead remaining content in their posture of "concerted ignorance" (p. 379; see also Katz 1979).

Citron pled guilty to multiple criminal counts, "including misappropriation of public funds and making false material statements in connection with the sale of securities," and received a one-year jail term and a $100,000 fine (Will, Pontell, and Cheung 1998:377). Assistant County Treasurer Matthew Raabe was also convicted, on charges related to his involvement in concealing Citron's failed investments, but his three-year prison sentence was overturned on appeal due to a conflict of interest stemming from the fact that the prosecutor's office had suffered financial losses from the bankruptcy. Merrill Lynch, which denied any culpability, settled lawsuits totaling $430 million (Rosoff, Pontell, and Tillman 2007).

Corporate Fraud

Criminal fraud, of which corporate fraud is a part, is the deliberate misrepresentation of truth or fact by which someone attempts to induce another into taking action that is financially disadvantageous to them. A national survey of adults conducted by the Federal Trade Commission (2004) found that over 10 percent of respondents reported being victimized by fraud each year. Topping the reported types of fraud were those involving *advance-fee loans,* in which consumers pay a fee for a "guaranteed" loan or credit card they do not receive; *buyers clubs,* in which consumers are billed for memberships or goods they did not order; *credit card insurance,* in which consumers are told that they face significant risk if their cards are misused by others (federal law limits consumer liability for fraud to $50); and *credit repair,* in which consumers pay fraudsters for falsely promising to remove negative (truthful) information from their credit reports or help them establish new credit records. Other types of reported fraud included those related to prize promotions, Internet services, pyramid schemes, business and job opportunities, and lottery scams (Brightman 2009; Coleman 2006; Friedrichs 2007; Rosoff, Pontell, and Tillman 2007).

Although these types of fraud are typically associated with scam artists and organized criminals, they are often committed by legitimate corporations as well. Indeed, fraud is an element in much of the corporate malfeasance discussed in this chapter. Our review of these incidents could lead to the impression that fraud is an American way of life, an impression that is reinforced when one considers the massive amount of fraud perpetrated by some of the largest US corporations in recent years, aided and abetted by numerous accounting, stock brokerage, and investment banking firms. The billions of dollars involved in corporate fraud make the Martha Stewart insider-trading case pale in comparison.[13]

Enron

Enron is arguably the "poster child" company for the multibillion-dollar problem of corporate fraud that came to light in the early 2000s. The corporation was formed in the 1980s through the merger of two gas pipeline companies. By the early 1990s, under the direction of its first CEO, Kenneth Lay, the Houston-based company became the dominant player in the natural gas and electricity industry, with plants and pipelines operating in the United States and abroad. Lay was a substantial contributor to the political campaign coffers of Republican senator Phil Gramm, a champion of deregulation (Gramm's wife was also awarded with a well-paying position on Enron's board of directors). He was also a major contributor to then-governor George W. Bush's 2000 presidential campaign and was known to have Bush's ear on energy policy. Although Bush tried to distance himself from Lay when the scandal became public, Lay was in fact an old family friend whom Bush affectionately called "Kenny Boy" (McLean and Elkind 2004; Reiman 2007; Rosoff, Pontell, and Tillman 2007).

Enron claimed to be making billions of dollars, and Lay and his executive cohorts—including Jeffrey Skilling, Lay's protégé, who took over as CEO in 2000, and Andrew Fastow, the chief financial officer—were raking in millions for themselves. The problem was that Enron was hiding massive debt. Barbara Ley Toffler (2003) was working at Arthur Andersen, Enron's accountant, at the time (see Chapter 2). She recalls that "Enron's basic strategy had been to buy an asset such as a power plant or water source and then create markets around it. To create these markets required taking on a lot of debt—debt which, if held on Enron's balance sheet, could have crippled the company's expansion plans and its high-flying stock" (p. 211).

To disguise this debt and other business losses, Enron created an interlocking network of some 3,000 corporate subsidies.[14] Most notable among these were the companies run by Fastow, which he apparently used to "funnel millions of company dollars to himself and a few carefully selected associates" (Toffler 2003:211). While some Arthur Andersen auditors were concerned about being embroiled in a fraud, the top executives at the firm feared losing Enron's multimillion-dollar annual business, which had reached $52 million in fees in 2000 and was expected to go higher, and did nothing about it (Rosoff, Pontell, and Tillman 2007).[15]

At the same time, as noted in Chapter 1, Enron created artificial energy shortages that inflated prices, most notably in California, where citizens held hostage to corporate greed suffered from energy blackouts. When the bubble finally burst, in the latter part of 2001, Enron investors lost billions, including the pensions and retirement savings of thousands of people. Although top executives at Enron sold their stock before its value collapsed, over 30 executives (Lay, Skilling, and Fastow among them) were prosecuted on charges that included fraud, insider trading, and money laundering. Lay died before sentencing and had his conviction posthumously vacated by a judge. Skilling was required to pay about $50 million into a restitution fund for Enron victims and was sentenced to 24 years in prison, a sentence he is appealing while serving time. Fastow was sentenced to six years in prison and two years on probation (Pasha 2006; Reiman 2007; Rosoff, Pontell, and Tillman 2007).

It's Not Just Enron

Unfortunately, Enron was not an isolated example, as the case of Bernard Ebbers and WorldCom suggests. In the early 1980s, with the breakup of the telephone monopoly AT&T, Ebbers saw an opportunity to sell cheap long-distance telephone service. Starting with a $650,000 loan from a local Mississippi bank, Ebbers built his Long Distance Discount Service company into a wildly successful telecom business, which was renamed WorldCom in 1995 and merged with rival MCI in 1997 (Prins 2004; Reiman 2007; Rosoff, Pontell, and Tillman 2007; Smith 2003).

On the surface, WorldCom was another capitalist success story, but like Enron, the corporation was riddled with debt, including debt incurred by Ebbers to pay for his personal extravagances, including a shipyard of yachts, acres of farm- and timberland, and the largest ranch in Canada. Ebbers also had overbuilt the business, which could no longer service the debt, and had overstated the company's earnings to try to attract investors. When the company declared bankruptcy in 2002, the largest in US history, Ebbers negotiated a $1.5 million yearly lifetime severance package. Two years later, however, he was indicted on criminal charges and received a prison sentence of 25 years (Pulliam, Solomon, and Mollenkamp 2002).

Once again, Arthur Andersen was implicated in the fraud, since WorldCom was one of its clients. Indeed, the accounting firm's client list read like a "who's who" of corporate fraudsters with whom it was complicit, including Global Crossing, Qwest Communications, Sunbeam, Waste Management, and Halliburton.[16] It was Enron, however, that was most responsible for Arthur Andersen's downfall (Rosoff, Pontell, and Tillman 2007; Toffler 2003).

According to the accounts of Toffler (2003) and others, Arthur Andersen officials shredded boxes of Enron documents and deleted numerous e-mails, allegedly at the behest of company executives, which implicated the accounting firm in Enron's malfeasance. This was not the first time Arthur Andersen personnel had shredded documents regarding a client that had been involved in fraud, and in 2002 the firm was convicted of obstruction of justice. Although the verdict was overturned on appeal on the grounds that the judge's instructions to the jury had been unclear on the requisite "consciousness of wrongdoing" that was required for conviction, the formerly prestigious but now tarnished accounting firm, which had once employed thousands of people in the United States and worldwide, became a mere shadow of itself, fending off civil lawsuits as it withered away (Prins 2004; Reiman 2007; Rosoff, Pontell, and Tillman 2007; Smith 2002).

The wrongdoings of the Rigas family, though not a client of Arthur Andersen, are worth mentioning as well. Adelphia Communications, owned by the Rigas family and headed by company founder John Rigas, was one of the largest cable companies in the country before it went bankrupt. The crimes of Adelphia illustrate the point made by Calavita and Pontell (1993) about elements of the S&L scandal: they appear to resemble the workings of organized crime. Evidence indicates that the Rigas family used the company as their personal piggybank and improperly took off-the-books loans and other payouts amounting to $2.3 billion. Several Adelphia executives were convicted, including members of the Rigas family, two of whom received prison terms (Prins 2004; Reiman 2007; Rosoff, Pontell, and Tillman 2007).

Dennis Kozlowski, CEO of Tyco, a corporate conglomerate whose products include fiber-optic cable, was also convicted and sentenced to a lengthy prison term for actions that were similar to those of the Rigas family. Kozlowski looted millions of dollars from the company, which was mired in fraud, for his own personal use (Prins 2004; Reiman 2007; Rosoff, Pontell, and Tillman 2007).

Halliburton is particularly noteworthy because of the notoriety of its former CEO Dick Cheney. Halliburton is an energy services and supply company with scores of subsidiaries that operate in countries around the globe. During the time Cheney was CEO, from 1995 to 2000, the company engaged in some of the same questionable accounting practices as had Arthur Andersen's other clients, practices that according to Stephen Rosoff, Henry Pontell, and Robert Tillman "may have tip-toed right up to the fraud line but never crossed it" (2007:325). These included overstating accounts receivable from customers, understating accounts payable to vendors, overbilling for services, and misleading investors about liabilities faced through litigation (Bussey 2002; Morgenson 2004; Rothe 2006).

Cheney cashed out company stock worth about $30 million before he resigned to run for vice president and just prior to the plummeting of Halliburton's stock amid allegations that the company had engaged in fraud.[17] Halliburton and its subsidiaries, most notably Kellogg, Brown, and Root, were also accused by the Pentagon of overcharging for fuel it had purchased as part of the "no bid" multibillion-dollar contracts it had awarded to Halliburton without competitive bidding from other companies (Bussey 2002; Gordon 2002; Rosoff, Pontell, and Tillman 2007).

Additionally, scores of other corporations in what Naomi Klein (2007) calls the disaster-capitalism complex (see Chapter 2) have collectively reaped billions of dollars through unethical and illegal practices such as fraudulent overcharging, the provision of shoddy products and services, outsourcing contracted work for profit, noncompetitive contracts, and open-ended contracts that allow companies to keep coming back to the government for more and more money (see Chapter 5). Such practices were especially apparent during the Iraq War and the aftermath of Hurricane Katrina (Fineman 2005; Roche and Silverstein 2004; Scahill 2007; Simon [1982] 2006). Jeremy Scahill points to three major war contractors alone—Boeing, Lockheed Martin, and Northrop Grumman—that have "engaged in 108 instances of misconduct since 1995 and have paid fines or settlements totaling $3 billion" but were still awarded $77 billion in government business in 2007 (2009a:4).[18]

Finally, in April 2010 the Securities and Exchange Commission filed civil charges against investment bank Goldman Sachs, alleging a fraud that had bilked investors out of about $1 billion. The civil suit alleges that Goldman Sachs hired a third party, ACA Management, to select pools of risky mortgages that were marketed as good investments, without disclosing to the investors that the securities were also crafted with input from another client, Paulson & Co., that took out insurance derivatives betting on them to fail; when the investments did in fact fail, Paulson & Co. made billions of dollars. As SEC enforcement director Robert Khuzami said, "Goldman wrongly permitted a client that was betting against the mortgage market to heavily influence which mortgage securities to include in an investment portfolio, while telling other investors that the securities were selected by an independent, objective third party" (quoted in Gordon 2010:B5).

Summary

In this chapter we examined several types of corporate financial crime: antitrust violations, crimes of high finance and banking, and corporate fraud. Antitrust violations, of which price-fixing is the most well-known example, undermine competition in ways that artificially inflate the prices consumers pay for products. The federal cases against the Archer Daniels Midland and Microsoft corporations in the 1990s stand out as among the most notable examples in recent history.

Crimes of high finance and banking include insider trading, a practice that gives some investors an unfair advantage over others, yielding high returns with little or no risk. Other financial schemes, both illegal and legal, bilk naive investors through intentional manipulation of stock prices; and the savings and loan debacle of the 1980s alone cost taxpayers billions of dollars. In the late 1990s, regulatory controls that were enacted during the financial crisis of the 1930s were repealed, freeing

Box 3.4 Tobacco Smuggling

Another way that citizens bear the costs of corporate crime is through tax evasion. Each year in the United States, corporations avoid paying the federal government untold billions of dollars through fraud, funneling money into dubious tax shelters and offshore banks, and reincorporating abroad (Friedrichs 2007; Komisar 2001; Simon [1982] 2006). The tobacco industry has been especially notorious, engaging in actions that blur the boundaries between corporate and organized crime. As a result of the general public health movement in the United States, as well as the $250 billion settlement reached between the industry and state attorneys general in 1998 to recoup public funds for treating tobacco-related illnesses (see Chapter 4), cigarette sales have been declining in the United States. Increasingly, tobacco companies have looked to foreign markets to sustain their profits, and evidence indicates that illegal (tax-free) smuggling is a significant way that tobacco products make their way into these markets. This occurs through criminal organizations, which are sometimes aided and abetted by tobacco companies themselves (Dickey and Nordland 2000; Schapiro 2002).

Take the case of British American Tobacco, the parent company of Brown & Williamson. One British American Tobacco salesman responsible for marketing the company's products in Colombia estimates that, at one time, 95 percent of its cigarettes in that country were contraband. He says that British American Tobacco encouraged and benefited from smuggling as a way to establish market dominance for its own products and those of its parent company. Evidence suggests that Philip Morris did the same—for example, by heavily advertising its cigarettes in Colombia at a time when its legal imports were next to zero. Both British American Tobacco and Philip Morris also initiated mass advertising campaigns and provided local distributors with favorable wholesale prices at a time "when their sales were almost entirely illegal" (Schapiro 2002:13). Additionally, the companies launched a rather cynical ploy, pressuring and bribing Colombian government officials to "lower taxes as a means of reducing the incentive for smuggling" (p. 15). With the lower tax rates in place, the companies gradually increased their legal imports. On top of all this, evidence suggests that criminal organizations within Colombia used drug profits from their US sales to purchase the contraband tobacco, making the tobacco companies complicit in the laundering of drug proceeds.

This is a global problem, and several countries in Latin America, Europe, and Canada have filed racketeering lawsuits against tobacco corporations. Most of the suits have been dismissed on technical grounds, but some are ongoing. Les Thompson, the former president of Northern

continues

FURTHER EXPLORATION

Box 3.4 continued

Brands, a Canadian affiliate of US-based tobacco corporation R.J. Reynolds, pled guilty to criminal charges in 1999. According to Thompson, Northern Brands engaged in a scheme to avoid paying Canadian taxes by shipping 5 billion cigarettes a year to a small Indian reservation on the US side of the US-Canadian border, with the explicit intention of smuggling them back into Canada for illegal resale. Thompson added that R.J. Reynolds set up Northern Brands expressly for this purpose (cited in Pelley 2000).

the highly speculative derivatives market, an exotic arena of finance capitalism whose cumulative losses spiraled out of control in the late 2000s.

Enron is arguably the most well-known case of corporate fraud in recent history, but Enron is not alone. The wave of corporate fraud cases that came to light in the 2000s implicated some of the most well-known, even venerated, institutions of US capitalism. All told, the instances of corporate financial crime reviewed in this chapter illustrate the devastating economic impact of white-collar crime on American society.

Notes

1. Several members of Madoff's family (including his wife, sons, brother, and niece), as well as business associates, appear to have been complicit in the scheme, raking in millions of dollars themselves (Arvedlund 2010; Foley 2009).

2. For example, Stephen Rosoff, Henry Pontell, and Robert Tillman (2007) note the mergers of AOL and Netscape, BP and Amoco, Chemical Banking and Chase Manhattan, Chevron and Texaco, Disney and Capitol Cities/ABC, Dow and Union Carbide, Exxon and Mobil, IBM and Lotus, Kimberly-Clark and Scott Paper, Time Warner and Turner Broadcasting, Union Pacific and Southern Pacific Railroads, and Westinghouse and CBS.

3. Price-gouging is another practice whose effects are similar to those of price-fixing. Price-gouging involves taking extraordinary advantage of consumers by exploiting loopholes in the law, monopolizing or manipulating the market, or contriving or exploiting product shortages. The most notable cases in recent years have involved the food, pharmaceutical, energy (e.g., Enron), and credit card industries (Friedrichs 2007; Rosoff, Pontell, and Tillman 2007; Simon [1982] 2006).

Still another practice that adversely affects the pocketbooks of consumers is false and deceptive advertising. The advertising industry claims that it serves as "a conduit between businesses' need to inform and the public's need to know," but in practice it "provides very little useful information to consumers, whose desire to evaluate products and services in a knowledgeable way remains largely unfulfilled" (Rosoff, Pontell, and Tillman 2007:64; Simon 2006).

4. Simply put, a financial security is a certificate that represents something of financial value that can be bought and sold.

5. Corporate executives who receive stock options as a part of their compensation also benefit from a practice known as "backdating," whereby their options are priced at a lower price from an earlier date rather than the price on the date they were actually issued, hence increasing their profit when they sell (Sloan 2006).

6. Neil Bush, son of George H. W. Bush and younger brother of George W. Bush, had been given a job on the board of directors of Silverado savings and loan in Colorado while his father was vice president, without any previous experience in banking. He used that position to approve Silverado loans to business associates in exchange for financial remuneration. While vice president, Bush Sr. also intervened to forestall the closing of the failing S&L until after the 1988 presidential election, in which he became president. Neil was given a mere reprimand by the federal Office of Thrift Supervision for engaging in "multiple conflicts of interest" and ordered to desist from any similar activities in the future. As part of a civil lawsuit against Silverado, he also paid a $50,000 fine, which was apparently covered by Republican donors (Carlson 2003; Jackson 1990; Phillips 2004).

7. The state conviction was overturned on appeal on the grounds that the trial judge, Lance Ito (of O.J. Simpson fame), had improperly instructed the jury about the law regarding fraud. The federal conviction was overturned on the grounds that the jury had been influenced by their prior knowledge of the state case.

8. Federal regulators permitted Citigroup to ignore the Glass-Steagall Act even before it was repealed (Greider 2009; Prins 2004).

9. During this time, Brooksley Born, head of an obscure federal regulatory agency called the Commodity Futures Trading Commission, tried to warn the Clinton administration and the US Congress of the risk and fraud associated with the derivatives market and of the danger of financial collapse. Her calls for investigating the fraud and regulating this market were dismissed. Federal Reserve Bank chairman Alan Greenspan reportedly told her that he did not believe in government regulation of fraud; rather, the market would regulate itself (Kirk 2009; Smith 2010).

10. By 2008, the unregulated US derivatives market, including mortgage-backed securities, reached $684 trillion (Prechel and Morris 2010).

11. Business analysts also implicate various rating agencies in the fiscal crisis of the late 2000s. As Nomi Prins explains, "Rating agencies are independent corporations that analyze the debt and corporate structure of [publicly traded] companies and assign a level of creditworthiness to each company based on the company's probability of defaults on its debt" (2004:48). Through collusion with risky investors, or simply being "chronically short-staffed and underfunded," these agencies too often gave low-risk ratings to companies that were, in

fact, involved in high-risk investments (p. 49; see also Cohan 2009; Lardner 2010; Leopold 2009a; Stiglitz 2010).

12. Grubman also was embroiled in a well-publicized conflict of interest with AT&T, upgrading his recommendation from "neutral" to "buy" just prior to the corporation's announcement of a deal that netted Citigroup $63 million in fees. Grubman apparently changed his recommendation at the request of Sandy Weill, the CEO of Citigroup at the time.

13. For reviews of the extensive fraud that occurs in the healthcare, pharmaceutical, insurance, and telemarketing industries, as well as in charity, religious, and media organizations, see Coleman 2006, Friedrichs 2007, and Rosoff, Pontell, and Tillman 2007.

14. Harland Prechel and Theresa Morris (2010) note that the expansion of the "multilayer-subsidiary" corporate structure is an important factor in contemporary corporate malfeasance. By 2004, about 85 percent of Fortune 500 companies were structured in this way. Prechel and Morris also implicate the practice of "off-balance-sheet" accounting, whereby the assets of subsidiaries do not appear on the parent company's financial statements. This practice is legal as along as the subsidiaries "hold passive assets, that is, assets that are not actively managed and are held over the longer term and are expected to generate predictable returns," but it has allowed managers to exploit this "black box" of information to disguise debt and avoid accountability to investors and government regulations (p. 340). Moreover, in the 1990s, managerial accountability was undermined when investors' rights were weakened by a series of court decisions and conservative legal reforms that reduced their capacity to bring class action lawsuits against corporate personnel "responsible for directly engaging in or collaborating on financial malfeasance" (p. 338). Finally, the practice of compensating executives with stock options, which was initially intended as a way to align executives' interests with investors' interests, created "incentives for executives to [artificially] inflate corporate balance sheets to increase the value of their stock" (p. 333).

15. Toffler (2003) notes that Arthur Andersen was founded as an auditing firm, and it was its integrity in this area that built its onetime stellar reputation. She indicts the company's increasingly influential consulting division, which accounted for 40 percent of the company's revenues by 1988 (and was its largest growth area), for fueling the pressure to increase revenues.

16. The fraudulent practices in Global Crossing and Qwest Communications were linked, because these two telecom companies engaged in swaps of their fiber-optical network capacities both between themselves and with other companies, thereby booking "paper" revenue that they did not really earn. Other notable companies implicated in Enron-like scandals include AOL–Time Warner, Boston Chicken, Kmart, Rite Aid, and Xerox (Prins 2004; Reiman 2007; Rosoff, Pontell, and Tillman 2007; Toffler 2003).

As a result of the fraudulent accounting practices implicated in these scandals, the US Congress passed the Sarbanes-Oxley Act in 2002, which "increased reporting requirements, penalties, and oversight over audits, financial reports, corporate counsels, senior executives, and Boards of Directors" (Snider 2010:572; see also Prins 2004; Reiman 2007; Toffler 2003). But by the time of the 2008–2009 financial crisis, many of these reform initiatives had been rolled back.

17. Cheney also was able to defer payments (plus interest) on his compen-

sation for 1999 for five years, thereby remaining financially linked to Halliburton through much of his vice presidency (Prins 2004; see Chapter 5).

18. Scahill also singles out the pharmaceutical giant Pfizer, which settled "a slew of criminal and civil cases, including Medicaid fraud" for $2.3 billion in 2009, yet "continues to do a robust business with the government" (2009a:4). As late as 2010, federal investigators were also still uncovering massive fraud in Iraq that has led to "dozens of indictments and convictions for corruption" (Glanz 2010:A3). Some of the cases even "involve people who are suspected of having mailed tens of thousands of dollars to themselves from Iraq, or of having stuffed the money into duffel bags and suitcases when leaving the country." As Stuart Bowen, head of the Office of the Special Inspector General for Iraq Reconstruction, said, "I've had a continuing sense that there is ongoing fraud that we have not been able to nail down" (quoted in Glanz 2010:A3).

4

Corporate Crime Against Workers, Consumers, and the Environment

IN *UNSAFE AT ANY SPEED*, PUBLISHED IN 1965, RALPH NADER exposed the structural design defects in General Motors' Corvair automobile that caused it to become unstable and overturn at high speeds. Nader offered the Corvair not as an isolated case but as an example of all-too-common corporate misconduct that sacrifices "human well-being for profits." His critique of the automobile industry established him as the leading spokesperson of the contemporary consumer rights movement, which seeks "to control the power of economic interests [that] ignore the harmful effects of their applied science and technology" ([1965] 1972:ix). It also gave impetus to federal legislation that established the National Highway Traffic Safety Administration, a division of the Department of Transportation, to regulate the automobile industry in the United States.

Several years later, in 1971, Ford Motor Company chairman Henry Ford II and Ford president Lee Iacocca met with President Richard Nixon in the White House to express their concern about NHTSA safety standards. Excerpts from White House tapes reveal that Ford told the president: "[I]f the price of cars goes up because emission requirements is gonna be in there, . . . safety requirements are in there, bumpers are in there, . . . people [will] stop buying [our] cars . . . [and] buy more foreign cars" (quoted in Cullen et al. 2006:142–143). Iacocca added that he had repeatedly complained to Department of Transportation officials that the automotive industry could not withstand further regulation: "[T]he Japs are in the wings ready to eat us up alive. So I'm saying . . . 'Would you guys cool it a little bit? You're gonna break us.' . . . And they talk about Naderism, and . . . the great pressure on them. . . . And they say, 'Hold it. People want safety.' I say, 'Well . . . what do you

87

mean they want safety? We get letters. . . . We get thousands on customer service. You can't get your car fixed. We don't get anything on safety!'" (pp. 143–144). President Nixon was very sympathetic to Ford and Iacocca's antiregulatory stance: "[W]e can't have a completely safe society or safe highways or safe cars and pollution-free and so forth. Or we could . . . go back and live like a bunch of damned animals. . . . But . . . the environmentalists and . . . the consumerism people . . . aren't really one damn bit interested in safety or clean air. What they're interested in is destroying the [capitalist] system" (p. 142).

This conversation took place around the time that Ford Motor Company was manufacturing the Pinto, which, as explored in Chapter 2, had a structural design defect that made it an incendiary device if hit by another vehicle from the rear, even in a low-speed collision. Ford managers and engineers knew about the design problem before the Pinto was put on the market, and had considered alterations that could have prevented the gas leakage, yet decided against making any of these changes. Eventually, the NHTSA did force Ford to recall the Pinto and fix the problem, but only after considerable resistance and delay by the company. In the meantime, many people suffered serious burn injuries and some died. After the controversy was made public, Ford also was forced to pay many millions of dollars as a result of civil lawsuits brought against it, and was even prosecuted in an Indiana criminal court for "reckless homicide" in the 1978 deaths of three teenagers—Judy, Lyn, and Donna Ulrich. This was the first time in history that a homicide indictment had been brought against a corporation for manufacturing a defective product (corporations may be considered "persons" for the purpose of criminal prosecution). But the jury found reasonable doubt as to Ford's criminal intent, a rather abstract concept when it comes to an organizational entity, and it acquitted the company (Cullen et al. 2006).

An incident that occurred in the wake of the reckless homicide trial is worth noting as well, because it entailed charges of murder and manslaughter brought against individual perpetrators. The case involved a Chicago-area firm called Film Recovery Systems (FRS), a multimillion-dollar company that salvaged silver from used x-ray plates. The process of silver extraction involves soaking the plates in a cyanide solution. Most of the employees at the FRS plant were immigrant workers from Mexico and Poland who could not speak or read English very well and who thus did not understand the labels on the 140 cyanide tanks. The employees were required to add and remove plates from the tanks manually, but they were not given proper protective gloves, boots, or aprons. And although inhaling cyanide fumes can be deadly, the workplace was not properly ventilated, and the workers were not given respirator masks. In 1983, Stefan Golab, a 59-year-old Polish immigrant, died from cyanide exposure. A week later, the company was cited for 17 OSHA violations. The Occupational Safety and Health Administration also learned that the company had not warned its workers about the dangers of cyanide and that other workers had suffered recurring bouts of vomiting, headaches, and dizziness. One employee had lost 80 percent of his eyesight from a splash at his tank (Frank and Lynch 1992; Rosoff, Pontell, and Tillman 2007).

As a result of Golab's death, the FRS president, plant manager, and foreman were convicted of murder and received 25-year prison sentences. The company itself was also convicted of manslaughter and fined $24,000. Due to a minor technicality, however, the convictions were overturned on appeal when an appellate court ruled that the defendants and the company had been convicted of two mutually inconsistent offenses (murder and manslaughter). Nevertheless, the FRS prosecution was a precedent-setting workplace injury case. While there had been prior corporate manslaughter cases, there had never before been an indictment for murder. Stephen Rosoff, Henry Pontell, and Robert Tillman (2007) favor more prosecutions of this nature, hoping they will deter work-related deaths. The stigma of criminal penalties, they believe, may potentially be more effective than civil or regulatory sanctions.

The criminal prosecutions of the Ford Pinto and FRS cases were unusual, but the physical harms that people suffer as a result of such corporate malfeasance are not. In this chapter, we consider corporate crime against workers, consumers, and the natural environment.

Crimes Against Workers

Corporate crime against workers falls into two general categories of hazardous conditions: workplace accidents and exposure to disease-causing substances. The injurious consequence of the former is immediate, while the impact of the latter may not become apparent for years, even decades.

Workplace Accidents

When considering the problem of workplace accidents, the term "accident" should be used advisedly, because in many cases these accidents could have been avoided. During the 1980s, for example, the state of

Texas recorded 1,436 deaths in the construction industry, more than any other state in the nation. In one illustrative Texas case, a crane operator was electrocuted to death when his crane hit an overhead power line. When the company, Baytown Construction, was cited by OSHA for violating regulations that require cranes to be operated with at least 10 feet of clearance between power lines and any part of the crane, Baytown blamed the accident on employee misconduct. OHSA argued, however, that Baytown was responsible, because it had not provided its employee with proper training or safety protection (Rosoff, Pontell, and Tillman 2007).

In another case, in North Carolina in 1991, an explosion and fire at a chicken-processing plant, Imperial Food Products, caused the deaths of 25 workers and injured 56 others. According to Judy Aulette and Raymond Michalowski's account, the fire "started because of the unsafe practice of repairing hoses carrying hydraulic fuel while continuing to maintain cooking temperatures with gas flames under large vats of oil. To minimize downtime, Imperial Food Products routinely left its gas-fired chicken fryer on while repairing adjacent hoses carrying flammable hydraulic fluid" (2006:61). An investigation by North Carolina's state insurance department also found "that during a repair operation, the incoming hydraulic line separated from its coupling . . . and began to discharge the fluid at high pressure. This high pressure and subsequent flow resulted in the hydraulic fluid being sprayed . . . onto the nearby cooker. Ignition of the fuel was immediate" (cited in Aulette and Michalowski 2006:62).

Aulette and Michalowski add that there was only one fire extinguisher in the plant and no sprinkler system or "automatic cutoffs on the hydraulic or gas lines" (2006:62). On the day of the fire, neither were there any "working telephones to call the fire department. . . . An employee had to drive several blocks to the fire station to inform them that there was a serious fire in the plant" (p. 62). All but one of the workers who were killed died from smoke inhalation; the other died from burn injuries. Workers at the plant claimed that the company deliberately kept exits locked to keep workers from stealing chicken nuggets. "In addition to locked doors, exits were unmarked and . . . [t]here had never been a fire drill in the plant or any fire safety instruction of employees" (p. 61). Aulette and Michalowski conclude:

> [T]he single most important factor . . . [in] the 25 deaths was the lack of readily accessible routes to safety. . . . Particularly telling is the fact that a number of the dead were found in a large freezer where they had retreated to escape the fire. Once inside the freezer they were protected from the heat and fire, but they were unable to close the door tightly

enough to keep out the toxic smoke. The fact that these workers had sufficient time to reach the freezer indicates that in all likelihood they would also have had sufficient time to escape the building if there had been adequate pathways to safety. (p. 60)

Moreover, the state of North Carolina was implicated in the incident because elected officials had refused to use federal OSHA money to help fund state safety inspections, which "had fallen to their lowest level in 16 years" (p. 46). One reason for this was that the state would have had to provide matching funds, which a majority of North Carolina legislators did not want to do. This practice was also consistent with a long-standing policy in the state of encouraging corporate investment by "limiting unionization and blocking the power of regulatory agencies" (p. 47).

Often the companies involved in industrial accidents have a history of OSHA violations, although the penalties that are issued are often too inconsequential to deter them from further misconduct, resulting in continued preventable injuries and deaths. McWane Inc., based in Birmingham Alabama, has been one of the most egregious corporate violators. Employing about 5,000 workers in a dozen metal-foundry plants around the country, McWane has been cited for nearly 500 safety violations since 2005, four times more than all of its six major competitors combined (Rosoff, Pontell, and Tillman 2007). Workers have been seriously burned, maimed (including severed limbs), and even killed. They labor in "dim, dirty, hellishly hot" conditions and have been forced to suffer indignities such as urinating in their pants because they are denied bathroom breaks (Barstow and Bergman 2003:1).

Another dangerous occupation in which workers are vulnerable to death and injury from explosions, fires, and cave-ins is mining. During the first six years of the George W. Bush administration, mining deaths increased to a 10-year high, reaching 47 in 2006 (Frank 2007). Critics blamed this increase on the administration's rollbacks of mine safety regulations, the appointment of former mine industry executives and lobbyists to important regulatory positions, the dramatic cutting of agency budgets and enforcement staff, and the reduction in penalties for law violators. They also noted the administration's opposition to proposals that would "require stronger standards on oxygen availability for mine emergencies, mine rescue teams, communications and tracking devices; . . . immediate notification of accidents and rapid emergency response; . . . [and] mandatory minimum penalties for egregious and repeated violations" (Dreier 2006:6; Kennedy 2004).

The explosion at Sago Mine in West Virginia in January 2006, which killed 12 miners, was particularly noteworthy for drawing public attention to the problem, especially because the operator of the mine, International Coal Group, had been cited 273 times for safety violations since 2004, although none of the fines had "exceeded $460, roughly one-thousandth of 1 percent of the $110 million net profit" earned by the company in 2005 (Urbina and Lehren 2006:1). Congress responded by passing new mine safety legislation, which took effect in 2009, to implement provisions that had been previously resisted by the Bush administration (Huber 2007). Nonetheless, in April 2010 in West Virginia, an explosion at the Upper Big Branch mine, operated by Performance Coal Company, killed 29 workers, the largest mining disaster in a quarter century. Performance Coal, a subsidiary of Massey Energy Company, also had a significant history of safety violations, including 57 alone in the month preceding the explosion. In 2009, Massey Energy had paid federal fines totaling $168,393, an amount too small to deter the negligent conduct of a corporation that earned a net income of $24 million in the fourth quarter of that year alone (Cooper 2010; *Huffington Post* 2010).

Insidious Injuries

Unlike the workplace accidents discussed so far, many occupational hazards experienced by workers are not immediately observable. Rather, they involve debilitating diseases that take a long time to develop. Craig Calhoun and Henryk Hiller (1988) label these types of diseases **insidious injuries**, which Rosoff, Pontell, and Tillman (2007) call **postponed violence**. These injuries entail diseases for which the link between the cause of the malady and its manifest symptoms is obscure. They have a long gestation period and "strike only a segment of the exposed population, either randomly or patterned by varying individual vulnerabilities." Moreover, they "manifest themselves by raising . . . risk for diseases that also have other causes" (Calhoun and Hiller 1988:163). Occupational exposure to workplace toxins, for instance, may multiply the risk of cancer from other sources such as cigarette smoke and air pollution.[1]

Exposure to asbestos has been one of the most publicized sources of insidious injuries, affecting millions of workers in the United States. Asbestos is a fibrous mineral mined from rock, and has been used mainly as a fire retardant in products such as textiles, brake linings, and especially construction materials (insulation, ceiling and floor tiles, pipe wrap, shingles, textured paint, cement). Asbestos fibers can crumble and become airborne. Long-term inhalation of these fibers can cause several debilitating if not fatal lung diseases, as well as damage to other internal organs.[2]

The Johns-Manville Corporation has been a major manufacturer of asbestos over the years. Internal company documents going back to the 1930s and 1940s indicate that Johns-Manville had full knowledge of the harmful effects of its product. To protect itself from financial liability, Johns-Manville had a policy of negotiating settlements with sick workers if they agreed to drop all other claims against the company. In addition, a Johns-Manville medical director advised that workers who had contracted illnesses but who had not yet manifested debilitating symptoms should not be informed of their condition. It was not until 1964 that Johns-Manville finally warned workers of the dangers of asbestos exposure. By 1972 it was still refusing to install a dust-control system to protect them. Company executives had calculated that it was more profitable to pay worker compensation to disabled employees or to the families of the deceased than to install the system (Calhoun and Hiller 1988).

In 1973 the federal government began implementing various policies to ban some asbestos applications and to ensure that asbestos in schools would be replaced if it did not meet safety requirements.[3] Several asbestos manufacturers have lost civil lawsuits and have been forced to pay millions of dollars in damages to injured or deceased workers or their families. In 1982 Johns-Manville negotiated a bankruptcy settlement with the government and was allowed to reorganize. The settlement called for the company to set up a trust fund of nearly $3 billion to settle claims with injured parties in exchange for immunity from further lawsuits (Calhoun and Hiller 1988; Rosoff, Pontell, and Tillman 2007).

Mining is another industry in which exposure to asbestos occurs, but here pneumoconiosis, or black lung disease, is a concern as well. Black lung disease is caused by long-term exposure to coal dust, which accumulates in the lungs, reducing lung capacity and leading to respiratory disease. During the 2000s, black lung disease was on the rise, even among younger workers, which health officials attributed to longer working hours and the drive to extract coal from more difficult locations. One study attributed the rise to increased exposure to airborne crystalline silica, a rock byproduct that causes scarring of lung tissues, which can be fatal (Davidson 2010; Maher 2009).

Textile manufacturing is another industry in which workers are victimized by insidious injuries. Exposure to cotton dust causes an irreversible lung disease called byssinosis, or brown lung. The industry's history of denying harm and suppressing information parallels that of the asbestos industry. J.P. Stevens, the second largest textile manufacturer in the United States, is one of the most notorious perpetrators of workplace-induced byssinosis, and it has been singled out by the National Labor Relations Board as "the greatest labor-law violator" in the country (Rosoff, Pontell, and Tillman 2007:180).

Workers also have been exposed to dangerous workplace conditions in the nuclear weapons industry. Beryllium, a metal that is used to encase nuclear weapons, creates a dust byproduct that, when inhaled, can cause berylliosis, an incurable and potentially fatal lung disease. Workers at weapons plants in Ohio and Pennsylvania claim to have been exposed to levels of beryllium dust that were a hundred times the federal safety limit (Rosoff, Pontell, and Tillman 2007).

The nuclear power industry, too, has been a source of insidious injuries, as brought to public attention by the 1983 film *Silkwood*, based on a true story. In the early 1970s, Karen Silkwood was employed by the Kerr-McGee Corporation, a company in Oklahoma that manufactured highly radioactive (and carcinogenic) plutonium fuel for nuclear reactors. Kerr-McGee had a history of careless handling of plutonium—for example, storing the material in leaking drums and shipping it in improper containers. Inside the plant, a number of workers, including Silkwood, were contaminated. After Silkwood was elected to be a union representative, she decided to go public in an effort to pressure Kerr-McGee to take measures to protect its employees. She contacted a *New York Times* reporter, saying she had obtained internal company documents indicating that Kerr-McGee had falsified records regarding levels of plutonium exposure in its plant. On her way to deliver the documents to the reporter, she was killed in a car accident. Investigative journalist Jack Anderson claimed there was evidence that Silkwood's car had been run off the road and that the documents she was carrying had been stolen.[4] A 1977 congressional investigation, however, concluded that her death had been an accident. The following year a civil jury ruled that Kerr-McGee was liable for having exposed Silkwood to plutonium and was ordered to pay $10.5 million in damages to her estate (Rashke 1981; Rosoff, Pontell, and Tillman 2007).

In spite of incidents such as these, work-related injuries and illnesses continue to be underreported in the United States. In a recent survey of occupational health practitioners (including company doctors and nurses) by the US Government Accountability Office, more than half said they had been pressured to downplay injuries or illnesses, and more than a third said they had been pressured to provide insufficient medical treatment, because their employer wanted to reduce worker-compensation costs or feared hurting its chances of winning contracts. More than two-thirds also said that they knew of employees who were reluctant to report injuries due to fear of disciplinary action (Greenhouse 2009).

Crimes Against Consumers

We now turn to a consideration of additional physical harms associated with the motor vehicle industry, as well as the airline industry, another part of the transportation sector that has unnecessarily put consumers at risk. We also consider consumer harms associated with the food, pharmaceutical, and tobacco industries, as well as those that have had a particular impact on women.

The Transportation Industry

In addition to the Pinto fires, Ford Motor Company was responsible for as many as 300 deaths and even more injuries from the mid-1960s to the mid-1980s because of malfunctioning transmissions that slipped from "park" to "reverse" after the driver and passengers had exited the vehicle. Ford knew about this problem for years but did nothing about it (Barkan 2006; Center for Auto Safety 2010b).[5]

Ford, of course, is not alone in endangering consumers by knowingly allowing dangerous motor vehicles onto the market. The "sidesaddle" fuel tanks on General Motors pickups and trucks built between 1973 and 1991, for instance, which were vulnerable to fuel leaks in accidents, are estimated to have caused more than 1,800 deaths, making this "the worst auto crash fire defect in the history of the United States" (Center for Auto Safety 2010a:1). And faulty rear-end latches on Chrysler minivans built between 1984 and 1995 caused passengers (especially children) in moderate-speed rear-end collisions to be thrown out of the vehicle, killing an estimated 37 people (SafetyForum.com 2003).

At the beginning of the new millennium, Ford once again became embroiled in a major product-defect case, this time involving defective tires manufactured by the Bridgestone Corporation, which were commonly used on Ford's bestselling Explorer sports utility vehicle (SUV) as well as its Ranger and F-series pickup trucks. The tires, which were prone to tread separation that caused blowouts at high speeds, are estimated to have caused more than 270 deaths and more than 800 injuries. The tragedies are made even more egregious by the fact that both Bridgestone and Ford knew about the problem but failed to do anything about it. Bridgestone's initial response to the revelation of the defect was to blame Ford, since the Explorer was dangerously prone to rollover accidents because of its top-heavy design: "a relatively narrow wheel base in proportion to the height and weight of the vehicle" (Mullins 2006:138). Indeed, prior to production of the Explorer, Ford officials knew that their Bronco SUV also had rollover problems and that the

Explorer was potentially even less stable. They also knew about problems with the front suspension that could contribute to poor vehicle handling during a tire blowout or potential rollover, even though Ford had advertised the vehicle as handling like a car. Additionally, Ford had not notified the NHTSA that it had replaced the tires on SUVs sold in other countries. Some 20 million tires were eventually recalled as both companies settled lawsuits in the millions of dollars (Mullins 2006; Naughton 2000; Rosoff, Pontell, and Tillman 2007; *Wisconsin State Journal* 2002).

In the early months of 2010, Toyota was the automobile company that dominated the news, primarily for problems with sticking gas pedals and sudden acceleration of its vehicles. The Japanese automaker, like other companies before it, withheld information about manufacturing defects that would have alerted consumers, and ignored court orders to produce documents. The NHTSA levied a $16.4 million fine for its delaying tactics, the largest ever given to an automobile manufacturer, and forced the company to recall and repair more than 2 million vehicles. At the time of this writing, scores of death and injury lawsuits were under way, with the NHTSA confirming at least 52 deaths (Anderson and Robbins 2010; Booth 2010; Gibb 2010; Von App 2010).

Like the motor vehicle industry, the airline industry also has a reputation for unnecessarily putting consumers at risk. One notable incident involved ValuJet flight 592, which crashed in the Florida Everglades in 1996, killing over a hundred passengers and crew members. According to Rick Matthews and David Kauzlarich's account, the crash was the result of "a fire that erupted after one or more oxygen generators exploded in a cargo compartment" (2006:82). Postcrash investigations indicated that both ValuJet and SabreTech, a maintenance company that did work for the airline, had failed "to comply with a host of regulations concerning the presentation, storage, and transportation of hazardous materials by air" (p. 82). Moreover, the Federal Aviation Administration (FAA) was implicated for its failure to monitor "the general safety of commercial aircraft as well as . . . its refusal to institute safeguards and guidelines that would have protected passengers and crews from crashes like that of flight 592" (p. 82).

ValuJet, an Atlanta-based company, was started in 1992 and grew rapidly, from 2 to 50 aircraft at the time of the flight 592 crash. It was able to offer passengers low-cost airfare by employing a "lean and mean" nonunion work force and outsourcing maintenance tasks to various certified facilities such as SabreTech. One of the functions outsourced to SabreTech was the inspection of aircraft oxygen generators "to determine if they had exceeded their allowable service life of 12 years" (Matthews and Kauzlarich 2006:84).

> Oxygen generators are cylindrical tubes that provide oxygen in emergency situations, when cabin pressure is lost. The generators, along with the oxygen masks, are mounted behind panels above or adjacent to passenger seats in the plane. The generator cannot be activated until the spring-loaded mechanism strikes a percussion cap containing a small explosive charge at the end of the generator. When struck, this cap provides the necessary energy to create an exothermic chemical reaction, which then causes the generator to expel oxygen and tremendous amounts of heat. When [properly] mounted in planes, however, the generators should not cause fires, because they are mounted on top of heat shields. (pp. 84–85)

Guidelines for properly removing and disposing of oxygen generators require that they be stored in a safe, combustible-free environment and secured with safety caps until any remaining oxygen residues are fully expended. Expenditure of the generators is accomplished "by securing them on a nonflammable surface in an area free of combustible substances. Once the chemical reaction has occurred and the canister has cooled, it may be [safely] disposed" (p. 85).

Just prior to the flight 592 crash, three ValuJet planes were brought to the SabreTech facility in Miami for servicing, where SabreTech crews removed the old oxygen generators from the planes and replaced them with new ones. Although ValuJet used its own technical staff to supervise the work, the discarded and mostly nonexpended canisters were improperly marked as "aircraft" parts and placed in cardboard boxes without safety caps and protective packing material as they were prepared for shipping to Atlanta. They were loaded onto the forward cargo bin of flight 592 and stacked on top of each other without being properly secured. Ten minutes after takeoff, the plane exploded and crashed.

While ValuJet and SabreTech were clearly responsible for the crash, so was the FAA, for it has responsibility to oversee the airline industry. The FAA, established in 1958 to regulate civil aviation, had undergone deregulation through the **Airline Deregulation Act** of 1978. The purported intent of the legislation was to increase competition that would reduce costs to consumers, but it also undermined the FAA's authority to regulate industry malfeasance. Prior to the crash of flight 592, FAA inspectors had concerns about the safety of ValuJet's operations. Top FAA officials, however, ignored these warnings, even though ValuJet's accident rate was 14 times higher, and its serious accident rate 32 times higher, than the rates of the major airline carriers. It also had a documented record of "planes skidding off runways, planes landing with nearly empty fuel tanks, oil and fuel leaks that were left unfixed for longer periods of time, and inexperienced pilots making errors of judgment" (Matthews and Kauzlarich 2006:91). Nevertheless, the FAA did nothing about ValuJet until after the flight 592 crash, when its operations were shut down.[6]

The negligence of the airline industry and the FAA is also implicated in the problem of airline security, including the infamous terrorist attacks of September 11, 2001, against the World Trade Center in New York City and the Pentagon in Washington, D.C., which killed more than 3,000 people. The threat of terrorist attack was first brought home to the American public with the tragedy of Pan American flight 103, which exploded over Lockerbie, Scotland, on its way from London to New York in 1988, killing over 260 people. The explosion was attributed to Libyan terrorists who had managed to smuggle aboard a bomb with an electronic timer in a cassette player. Even before then, in the 1960s and 1970s, the FAA had been taking a closer look at the security of airline travel after a series of hijackings by Cuban refugees seeking to return home, but the "risks to the 'flying public' were swept under the rug" (Ridgeway 2005:18). Following the Pan American crash, the FAA was directed by Congress to create a "Red Team," which used simulated "real-time" exercises to test airport security against hijackings and the smuggling of explosive devices onto planes. In the early 1990s, the Red Team reported a security failure rate of 90 percent, but little was done to remedy the problem.

In the years leading up to 9/11, the FAA, as well as other agencies of the US government such as the Federal Bureau of Investigation and Central Intelligence Agency, had knowledge of terrorist plots to blow up planes and even crash them into buildings (Graham 2004; Ridgeway 2005; Shenon 2008; see Box 6.3). But FAA officials "appeared more concerned with reducing airline congestion, lessening delays, and easing airlines' financial woes than deterring a terrorist attack" by taking measures such as toughening airport screening procedures, securing cockpit doors, or expanding the use of on-flight air marshals (Lichtblau 2005:1). In 1999 alone, the three major air carriers—American, Delta, and United—were fined for a total of 1,945 security violations, although by then the penalties had "simply become part of the cost of doing business and . . . cheaper than implementing better security practices" (Ridgeway 2005:27). During the first half of 2001, "the FAA's Office of Civil Aviation Intelligence conducted a series of classified briefs for security officials at 19 of the nation's largest airports," including the airports used by the 9/11 hijackers, which "highlighted the threat posed by terrorists in general and [Osama] bin Ladin in particular, including his threats against aviation," but nothing was done to change security practices (p. 35). On that fatal day, all 19 of the 9/11 hijackers passed through airport security checkpoints that were run by private security firms hired by the airlines, "which had long been held to lower performance standards by airlines that claimed they lacked the money to demand better" (p. 38). And communication breakdowns between the FAA and the North American Aerospace Defense Command (NORAD) prevented the deployment of military aircraft to shoot down the planes before they crashed into the World Trade Center and Pentagon (Farmer 2009; Griffin 2008; Shenon 2008; Thomas 2003).[7]

Foods, Pharmaceuticals, and Tobacco

Decades after Upton Sinclair's exposé of the meatpacking industry (see Chapter 1),[8] millions of Americans continue to get food poisoning and some 5,000 die each year from diseased meat and poultry products, some as a result of corporate malfeasance (Moss 2009; Rosoff, Pontell, and Tillman 2007). In 1998, for example, the press reported that the Department of Agriculture had been "permitting hundreds of meat and poultry plants to operate virtually uninterrupted even while federal inspectors [filed] tens of thousands of citations against them for unsanitary conditions and food contamination" (Jaspin and Montgomery 1998:7A). One Arkansas plant operated by Tyson Foods was cited for 1,753 "critical" violations in 1996 alone, yet it did not lose a single day of production ("critical" is defined by the Department of Agriculture as a condition "certain" to cause contamination, "certain" to reach consumers, and "certain to have a detrimental effect" on consumers [cited in Jaspin and Montgomery 1998:7A]). Clearly, law enforcement against food industry violators was not one of the priorities of the Bill Clinton administration, perhaps because of Clinton's ties to Tyson, which go back to his earlier political career in Arkansas (Fritz 1994; Hitchens 1999).

More recently, concerns about food have focused on tainted ground beef that has been contaminated with the virulent E. coli bacteria. Ground beef is particularly vulnerable to contamination because it often consists of "an amalgam of various grades of meat from different parts of cows," with the low-grade ingredients "cut from areas of the cow that are more likely to have had contact with feces, which carries E. Coli" (Moss 2009:1). Moreover, the components of ground beef often come from different slaughterhouses from different states and even different countries, making it especially difficult to ensure the quality of the meat and identify the source of problems should they occur. Too often, meat producers' attempts to test for product safety are meager, and we do not learn of the problem until people get sick. In one case, a 22-year-old woman suffered kidney failure, seizures, and paralysis from infected meat she ate at a fast-food restaurant. In the summer of 2009, the Department of Agriculture initiated a recall of beef from nearly 3,000 grocers in 41 states.[9]

Disconcertingly, even foods produced for infant children have been found to be contaminated, with studies conducted in the mid-1990s finding traces of pesticides in over half of baby foods tested, including pesticides with neurotoxins and known carcinogenic effects (Rosoff, Pontell, and Tillman 2007). According to the National Academy of Sciences, "Children are more susceptible than adults to most pesticides. . . . [If they] are exposed to compounds that act in the nervous system during periods of vulnerability, they can be left with lifelong deficits. If they're exposed to carcinogens, it can set the stage for cancer later" (cited in Rosoff, Pontell, and Tillman 2007:121).[10]

Concerns about the safety of consumer products have also been directed against the pharmaceutical industry. During the 1980s, for instance, the Eli Lilly pharmaceutical corporation marketed Oraflex, a painkiller intended for arthritis patients. When the company asked the Food and Drug Administration to approve the sale of the drug in the United States, it did not inform the FDA of at least 26 deaths that had been linked to Oraflex overseas. The drug was sold in the United States for about six months, but withdrawn after reports of deaths began circulating in the news. The company and one executive were criminally prosecuted, pled guilty, and were fined (the company was fined $25,000 and the executive $15,000). Some observers estimate that Oraflex caused the deaths of about 50 people overall, as well as serious liver and kidney damage in more than 900 others (Coleman 2006; Rosoff, Pontell, and Tillman 2007).

Although the FDA requires foods, drugs, medical devices, and cosmetics to be tested to ensure safety before they are sold to the public, these tests "are seriously weakened by the fact that the manufacturer, not the FDA," typically conducts the tests (Coleman 2006:145). In the case of pharmaceuticals in particular, "drug companies often have an enormous financial stake" in the testing process, and they have powerful incentives "to bias the testing procedures or even falsify the data" (p. 145). Moreover, much of the FDA budget relies substantially on "user fees" provided by the drug companies themselves, and some 30 percent

Box 4.1 The China Connection

The problem of toxic products imported from China has recently received much media attention in the United States. The initial concern was over dog and cat food. David Goldstein describes the early signs of the problem, which were first publicized in the latter part of 2006:

> America's dogs and cats started dying painful, mysterious and sometimes gruesome deaths. . . . Previously healthy pets would suddenly vomit blood and bile, produce bloody diarrhea and lose control of bladder and bowel. Some animals displayed unquenchable thirst, while others refused to eat or drink at all. Victims became lethargic and withdrawn, their limbs wobbly, eyes cloudy and stomachs painfully distended. Then seizures set in. (2007:5)

It is estimated that between December 2006, when food importers first began monitoring the problem, and February 2007 alone, as many as 39,000 pets were sickened or killed. The problem was finally traced to contaminated wheat gluten in the pet food.

In the ensuing months, we then learned about "antifreeze in toothpaste, banned antibiotics in farmed seafood and lead paint on Thomas the Tank Engine toys—all imported from China and all unwittingly consumed or otherwise used by Americans for months, if not years" (Goldstein 2007:5). Problems with lead in other Chinese-manufactured toys, children's necklaces, and fake Halloween teeth soon came to light. We also learned of Chinese-manufactured baby cribs, some of them best-selling models in the United States, causing the deaths of at least three children who suffered falls resulting from faulty rail design (Possley 2007; Simmons 2007).

Questions were raised as to why the US government was not protecting the public from these harmful products, and the deregulation policies of the Bush administration were harshly criticized. It was actually the *Chicago Tribune,* not the Consumer Product Safety Commission (CPSC), for example, that discovered the problems with the cribs and pressed the reluctant safety commission to issue a recall. Indeed, Nancy Ford, head of the CPSC, had throughout her term of office resisted congressional efforts to increase the commission's staff and responsibility so that it could more effectively monitor problems like this. As a result of the China controversy, however, public pressure to make the CPSC a more effective instrument of public safety will likely increase (Possley 2007; Tankersley and Possley 2008).

of individuals who serve on the numerous advisory boards that are used by the FDA to purportedly "provide objective and detached advice on awarding FDA approval" have direct ties to the companies whose products are being evaluated (Alonzo-Zaldivar 2006; Singer and Baer 2009:22).

The circumstances surrounding the "blockbuster" drug Vioxx, manufactured by Merck & Co., is a case in point (Vioxx is the brand name for rofecoxib, which has also been marketed as Ceoxx and Ceeoxx). Vioxx is an anti-inflammatory drug designed to treat arthritis, acute pain conditions, and dysmenorrhea. Merck put the drug on the market in 1999 until it was withdrawn in 2004 due to reported adverse side effects experienced by thousands of users—including heart attacks, strokes, blood clots, and sudden deaths. Merck had spent over $160 million marketing the drug, which was prescribed to millions of people worldwide, and had earned a profit of about $2.5 billion annually. A subsequent FDA investigation and civil lawsuits brought against Merck revealed that the company had withheld test data showing some of these adverse effects. In 2007 Merck settled the pending lawsuits for $4.85 billion (NewsInferno.com 2007; Singer and Baer 2009; *Wisconsin State Journal* 2007c).

In another pharmaceutical case that came to light in 2004, Warner-Lambert, a division of Pfizer Inc., agreed to plead guilty to two felony counts and pay $430 million in criminal and civil penalties for fraudulently promoting Neurontin, an FDA-approved epilepsy drug, for unapproved purposes such as bipolar disorder, pain, migraine headaches, and drug and alcohol withdrawal (Tansey 2004). It is estimated that up to 90 percent of prescriptions for Neurontin were issued for unapproved uses, helping to boost sales of the drug from $97.5 million in 1995 to nearly $2.7 billion in 2003. Warner-Lambert engaged in such illegal tactics as paying doctors to listen to sales pitches for unapproved uses; treating doctors to trips to Hawaii, Florida, and the 1996 Atlanta Olympics; paying doctors to allow sales representatives to sit in on patient visits; and planting company operatives in audiences at medical education events to contradict unfavorable comments about the drug. Five years later, in 2009, parent company Pfizer was fined $2.3 billion in criminal and civil penalties for fraudulently promoting the painkiller Bextra, which had been removed from the market in 2005 because of concerns about increased risk of heart attack and stroke, as a way to relieve symptoms of osteoarthritis and rheumatoid arthritis (Guilloton 2009).[11]

The tobacco industry is yet another business marked by corporate malfeasance. Smoking has been recognized for decades "as the primary preventable cause of death in the United States" (Rosoff, Pontell, and

Tillman 2007:108). Its role in heart disease and lung cancer is incontrovertible. Even research conducted by the tobacco industry itself, dating back to the 1960s, recognized these adverse effects, although this information was not disclosed until it was leaked three decades later. And it was not until the mid-1990s that we learned that the industry had been manipulating the level of nicotine beyond the amount that occurs naturally in tobacco in order to increase the addictive quality of the product. Internal corporate memos indicate that tobacco company officials viewed cigarettes as nothing more than "nicotine-delivery systems" and saw themselves as being "in the business of selling nicotine" (cited in Rosoff, Pontell, and Tillman 2007:109). Yet they continued to deny that they were manipulating nicotine levels, and they repeatedly suppressed research that demonstrated nicotine's addictive properties (Wiener 2010).

It is now also clear that tobacco corporations, in spite of their denials, intentionally marketed their products to teenagers. Internal documents from Philip Morris, for example, show that in the 1970s the company commissioned a poll to ascertain the smoking habits of youths as young as 14 years of age. Philip Morris wanted to know which competing brands were discouraging the use of its Marlboro cigarettes among the young. An R.J. Reynolds memo indicates that company officials felt "unfairly constrained from directly promoting cigarettes to the youth market," but they believed it was imperative nevertheless to "offer . . . the '21 and under' group . . . an opportunity to use our brands" (cited in Rosoff, Pontell, and Tillman 2007:112).

Much of our current knowledge of industry suppression of information comes from the Liggett Group, one of the smallest of the main tobacco corporations, which broke ranks with the industry by agreeing to settle claims against itself and by releasing what it described as a "treasure trove of incriminating documents" from 30 years of meetings with other tobacco companies (cited in Rosoff, Pontell, and Tillman 2007:111). Although most individual lawsuits against tobacco companies have been unsuccessful, in 1998 the attorneys general of all 50 US states settled lawsuits totaling some $250 billion to recoup public funds that have been spent treating tobacco-related illnesses.[12]

Additionally, in 2006 a federal district judge found the nation's top tobacco companies guilty of racketeering and fraud for deceiving the public about the health impact of smoking (including secondhand smoke), the addictiveness of nicotine, the safety of so-called light cigarettes, and the targeting of youths. This ruling was upheld by a federal appeals court in 2009. At the time of this writing, the tobacco companies were negotiating with the US Justice Department about potential remedies for their crimes. Individual civil suits remain ongoing as well (Wiener 2010; *Wisconsin State Journal* 2009a; Yost 2010).

Crimes Against Women

Over the years, corporate crime against consumers has had a particular impact on women, especially in areas related to reproductive issues.[13] One of the noteworthy cases involved the drug thalidomide. In the early 1960s, thousands of pregnant (mostly European) women who had taken thalidomide, which was prescribed for morning sickness and sleeping disorders, had given birth to severely deformed infants. Although thalidomide was first developed in Europe, Richardson-Merrell, a US corporation, purchased the rights to sell it in the United States even though it knew the drug had already been withdrawn from the German market because of suspected birth defects. The FDA did prohibit the sale of thalidomide in the United States, despite heavy lobbying from Richardson-Merrell, but not before the corporation had distributed free pills for doctors to pass out to patients (Dowie and Marshall 1980).

In the early 1970s, another pharmaceutical corporation, the A.H. Robbins Company, marketed an intrauterine device (IUD), a method of birth control, called the Dalkon Shield to about 2.2 million women in the United States and another 2.3 million worldwide. Sold without adequate premarket testing, the Dalkon Shield turned out to be both ineffective and harmful. A design defect in the wick used to insert and remove the IUD allowed bacteria to travel up into the uterus, where it caused infection. Thousands of women who used the device were rendered sterile, suffered miscarriages, or gave birth to stillborn or premature babies with congenital birth defects. At least 18 women in the United States alone died from its use before the FDA forced its withdrawal from the US market. A.H. Robbins, however, continued to sell the Dalkon Shield abroad for at least another nine months. The company even persuaded the US Agency for International Development (USAID) to distribute it in over 40 countries overseas. One USAID official reported that the IUD was still being used in Pakistan, India, and possibly South Africa five years later. In the late 1980s, after paying millions of dollars to settle thousands of lawsuits, A.H. Robbins agreed to a settlement and declared bankruptcy, reorganized, and established a $2.5 billion fund to compensate victims (Ehrenreich, Dowie, and Minkin 1979; Mintz 1985; Perry and Dawson 1985).

In 1980, women bore the costs of another harmful product when Procter & Gamble sent 60 million sample packages of its superabsorbent Rely tampon to consumers in 80 percent of US households. Unfortunately, Rely not only contained cancer-causing synthetics such as polyurethane, but also allowed potentially deadly bacteria to grow and move from the vagina or cervix into the uterus and then the bloodstream, causing a possibly fatal condition known as **toxic shock syndrome.** Symptoms of this disease include high fever, vomiting, sunburn-like skin rash, peeling skin on hands and feet, and damage to internal organs, including the lungs, which fill with fluid until respiratory or cardiac failure ensues. At Procter & Gamble, complaints about such problems were considered routine—the company had been receiving over a hundred per month—and company officials first attributed them to allergies. In just the first year of distribution, however, the Centers for Disease Control documented 55 fatal and over 1,000 nonfatal cases of toxic shock syndrome. Procter & Gamble did bow to FDA pressure to pull Rely off the market, and agreed to pay for a mass advertising campaign to warn women to stop using the product. But the corporation never admitted that the product "was defective or that they had done anything wrong" (Rosoff, Pontell, and Tillman 2007:134; Swasy 1993).

Another notable case, which came to light in the 1990s, involved the silicone-gel implants used for breast enlargements. Although scientists working for Dow Corning, the leading implant manufacturer, had been concerned about implant leaks and ruptures since the 1970s, Dow falsified some of its quality-control tests and continued to sell the product to some 150,000 women annually for three decades. Dow claims that its critics have not proven any adverse effects from the silicone implant. However, thousands of women have filed legal claims against Dow, alleging that silicone released into their bodies caused tremors, extreme fatigue, and connective-tissue diseases such as rheumatoid arthritis, scleroderma, and lupus. Plaintiffs also believe that children breast-fed by mothers with silicone in their system have suffered similar symptoms. Dow and other breast-implant manufacturers have lost several multimillion-dollar civil lawsuits. In 1995 Dow entered bankruptcy after determining that an agreement it had made the year earlier to pay over $4 billion in liability costs would not cover the claims against it (Rosoff, Pontell, and Tillman 2007).

Crimes Against the Environment

One does not have to work under hazardous conditions or consume dangerous products to be physically harmed by corporate crime. Toxic

FURTHER EXPLORATION

Box 4.2 Fertility Fraud

One of the most noxious areas of white-collar crime is the practice of fertility fraud, "perpetrated against women and couples who are having problems trying to conceive" (Rosoff, Pontell, and Tillman 2007:487). Unscrupulous physicians are sometimes willing to exploit such vulnerable women and couples, who pay an average of $8,000 for fraudulent fertility services. The first known case of fertility fraud, revealed in the early 1990s, involved Cecil Jacobson, a renowned geneticist. Jacobson deliberately deceived a number of his patients by administering "hormone treatments that simulated the effects of early pregnancy" and then telling them they were pregnant when, in fact, they were not (p. 487). He also impregnated women with his own sperm when they thought it was the sperm of their spouses. In 1992, Jacobson was convicted on 52 felony counts of fraud and perjury and received a five-year prison sentence. DNA evidence presented at trial documented at least 15 women who gave birth to children fathered by him; this number may actually be as high as 75 according to some estimates, but many patients declined to come forward for testing.

Another fertility fraud case that became public around this time involved three physicians at the Center for Reproductive Health at the University of California–Irvine, including its director, Ricardo Ash. These doctors conducted unauthorized research on patients with an unapproved fertility drug without their consent, "stole" eggs or embryos from some patients and implanted them in others without their knowledge, and failed to report nearly $1 million in income. The doctors were dismissed from the university. Ash and colleague Jose Balmaceda fled the country to avoid criminal charges. The third physician, Sergio Stone, served two months in jail prior to his release on a $3 million bail bond, after which he was convicted of several counts of fraud and ordered to pay a fine of $50,000 (Dodge and Geis 2003; Rosoff, Pontell, and Tillman 2007).

industrial byproducts such as carbon dioxide emissions, mercury, and countless synthetic chemicals and gases continue to pollute the air, land, and waterways. These industrial byproducts poison fish and wildlife and enter the food chain with deleterious consequences that may not be fully recognized for years. Overall, human exposure to environmental toxins may account for as much as 70 to 90 percent of all cancers (Friedrichs 2007; Reiman 2007; South and Bierne 2006; Szasz 1986a).

Corporate polluters—who constitute what Daniel Faber (2008) calls the **polluter-industrial complex**—continue to view these costs of production as "externalities" they can pass on to the public, rather than as "internalities" to be deducted from their profits by finding ways to change their business operations. In a practice known as **corporate dumping**, some of these externalities—hazardous products and toxic waste that cannot be sold or disposed of in the United States—are shipped abroad to developing countries with weak regulatory structures.[14] In other instances, entire production operations are relocated abroad. These practices can have a **boomerang effect** when, for example, pesticides that are banned in the United States are shipped "overseas for use on foreign crops" and are then "reimported into the US in the foods that we eat" (Frank and Lynch 1992:89; see also Michalowski and Kramer 1987; Mokhiber 1988; South and Bierne 2006).[15]

Toxic Communities

One of the most infamous cases of corporate environmental malfeasance in the United States involved the Hooker Chemical Corporation. During the 1940s and early 1950s, in Love Canal, an abandoned waterway near Niagara Falls, Hooker burned and stored millions of pounds of chemical waste that contained carcinogenic substances such as dioxin and benzene. The canal was subsequently back-filled and turned into a housing development. By the late 1970s, contaminated black sludge began seeping into the basements of homes, and residents reported an unusually high number of miscarriages, stillborn babies, and babies with birth defects. A 1980 study found that over 900 Love Canal children were suffering from "seizures, learning problems, eye and skin irritations, incontinence, and severe abdominal pains" (Griffin 1988:27). Internal Hooker documents indicate that the company had known about the problem as early as 1958 but failed to notify the residents. In 1984, Hooker settled a lawsuit and agreed to pay $20 million to residents who had been forced to move from their homes. In 1995, after 16 years of resistance, Occidental Petroleum, the parent company of Hooker, agreed to reimburse the federal government $129 million for cleaning up the site (Clifford 1998; Friedrichs 2007; Rosoff, Pontell, and Tillman 2007).

The 1996 film *A Civil Action*, based on a true story, depicted a similar situation in Woburn, Massachusetts, an industrial suburb of the city of Boston. Since the 1930s, residents had noticed the red coloring and nauseating odor of Lake Mishawum, the source of their water supply. By the 1970s, residents had become concerned about a growing number of childhood leukemia cases, which they suspected were associated with the discoloration and onerous smell and taste of their drinking water. In 1979 the presence of cancer-causing contaminants was confirmed by scientists from the Environmental Protection Agency; and in 1981 the

Massachusetts Department of Health released a report attributing the high incidence of leukemia as well as kidney cancer to the pollution (Harr 1995; Rosoff, Pontell, and Tillman 2007).

The following year, eight families filed a civil lawsuit against the Cryovac Division of the W.R. Grace Corporation for its negligent chemical waste disposal practices. A jury found in favor of the plaintiffs, but the judge "set aside the verdict on the grounds that the jury had not understood the highly technical data upon which the case had been based" and ordered a new trial (Rosoff, Pontell, and Tillman 2007:256). A few days later, Grace agreed to an $8 million settlement with the plaintiffs, but in a subsequent investigation was indicted in federal court on 12 criminal counts for providing false information to the EPA. The company agreed to plead guilty to one of the charges and pay the maximum fine of only $10,000.

Over the years, other US communities have suffered problems similar to those in Love Canal and Woburn, and in some cases residents have been forced to evacuate their homes because of leaks from hazardous waste sites or contamination of drinking water.[16] One recent case involves the poor, Latino farmworker town of Kettleman City, California, where residents have been reporting an unusual number of serious birth defects in children, primarily cleft lips and palates but also Down syndrome, brain damage, heart problems, and other life-threatening maladies. The cause of these health problems has yet to be verified, but residents and environmentalists implicate multiple environmental toxins. Scores of diesel trucks roll through the town spewing toxic fumes every day. The smell of the chemical pesticides that are sprayed in the fields fills the air. The town's "two municipal wells are contaminated with naturally occurring arsenic and benzene," and the biggest toxic waste dumpsite west of Alabama, operated by Waste Management Inc., lies just three miles away (Leslie 2010:50). In 2009 alone the Kettleman dumpsite "accepted 356,000 tons of hazardous waste, consisting of tens of thousands of chemical compounds including asbestos, pesticides, caustics, petroleum products, and about 11,000 tons of materials contaminated with PCBs [polychlorinated biphenyl compounds]—now banned chemicals linked to cancer and birth defects" (p. 50).

Because these types of problems disproportionately affect poor and minority residents, some researchers have raised concerns about environmental racism. One study estimated that about a third of the hazardous waste landfills in the contiguous United States were located in just five southern states and that 60 percent of the waste contained in these sites was located in three predominately African American zip code areas (Bullard and Wright 1989–1990). In the state of Louisiana in particular, the concentration of chemical plants near poor African American communities between New Orleans and Baton Rouge is referred to as "Cancer Alley" (Faber 2008). More generally, there is a large body of research documenting the extensive racial and ethnic disparities present in exposure to hazardous waste throughout the United States, with black and Hispanic residents more likely to be exposed than white residents (e.g., Cole and Foster 2001; Mohai and Saha 2007; Pulido, Sidawi, and Vos 1996; Stretesky and Lynch 1999). Of course, the displacement of environmental hazards onto developing countries is also a form of environmental racism (Faber 2008).

The animal waste from industrial factory farms, especially pig farms, is also a particular problem, and much more so per acreage compared to small family farms. The smaller operations are capable of using the waste they produce as manure to grow crops on their own land. The larger operations, however, concentrate a huge amount of waste—a "witch's brew" of toxic pesticides, hormones, antibiotics, and disease-causing viruses and microbes—that cannot safely be absorbed by the adjacent land. For this reason, industrial meat producers typically locate their factories in poor and minority communities, which are less able to mount opposition to these harmful environmental practices (Kennedy 2004; Seely 2010).

Other victims of unsafe environmental practices include the poor and working-class people of the coal-rich Central Appalachia region of the United States, ranging from Kentucky and Tennessee to West Virginia and Virginia, where strip-mining is used to "blow off hundreds of feet from the tops of mountains to reach the thin seams of coal beneath. Colossal machines dump the mountains into adjacent valleys, destroying forests and communities and burying free-flowing mountain streams in the process" (Kennedy 2004:114). Massey Energy, which controls almost one-third of the total coal reserves in Central Appalachia, has been involved in civil litigation with residents who claim that their water supply has been poisoned by the oily toxic sludge that seeps into the groundwater (SourceWatch.org 2010b). In one case in 2000, a storage pit in Kentucky that is owned by Martin County Coal, a subsidiary of Massey Energy, spilled 300 million gallons of "thick black lava-like toxic sludge," the largest coal-related spill in US history, "containing 60 poisonous chemicals that choked and sterilized 100 miles of rivers and creeks and poisoned the drinking water of 17 communities" (Kennedy 2004:121). The unfortunate residents in these communities are often forced to choose between the jobs provided by the coal industry and the health of their families.

Box 4.3 Organized Crime and Hazardous Waste

The blurred boundary between organized crime and corporate crime (see Chapter 3) is prevalent in the hazardous waste disposal industry, where disreputable haulers dump hazardous materials in landfills, sewers, and waterways, and along roadways or just about anywhere they wish. This illegal service saves millions of dollars for corporate manufacturers of waste who would otherwise incur far greater costs if they had to dispose of or treat the waste safely themselves (Szasz 1986a).

Corporations have benefited from elements of the **Resource Conservation and Recovery Act** of 1976 that protected them from legal liability for what happens to the waste they turn over to haulers. In his research on the creation of this law, Andrew Szasz (1986a) documented how corporations lobbied heavily for a regulatory structure that would place the burden of responsibility on those involved in the final stage of disposal. He notes that the federal government could have mandated "generators to treat all of their wastes themselves, or legislated that generators retain full responsibility for their wastes even if they assign them to other parties for shipping and disposal" (p. 12).

Corporate generators of hazardous waste argue that "they do not know they are dealing with organized crime" and that "they are in fact being cheated because they pay large amounts for treatment and disposal that are not performed" (p. 17). But since corporations "explicitly fought for [Resource Conservation and Recovery Act] language that entitled them to this state of ignorance," Szasz finds their claims unconvincing. He observes, for example, that "organized crime control of garbage hauling and disposal had been considered a fact of life in New Jersey for decades" and rational industrial managers "would have had ample reason to distrust the identity of their contractual partners" (p. 17). On the other hand, Szasz does not think that corporations consciously wished to create a regulatory structure that encouraged organized crime involvement in hazardous waste disposal. Rather, they simply acted out of a general attitude of indifference and resistance to accepting "social responsibility for . . . the environmental and public health consequences" of their operations (p. 19).

Drill, Baby, Drill

During the 2008 presidential campaign, we heard Republican vice presidential candidate Sarah Palin, among others, exhort the virtues of "drill baby drill" before cheering supporters when she advocated an expansion of oil and gas development. Environmentalists have been concerned about this approach, in part, because the burning of fossil fuels such as oil and coal creates gaseous byproducts that become trapped in the atmosphere—the "greenhouse" effect—that contributes to the problem of global warming.[17] These conditions threaten to dramatically disrupt Earth's ecosystems and patterns of human habitation by melting the polar ice caps and causing sea levels to rise (which can result in flooding of coastal communities and salinization of underground water supplies) and by altering rainfall patterns and moisture levels in soils (which can adversely affect agricultural production). With increased warming, some parts of the world can expect to experience more droughts, whereas other parts can expect intensified rainstorms, flooding, and blizzards as a consequence of increased evaporation from the ocean surface (Clifford 1998; Faber 2008; Heilprin 2006; Kennedy 2004).

Over the years, oil spills caused by offshore drilling also have been an unfortunate byproduct of energy production. The infamous oil spill that occurred off the coast of the once pristine city of Santa Barbara, California, was the first time this problem was brought home to the American public. In January 1969, at the site of a drilling operation that was jointly owned by the Union Oil, Mobil, Texaco, and Gulf oil companies, a viscous black mass erupted from the ocean floor, surging to the surface.[18] Three months later, according to S. Prakash Sethi's account, "the best estimate indicated that at least 3 million gallons" had spilled, spreading over more than 800 square miles of ocean and more than 40 miles of some of the finest beach area in the country (1982:240). Oceanographers described the effect on the fish and wildlife as a "dead sea," noting that it would take "years, even decades, before this area of the ocean returns to normal" (cited on p. 241).

The oil industry's response to the disaster, which outraged the people of Santa Barbara, was simply to note that "such risks are inevitable in major operations of this kind and must be borne in view of the economic returns and the country's growing petroleum needs" (Sethi 1982:247). Numerous lawsuits seeking compensation for damages from the oil companies were forthcoming from property owners, fishermen, boat owners, and other individuals; and the companies agreed to pay several million dollars in out-of-court settlements. Ironically, Union Oil, which had steadfastly maintained that the accident "had been unforeseeable and unpreventable, sued its drilling contractor, the Peter Bawden Company, for negligence," charging that it had caused the spill (p. 259).

In 1989, another notable oil spill involved the oil tanker *Exxon Valdez*, which released nearly 11 million gallons of oil when it struck a reef off the coast of Alaska, devastating the wildlife, environment, and economy of the region. Questions regarding Exxon Corporation's responsibility for the disaster arose as evidence surfaced that the company had known of the ship captain's drinking problem but had failed to take appropriate action. In addition, Exxon had reduced the size of the crew, causing the remaining crew members to work while fatigued. After the spill, the "clean-up response was slow, and it was clear . . . that nobody involved was adequately prepared to handle a disaster of that magnitude" (Cruciotti and Matthews 2006:154). Alyeska Pipeline Service Company, a consortium of seven oil companies that had the responsibility for developing and implementing cleanup plans, was ill-prepared to do so, causing delays that might have mitigated some of the damaging effects. And both the US Coast Guard and the Alaska Department of Environmental Control were lax in meeting their responsibilities to exert regulatory supervision to both prevent and respond to problems. In the end, Exxon was forced to pay $100 million in criminal fines, $1 billion in civil settlements, and $2.5 billion in punitive damages, the latter of which was reduced to about $500 million after a successful appeal (Friedrichs 2007; Oliphant 2008; *Wisconsin State Journal* 2006).

New Orleans, the city that was devastated by Hurricane Katrina in August 2005, is a place that has borne the costs of US dependence on oil. Much has been said about the ineffective response at all levels of government to the hurricane that caused the deaths of hundreds of people and displaced thousands from their homes (see Box 5.2). But too often missed is the fact that the tragedy itself was in large part a result of abusive environmental practices. Environmentalists had been worried for years about the destruction of the city's natural protection against flooding as a consequence of the oil industry's installation of more than 8,000 miles of pipeline canals to transport oil from its offshore drilling stations in the Gulf of Mexico. The installation of these pipeline canals eviscerated about 1,900 square miles of surrounding wetlands, undermining their natural capacity to absorb floodwaters and "storm surges"—the wind-fueled spikes in water level—associated with major hurricanes. But environmentalists' pleas for policies to restore the wetlands fell on deaf ears (Blumenthal 2005a; Faber 2008; Gilgoff 2005).

The city of New Orleans, which covers 364 square miles, including 265 square miles of inland water, lies along the Mississippi River about a hundred miles north of the Gulf. Much of the city, one of the oldest in the southern United States, was built below sea level and was protected from flooding by a 350-mile levee system. In the long term, however, these levees only exasperated destruction of the wetlands, because they prevented the Mississippi River from depositing the silt necessary for the natural replenishment of the area. Moreover, the levee system, decades old by the time of Katrina, was designed to withstand only a Category 3 storm; Katrina was a Category 5 hurricane. Once the levees breached, the water that surged to the other side became trapped in a "bowl"—what residents of New Orleans call "flooding the bowl" (Gilgoff 2005).

Louisiana authorities had long been aware of these problems, yet "they had no comprehensive plan to evacuate people from even the lowest parts of the city, whose virtually every corner lies below sea level" (Gilgoff 2005:27). Scientists at Louisiana State University, for instance, "had warned that even a Category 3 storm could dump up to 27 feet of water in some neighborhoods," and "officials in the New Orleans district office of the US Army Corps of Engineers, which built and administers the levees, pushed to raise the protection level from Category 3 to Category 5" (pp. 27–28). Regrettably, the $2–3 billion it would have taken to prevent the tragedy was deemed too expensive.

In April 2010 the state of Louisiana and the entire Gulf of Mexico region were hit by another devastating tragedy—this one caused by an explosion at the Deepwater Horizon oil-drilling rig, located 40 miles offshore. The explosion at Deepwater Horizon, a project of the London-based BP corporation,[19] killed 11 workers and released millions of gallons of crude oil from its well 5,000 feet below the surface. By mid-July the spill had exceeded 180 million gallons, far surpassing the *Exxon Valdez* disaster. The oil had penetrated the beaches and the already fragile coastal wetlands of the Gulf, and was causing irreparable harm to the fish and wildlife in the area. Ultimately, the cost of cleanup, lawsuits, and harm to the economy of the Gulf, including the devastation of the fishing industry, could be more than $14 billion (Bergin 2010; Kaufman and Berger 2010; Shapley 2010).

The disaster, regrettably, did not come as a surprise to environmentalists, who for many years have been cautioning against the "drill baby drill" mentality. As Tyson Slocum points out, BP has "one of the worst safety records of any oil company. . . . In just the last few years, [it] has paid $485 billion in fines and settlements to the US government for environmental crimes, willful neglect of worker safety rules, and penalties for manipulating energy markets" (2010:2).[20] At a congressional hearing held in May 2010, a BP executive claimed that Transocean, the owner of the Deepwater Horizon rig, which was contracted by BP, was responsible. A Transocean executive, in turn, blamed Halliburton, to which it had subcontracted some of its operations, for the explosion.

FURTHER EXPLORATION

Box 4.4 The Bhopal Disaster

In 1984, another well-publicized accident occurred at a US-owned Union Carbide pesticide plant in Bhopal, an impoverished city in India, when 27 tons of deadly methyl isocynate gas was leaked into the atmosphere, blanketing the city in a cloud of poisonous gas. The leak, which was attributed to a poorly designed safety system that either malfunctioned or was mistakenly turned off, is estimated to have killed as many as 5,000 people and injured 200,000 others, 20,000 permanently (Coleman 2006; Faber 2008; Friedrichs 2007).

Many people considered Union Carbide blameworthy for the "accident" because the pesticide plant had ignored previous warnings from its engineers about the inadequate safety equipment, maintenance practices, and employee training, all of which was made more dangerous by the decision to store an enormous amount of methyl isocynate on-site. Union Carbide officials, however, had ignored these warnings in order to save money. Civil lawsuits were brought against Union Carbide by injured parties and survivors of those who were killed, which the company settled for $470 million. Indian authorities indicted top Union Carbide executive Warren Anderson for manslaughter, but Anderson sought refuge in the United States and avoided prosecution. In 2010, a quarter of a century after the disaster, eight former executives of Union Carbide's Indian subsidiary (including one who had already died) were convicted of criminal negligence, which carries a two-year prison term. Victim advocates criticized the sentence as "the world's worst industrial disaster reduced to a traffic accident" (quoted in Polgreen and Kumar 2010:1). The 425 tons of hazardous waste at the site have yet to be cleaned up (Faber 2008; Polgreen and Kumar 2010; Venkatesan 2003; Vosters 2003).

And in the cascading chain of recrimination and denials, a Halliburton executive blamed the other companies, saying it had followed standard industry practices and federal guidelines. The truth of the matter is that everyone is to blame, including the Department of Interior's Mineral Management Service (MMS) (Bergin 2010; Crum 2010; Hebert 2010; Power, King, and Hughes 2010).

Critics of the MMS cite the conflict of interest in the agency, whereby it had the function of both regulating oil drilling *and* collecting some $13 billion annually from the leasing of rights to drill in federal waters and on federal lands, which amounts to about 95 percent of the revenue collected by the Department of the Interior as a whole.[21] The MMS had given BP a **categorical exclusion** for its Deepwater Horizon facility, which essentially amounted to a waiver of environmental review and a rubber stamping of its operations based on the (dubious) assumption that the project did not pose a significant risk to the environment. Thus BP and its corporate partners were allowed to begin drilling without installing properly functioning safety equipment, including a cement casing around the well that might have plugged a leak in the event of an explosion (Environment News Service 2010; Morrison 2010; Power, King, and Hughes 2010; Siegel 2010).[22]

Five weeks after the explosion, the press reported on an ongoing Coast Guard hearing that was being conducted in New Orleans (Kunzelman, Baker, and Donn 2010). Doug Brown, the chief rig mechanic aboard the Deepwater Horizon platform, testified about a meeting that had taken place just hours before the blowout, in which rig workers and one BP official skirmished over a BP decision "to replace heavy drilling fluid in the well with saltwater" (p. A11). The company wanted to remove the heavy fluid so it could use it for another project, but rig workers were concerned that the seawater would provide "less weight to counteract the surging pressure from the ocean depths." According to Brown, the BP official "overruled the drillers, declaring, 'This is how it's going to be.'" Another rig worker submitted a hand-written statement to the Coast Guard that added: "I overheard upper management talking, saying that BP was taking shortcuts by displacing the well with saltwater instead of mud without sealing the well with cement plugs, this is why it blew out" (p. A11).

In July, a Deepwater Horizon engineer, Transocean employee Mike Williams, testified that the safety system had been in ill repair for months, if not years (Lin and Boxall 2010). At one point, Williams said, he was chastised by a superior for having activated a gas safety valve that had been placed in bypass mode. Williams recalled his supervisor saying, "The damn thing has been in bypass for five years. . . . As a matter of fact, the entire fleet runs them in bypass" (p. A10). Williams also testified that "the pressure regulator valve, which automatically cuts off natural gas flow when it reaches a certain pressure point, was in bypass mode when a burp of gas shot up" from the Deepwater Horizon well into the rig, causing the explosion that set "in motion the worst offshore oil spill in U.S. history" (p. A10).

Additionally, a memo released by the House Committee on Energy and Commerce, which is also investigating the spill, revealed an internal BP inquiry stating that tests conducted by BP less than an hour before the explosion had detected a buildup of pressure that was an "indicator of a very large abnormality" (Kunzelman, Baker, and Donn 2010:A11).

Five hours before the accident, rig workers had detected an unexpected loss of fluid from a pipe that was indicative of a leak in the blowout preventer, a five-story device that is supposed to slam shut in an emergency. After the explosion, when an attempt was made to activate the preventer, there was no hydraulic power to operate the equipment.[23]

Going Nuclear

Over the years, the nuclear weapons industry, whose production peaked during the height of the Cold War in the late 1950s and early 1960s, has released untold gallons of dangerous nuclear waste into the environment.[24] One of its most notorious sites is the Hanford Nuclear Reservation in Washington State near the Columbia River, which contains "more than 1,300 nuclear waste sites within its perimeter." In this area, "[t]renches, tanks, ponds, sand-covered pits, and underground storage cribs hold over a billion cubic meters of hazardous materials," endangering the more than 13,000 people living near the site, who "are believed to have received significant dosages of radiation that [has] leaked out from the facility" (Coleman 2006:80; see also Clifford 1998; Kauzlarich and Kramer 2006).

One of the most egregious cases of willful criminality involving the nuclear weapons industry occurred at the Rocky Flats facility in Colorado, operated by Rockwell International. Rockwell, which had been contracted by the Department of Energy to build nuclear warheads, not only knowingly exposed its workers to dangerous levels of radioactivity but also dumped radioactive waste into local rivers. In 1992, Rockwell pled guilty to five felony violations of environmental law and agreed to pay an $18.5 million fine. Department of Energy officials were implicated, too, for complacency in fulfilling their obligation to protect the public. Astonishingly, around the time of the plea agreement, the Department of Energy actually awarded Rockwell a $22.6 million performance bonus (Clifford 1998; Kauzlarich and Kramer 2006; Rosoff, Pontell, and Tillman 2007).

Currently the problem of global warming has generated more interest in expanding the production of civilian nuclear power, which proponents believe is a clean source of energy. Environmentalists, however, have warned us about the potential hazards of moving energy policy in this direction. This concern was first brought home to the American public in 1979, when the cooling system that controlled temperatures in the reactor core at the Three Mile Island plant in Pennsylvania malfunctioned and released radioactive coolant into the environment.[25] While the long-term carcinogenic health effects of the accident, which was attributed to mechanical and human error, remain in dispute, it did halt the construction of new power plants in the United States, led to the imposition of new safety regulations, and give impetus to the anti–nuclear power movement (Gray and Rosen 2003; Walker 2004).

The costs of building state-of-the-art facilities that maximize public safety are very expensive, however, and according to Christian Parenti (2009), the most pressing issue is what happens to the older facilities that are still in operation. Parenti points out that most of the plants that are currently in operation were "opened in the early 1970s and designed to operate for only 40 years" (p. 26). Yet more than half of them have received new licenses to stay open for another 20 years.

The older plants, however, are plagued by all-too-common problems: deteriorating facilities, lax maintenance, and secrecy. Parenti notes, for example, that the Oyster Creek plant in New Jersey, slated to close in 2009, was granted a 20-year extension by the Nuclear Regulatory Commission on April 8, 2009. One week later, workers at the plant discovered a leak of radioactive water, and more significantly, in August, a leak of about 7,200 gallons a day that "contained 500 times the acceptable level of radiation for drinking water" (p. 26). The leak was caused by the deterioration of old pipes buried in a concrete wall, which become brittle over time and must be routinely replaced with new ones. The leaking pipes in question "had erroneously—or perhaps fraudulently—been listed in [Oyster Creek] paperwork as replaced" (p. 26). Moreover, nuclear facilities throughout the United States, as well as thousands of chemical facilities nationwide, continue to remain vulnerable to terrorist attack (Kennedy 2004; Marek 2006).

Robert Kennedy Jr. (2004) also has raised concerns about the security of nuclear (and chemical) plants in the face of a potential terrorist attack.[26] Indeed, security breaches have been uncovered at these facilities by both journalists and Nuclear Regulatory Commission agents who were able to enter the plants, but little has been done to remedy such life-threatening vulnerabilities. One power plant, Indian Point Nuclear, is located just 24 miles north of New York City and stores about 1,500 tons of highly radioactive fuel waste, which, if released, could expose some 21 million people to harmful radiation. On September 11, 2001, one of the planes that hit the World Trade Center came within a few thousand feet of the plant. Still, as of the time of this writing, the US government has not enforced a no-fly zone over the plant, which it does even for places like Disney World.

Summary

In this chapter we examined notable cases of corporate malfeasance in three broad areas of physical harm from white-collar crime: crimes against workers, consumers, and the environment. We noted that the injurious consequences of hazardous working conditions can be both immediate and delayed, from workplace accidents to environmentally induced diseases that gestate for years. Regarding crimes against consumers, we have reviewed notable cases in the motor vehicle and airline industries; cases in the food, pharmaceutical, and tobacco industries; as well as cases that have had a particular impact on women. And we noted how crimes against the environment, including oil spills and nuclear accidents, can expose entire communities to harmful toxic substances and destroy the natural environment.

Notes

1. To be sure, workers are also exposed to harmful chemicals that have immediate effects. In a well-known case that came to light in the 1970s in Virginia, workers at a pesticide plant operated by Life Sciences Products, a subsidiary of Allied Chemical Corporation, were exposed to highly toxic levels of Kepone and suffered dizzy spells, bodily tremors, and blurred vision after only a few weeks at the plant. The pesticide also contaminated the local waterways, all but destroying the fishing industry in the area (Coleman 2006; Rosoff, Pontell, and Tillman 2007).

2. Mesothelioma, a cancer that affects the linings of the lungs, heart, and abdomen, is the most well-known disease associated with asbestos exposure.

3. Although the use of asbestos in new construction projects has been banned in many countries, it is still used in the United States.

4. Workers at other plants also have reported harassment and threats from their employers for speaking out about problems at nuclear facilities (Rosoff, Pontell, and Tillman 2007).

5. Ford also has been cited by the federal government for "fraudulent concealment" of a faulty ignition system, installed on over 22 million vehicles sold from 1983 to 1995, that caused vehicles to stall (Mullins 2006).

6. At the time of this writing, the Federal Aviation Administration was seeking a $22.2 million fine against American Airlines for improper maintenance of wiring that could have put passengers in danger (Koenig 2010).

7. For detailed accounts of what transpired on that day, see Ahmed 2005, Farmer 2009, Griffin 2008, and Ridgeway 2005. For further discussion of 9/11 in this book, see Chapter 6, especially Box 6.3.

8. The meatpacking industry continues to remain one of the most dangerous workplace environments (Cohen 2006).

9. In 2010, "a salmonella outbreak at two Iowa egg plants sickened hun-

dreds of people and led to the recall of about 555 million eggs—one of the largest egg recalls in history" (Zajac and Hamburger 2010:A9). The owner of the egg farm, who has been at the center of the controversy, is Austin "Jack" DeCoster, an acknowledged "habitual violator" of government regulations (Foley 2010:A6). A survey of Food and Drug Administration scientists found that only half had full confidence that the FDA could protect consumers from food-borne illness in eggs (Zajac and Hamburger 2010).

10. The extensive use of chemical additives in the US food supply (such as preservatives, bleaching and color additives, hormones, and artificial sweeteners) has also raised health concerns, as has the excessive sugar and fat content of American diets. Critics of the food industry have been especially concerned about the way unhealthy food products are marketed to children on television. According to David Simon, the most serious "nutritional problem emanating from the television advertising blitz aimed at children is that the most advertised food products are sugar-coated cereals, candies, and other sweet snack foods" ([1982] 2006:142). These advertisements are very effective in influencing children's food preferences, which are typically honored by parents. Although some people have called for greater regulation of television advertising directed at children, the food and advertising industries have of course resisted. One advertising executive, cited by journalist Bill Moyers, told the Federal Trade Commission, "Children, like everyone else, must learn the marketplace. Even if a child is deceived by an ad at age four, what harm is done? Even if a child perceives children in advertisements as friends and not actors, selling them something, where's the harm?" But Moyers finds this attitude, which treats children "as members of a vast collective to be hustled" by corporations, rather "astonishing" (cited in Simon 2006:143–144).

11. In another recent drug case, Purdue Pharma and its top executives were fined $634.5 million for deliberately misleading the public about the risk of addiction from its painkiller OxyContin (*Wisconsin State Journal* 2007a).

12. Forty-six states received the bulk of this money, about $246 billion, through a collective settlement.

13. The elderly are another group of people whose vulnerability has made them targets for white-collar crimes (see Friedrichs 2007; Rosoff, Pontell, and Tillman 2007).

14. For a recent consideration of the problem of global trafficking in electronic waste—that is, irreparable or obsolete electronic equipment that, when improperly disposed, pollutes the environment with toxic metals—see Gibbs, McGarrell, and Axelrod 2010.

15. For a consideration of the emerging field of "green criminology," which addresses the concerns of environmental harm, see South and Bierne 2006.

16. More recently, in the late 1990s, residents in the Hickory Woods neighborhood of Buffalo, New York, 25 miles down the road from Love Canal, began complaining about "Love Canal symptoms" caused by toxic waste byproducts left over from the operation of a steel plant. Environmentalists cited delays and funding cuts in the federal government's Superfund cleanup program as part of the problem (Goldbaum 2000; Rosenberg 2003).

17. Other sources of global warming include methane, sulfur dioxide,

nitrous oxide, and chlorofluorocarbons (from refrigeration and aerosol sprays), the latter of which also reduce the stratospheric ozone layer that blocks a portion of the sun's radiant energy; as well as deforestation, which also undermines Earth's capacity to absorb heat-trapping gases (Clifford 1998; Faber 2008; Heilprin 2006; Kennedy 2004).

Those who doubt the human sources of global warming often fail to distinguish between "weather" and "climate change." Whereas weather refers to short-term atmospheric conditions, climate refers to how the atmosphere "behaves" over relatively long periods of time. There is little doubt that Earth's temperature has been rising over time, and the overwhelming consensus in the scientific community is that human activity is a significant contributor (Begley and Murr 2007). Still, there are a minority of scientists, some of whom work for corporate-sponsored think tanks, who seek to undermine the majority view (Kennedy 2004; Mooney 2005).

Recently, computer hackers broke into private e-mails of prominent scientists, revealing discussions that appeared to undermine the credibility of the case for human activity as the primary cause of global warming (Revkin 2009). The e-mails suggest that a handful of scientists discussed ways to present and interpret evidence in a couple of studies that examined data on long-term temperature trends. The scientists in question have said that the language they used in the e-mails has been misinterpreted by critics. One scientist admitted that what was said "sounds incriminating," but when you actually examine what they were talking about, "there's nothing there" (quoted in Revkin 2009:2). Indeed, the controversy over these e-mails has not dislodged the scientific consensus. Wherever one stands on this issue, however, there is little doubt that the polar ice caps are melting, and oil companies are taking advantage of this by buying up rights to explore Arctic and sub-Arctic lands that have already been exposed, or that are soon to be exposed, in order to drill for more oil (Kurlantzick 2006).

18. According to S. Prakash Sethi's account, the spill stemmed from the attempt to remove the drill pipe from a well depth of 3,479 feet: "Suddenly, mud began trickling up through the pipe; soon it became a geyser of natural gas and mud. With tremendous effort, the crew successfully sealed the well in less than 15 minutes. . . . [But immediately] the attempt to contain the pressure . . . caused a rupture in the ocean bottom" (1982:238).

19. BP, formerly called British Petroleum, changed its name to Beyond Petroleum to sound more environmentally friendly, but it remains one of the largest oil drillers in the world. The Deepwater Horizon site was run by its subsidiary BP America.

20. In August 2010, BP agreed to pay a record $50.6 million fine for failing to correct safety problems at its Texas City refinery, where an explosion killed 15 workers in 2005 (Plungis 2010).

21. To remedy this problem, Secretary of Interior Ken Salazar announced a restructuring of the MMS to divide its conflicting functions into separate independent entities with different responsibilities (Environment News Service 2010).

22. The question remains as to whether this backup safety mechanism will function properly at depths of 5,000 feet or more. At the time of this writing, MMS had given categorical exclusions to 20 other deepwater drilling projects (Morrison 2010; Siegel 2010). Initially intended to speed up the review of small

projects like the installation of stop signs, categorical exclusions were extended by an executive order during the Bush-Cheney administration to "massively complicated deepwater drilling projects" like Deepwater Horizon; and the Obama administration had done nothing to change this practice (Plumer 2010:9).

23. As BP worked furiously to cap the leaking well, little attention was given to the unknown long-term risks of further leaking from abandoned wells, which often repressurize over time like dormant volcanoes and whose exposure to underground pressure and seawater causes "cement and piping to corrode and weaken" (Donn and Weiss 2010:A9). Government officials estimate that the tens of thousands of abandoned wells in the United States and its coastal waters "are badly sealed, either because they predate strict regulation or because the operating companies violated rules." There are more than 27,000 abandoned wells in the Gulf of Mexico alone.

24. For a discussion of the human exposure to harmful fallout from the atmospheric testing of nuclear weapons in the Nevada desert by the US government in the 1950s and 1960s, see Fradkin 1989. Daniel Goldhagen (2009) also reminds us of President Harry Truman's momentous decision to drop atomic bombs on Hiroshima and Nagasaki at the end of World War II in August 1945. Goldhagen considers the bombings to be a state crime of mass murder, since "Truman knew that each would kill tens of thousands of Japanese civilians who had no direct bearing on any military operation" (p. 3). People in the United States commonly assume that the bombings were necessary to end the war and save the lives of US troops, but as Truman knew at the time, and as his advisers (including his military advisers) had told him, these rationales were not true (Alperovitz 1996; Goldhagen 2009). Even Dwight Eisenhower, then–supreme commander of Allied forces in Europe, voiced his "grave misgivings" to Secretary of War Henry Stimson:

> first on the basis of my belief that Japan was already defeated and that dropping the bomb was completely unnecessary, and secondly because I thought that our country should avoid shocking world opinion by the use of a weapon whose employment was, I thought, no longer mandatory as a measure to save American lives. It was my belief that Japan was, at that very moment, seeking some way to surrender with a minimum loss of "face." (Eisenhower 1963:312–313)

25. The worst civilian nuclear power accident in world history occurred in 1986 at the Chernobyl facility in Ukraine, then part of the Soviet Union. Scores of plant and cleanup workers were exposed to toxic levels of radiation, and 28 died within a few weeks of the accident. More than 336,000 people had to be evacuated from the affected area. The long-term cancer effects on those who were exposed to the radiation has been difficult to determine, but as many as 4,000 people are believed to have been affected (Medvedev 1990; World Nuclear Association 2010).

26. There are about 15,000 plants (chemical and nuclear) nationwide. If ever attacked, more than a hundred of these could each put a million or more people at risk (Kennedy 2004).

5

Political Corruption

WILLIAM MARCY TWEED WAS A MASTERFUL POLITICIAN OF THE nineteenth century. "Boss Tweed," as he was known, led a powerful coalition of local Democrats associated with New York City's infamous Tammany Hall, which essentially ran the city during that era.[1] Tweed, who held many positions simultaneously—including state senator, head of the city's public works department, and president of the county board of supervisors—portrayed himself as a social reformer, establishing public parks programs and city construction projects and supporting (largely Irish) workers' right to strike and form unions (Douglas 1977; Kolbert 2002). Tweed, however, also favored lower taxes. Although this agenda of social programs and tax cuts made him popular with voters, it produced a fiscal deficit. Tweed attempted to solve this problem by secretly selling short-term city bonds to raise money, but the plan went awry in the early 1870s as the bonds came due and there was no money to pay back investors. Investigation into this debacle revealed that Tweed and his associates (the Tweed Ring) had been exploiting their political power for financial gain by selling office supplies to the city through a private printing company and padding the bill, by paying phony city bills in order to receive kickbacks on the profits, and by demanding payoffs from contractors who did business with the city, among other schemes. Tweed's corrupt administration cost New Yorkers many millions of dollars. He was sent to prison, where he died, leaving a legacy that still haunts the United States today. As he said, "New York politics were always dishonest—long before my time. . . . This population is too hopelessly split up into races and factions to govern it under universal suffrage, except by the bribery of patronage and corruption" (quoted in Douglas 1977:84).

123

A few decades later, during the Republican administration of President Warren Harding (1921–1923), Secretary of Interior Albert Fall secretly leased US Navy oil reserves in Elk Hills, California, and Teapot Dome, Wyoming, to private oil companies owned by Edward Doheny and Harry Sinclair, respectively. Fall received a $100,000 loan from Doheny and more than $300,000 in cash, bonds, and livestock from Sinclair. In 1923 Fall resigned and joined Sinclair's business. The **Teapot Dome scandal**, which became one of the most well-known public corruption scandals of the twentieth century, was investigated for several years, and in 1929 Fall was convicted of bribery and sentenced to a year in prison. He was the first federal cabinet member ever sent to prison for a crime committed while in office (Dickenson 1977; Noggle 1965).[2]

The Tweed and Fall cases illustrate political corruption as a bipartisan phenomenon that is prevalent among members of both major political parties and occurring across all levels of government in the United States. Earlier we defined corruption as a form of governmental malfeasance undertaken by public officials and politicians for direct personal gain (see Chapter 1). This gain may be both financial and political—that is, it may involve the misuse of public office to accumulate personal wealth as well as to acquire, maintain, and exercise political power. These two domains of corruption, which we will call **financially remunerative corruption** and **abuse of power for political gain**, often overlap and mutually reinforce each other.

Financially Remunerative Corruption

We will first turn our attention to the misuse of public office for financial gain, considering corruption at the local and state levels and then the federal level of government. We will also focus specifically on corruption that occurs at the nexus between political and corporate power by considering the problem of financial profiteering from war and disaster.

Local and State Corruption

In July 2009, a two-year FBI probe into political corruption and money laundering in New Jersey culminated in the arrest of forty-four individuals, including three mayors (all Democrats), two state assemblymen (one Democrat, one Republican), and five Syrian-Jewish rabbis.[3] The investigation began when Solomon Dwek, a smooth-talking yet unsuccessful New Jersey real estate developer, self-styled philanthropist, and prominent member of the Syrian-Jewish community, was arrested for trying to pass a bad check worth $25 million. Dwek turned government informant and gave authorities entry into an extensive network of corruption. Operating under an assumed name, Dwek approached various local influence-peddlers and told them he was looking for help in obtaining government approval for various high-rise buildings and other construction projects. Upon making contact with public officials who had jurisdiction over projects in their area, Dwek offered each of them $5,000 in cash for an upcoming political campaign or simply as a straight-up bribe, with the promise of more to come. He then handed them the money from the trunk of his car. Many of these officials accepted his bribes, which amounted to more than $650,000 according to the criminal complaint (CNN.com 2009; Halbfinger 2009).

Observers of the New Jersey political scene were not particularly surprised by the scandal, since the state is notorious in this regard. Brad Parks notes, for example, the case of Frank "I Am the Law" Hague, "who never made more than $9,000 [a year] as mayor of Jersey City, and never held another job during his 30 years in office, yet died in 1956 with an estate estimated at $5 million" (2009:2). Of the more recent corruption case involving Dwek, Ralph Marra Jr., the acting US Attorney in New Jersey, said: "For these defendants, corruption was a way of life. They existed in an ethics-free zone" (Halbfinger 2009:1).

Not to be outdone, the state of Illinois, whose history of corruption rivals New Jersey's, has been in the news as well. In the latter part of 2008, now-impeached Democratic governor Rod Blagojevich became the seventh governor in the history of Illinois to be arrested or indicted for his misdeeds (Suddath 2008). His most recent predecessor, Republican George Ryan, who served as governor from 1999 to 2003, was convicted in 2006 on 18 felony counts (including racketeering, fraud, and obstruction) and sentenced to six years in prison for actions that go back to his tenure as secretary of state from 1991 to 1999. The investigation of Ryan, which began in 1994 when a fatal truck accident inadvertently exposed a statewide "scheme to trade truck operators' licenses for political contributions," took years to complete (Suddath 2008:2). Operation Safe Roads, as the probe was called, also resulted in the conviction of more than 70 former state officials, lobbyists, and truck drivers (Rosoff, Pontell, and Tillman 2007).

The wrongdoing for which Blagojevich is best known involves his alleged solicitation of bribes from potential candidates for Barack Obama's replacement in the US Senate seat after the 2008 presidential election, a decision that Blagojevich controlled. Blagojevich even floated a suggestion with the Obama campaign, which was forthrightly rejected, "to get a cabinet job in return for naming [Obama's] choice to be his Senate successor" (Saltonstall 2008:1). The federal indictment also alleges that Blagojevich tried to shake down the owner of the *Chicago Tribune,* who owns the storied Wrigley Field baseball stadium, by trying to force the newspaper to fire editorial writers who had been critical of him in exchange for a tax break for the stadium worth about $100 million. And he is accused of threatening "to revoke millions in funding for a Chicago children's hospital if its CEO did not pay his campaign a $50,000 tribute" (Scherer 2008:1). In the summer of 2010, a federal jury found him guilty on one count of lying to federal agents, but deadlocked on 23 other counts due to the dissenting opinion of one juror (Babwin 2010). The prosecuting attorney said he planned to retry the case.[4]

In a column reflecting on the Blagojevich case, journalist Jacob Weisberg (2008) notes that in spite of the boldness of Blagojevich's actions, corruption in the state of Louisiana is second to none. Between 1997 and 2006, he observes, Louisiana led the nation with 326 federal corruption convictions, for a per capita rate of 7.67 per 100,000 population. Illinois's 524 convictions during that period equate to a rate of only 4.64 per 100,000 population.[5] Traditionally, Weisberg argues, corruption in Illinois entailed petty patronage: "methodological rake-offs from the quotidian operations of government: liquor licenses, elevator inspectors, speeding tickets, and above all, hiring" (p. 1).[6] In Louisiana, on the other hand, corruption is more "flamboyant and shameless." Weisberg explains that with the discovery of oil and gas in Louisiana around 1912, "politicians in the dirt-poor state suddenly controlled a gold mine in tax revenue," and as long as they threw enough crumbs to the masses, they were able to spend the state's resources as they wished (p. 2). As Earl Long, who served three terms as governor between 1939 and 1960, once said, Louisiana voters "don't want good government, they want good entertainment" (quoted in Weisberg 2008:2).

In Edwin Edwards, who served four terms as Louisiana governor between 1972 and 1996, voters got both corruption and entertainment. When the flamboyant and wisecracking Democrat ran for governor in 1983, he said of the incumbent: "If we don't get Dave Treen out of office, there won't be anything left to steal" (quoted in Weisberg 2008:2). Edwards, an admitted high-stakes gambler, was tried twice in the mid-1980s "on racketeering charges related to questionable hospital and nursing home deals, for which he made $2 million," but a deadlocked jury on the first trial and an acquittal on the second "earned Edwards a colorful reputation for legal invincibility" (Rosoff, Pontell, and Tillman 2007:442). Edwards's luck ran out in 2000, however, when he was convicted on 17 counts of extortion and racketeering and sentenced to 10 years in prison. The government's chief witness in the case was Edward DeBartolo Jr., the owner of the San Francisco 49ers football franchise. DeBartolo had pled guilty to concealing Edwards's scheme and agreed to testify against the former governor in exchange for a reduced sentence. Stephen Rosoff, Henry Pontell, and Robert Tillman summarize DeBartolo's testimony:

> DeBartolo had won a license in 1997 for a floating casino along Shreveport's Red River. Edwards, out of office at this time but still politically influential, had demanded and received $400,000. DeBartolo handed Edwards his payoff in a brief-case stuffed with cash at the San Francisco airport. . . . Edwards also wanted a $50,000-a-month consulting fee, a per-head commission on every customer entering the casino, and 1 percent of the gross revenues. (2007:443)

After his conviction, an unrepentant Edwards compared his fate to a Chinese proverb: "If you sit by a river long enough, the dead bodies of your enemies will float by you. I suppose the feds sat by the river longer enough, and here comes my dead body" (quoted in Rosoff, Pontell, and Tillman 2007:443).[7]

Federal Corruption

In the aftermath of the Watergate scandal (discussed in more detail later in the chapter), federal investigators gave greater attention to the problem of political corruption. One of their most well-known investigations was called **Operation ABSCAM**, which was carried out in the late 1970s. Like the previously mentioned New Jersey scandal, Operation ABSCAM began when a convicted swindler and con artist, Melvin Weinberg, agreed to cooperate with the FBI in an investigation of corrupt politicians in exchange for a lighter sentence. Under the supervision of the FBI, Weinberg set up a phony investment company called Abdul Enterprises, purportedly owned by a wealthy Arab shaikh, to entice US business ventures. Weinberg introduced prospective targets of the investigation to FBI agents posing as Middle Eastern businessmen, offering them lucrative bribes in exchange for "greasing the wheels" on investments ranging from obtaining a casino license in Atlantic City to obtaining defense contracts and other federal government business.[8] Operation ABSCAM succeeded in snaring six members of the US House of Representatives (five Democrats and one Republican) and a US senator from New Jersey, Harrison "Pete" Williams, in addition to other local officials (Rosoff, Pontell, and Tillman 2007; SourceWatch.org 2010a).

Williams, one of the highest-ranking Democrats in the Senate, was arguably the biggest "catch" of the operation. Williams offered to arrange a business deal with his associates, including a man with ties to the aging organized crime boss Meyer Lansky, to purchase a titanium mine in Virginia, the largest in the country. Titanium is a rare metal used in the construction of submarines and other defense projects. Williams would then steer government contracts to benefit the owners of the mine (Rosoff, Pontell, and Tillman 2007).

The bribe-taking, which was captured on videotape, was a national embarrassment. One of the congressmen, Michael "Ozzie" Myers, a Democrat from Philadelphia, offered a pathetic explanation, claiming that the money was not a bribe because he had no intention of doing anything on behalf of Abdul Enterprises: "[I] saw it as a way to pick up some easy money for doing absolutely nothing" (quoted in Rosoff, Pontell, and Tillman 2007:432). Myers and the other disgraced congressmen were convicted and received prison terms of two to three years.

Following Operation ABSCAM, during the Republican administration of Ronald Reagan, another FBI investigation, **Operation Ill Wind**, focused on US Navy undersecretary Melvyn Paisley, who was responsible for procuring weapons systems for the government that were worth hundreds of millions of dollars.[9] Paisley sold classified information to defense firms competing for government business, granted contracts to firms that paid him bribes, and even awarded a contract to a company that he co-owned. Paisley and a number of other government officials, corporate executives, and defense consultants were convicted of bribery, tax evasion, and fraud. Paisley received a four-year prison term (Rosoff, Pontell, and Tillman 2007; Simon 2006).

Around the same time, the Department of Housing and Urban Development (HUD) became a center of influence-peddling and fraud, as HUD secretary Samuel Pierce and his aides steered lucrative government contracts to Republican Party benefactors and paid exorbitant consulting fees to Republican political insiders. Although Pierce himself was not prosecuted, a number of HUD officials were convicted in a scandal that cost taxpayers several billion dollars (Simon 2006).

Cataloging the numerous congressmen who have been embroiled in corruption scandals would fill a volume of its own, but a few over the past couple of decades are worth mentioning. Among Democrats, Dan Rostenkowski of Illinois, chair of the influential House Ways and Means Committee, stands out for his conviction in 1996 for misappropriating $640,000 of congressional funds for his own personal use during a corrupt political career that spanned three decades. He received a prison term of 17 months. In 2002, James Traficant of Ohio was convicted for soliciting bribes, tax evasion, and even extorting money from his own staff by forcing them to return part of their salary to him. He received a prison term of eight years, which at the time was the longest for a congressman who had been indicted while in office. In 2005, William Jefferson of Louisiana made the news when FBI agents investigating his involvement in bribery found $90,000 in cash stored in his freezer in his Washington, D.C., home. He received a prison term of 13 years, the longest ever imposed on a congressman for bribery (Courson 2009; Rosoff, Pontell, and Tillman 2007; *Wisconsin State Journal* 2009b).

Among Republicans, Randy "Duke" Cunningham of California stands out for receiving $2.4 million in bribes, the most lucrative in the history of congressional bribery, mostly from defense contractors looking for government business and other favors. In addition to cash, Cunningham's benefactors lavished him with a Rolls-Royce, a luxury yacht, museum-quality antiques, Persian rugs, and a mansion in one of the nation's wealthiest communities. In 2005 he received a prison term of eight years and four months (Rosoff, Pontell, and Tillman 2007; *Wisconsin State Journal* 2005).

The K Street Project

No account of political corruption would be complete without mentioning the web of scandal associated with lobbyist Jack Abramoff. As a former president of the College Republicans, Abramoff prided himself as a power broker, making deals between his corporate clients and the Republican-controlled Congress that came to power in 1994. Under the leadership of Georgia congressman Newt Gingrich, who served as Speaker of the House from 1994 to 1999, the Republicans advanced their "Contract with America," which was "aimed at restoring the faith and trust of the American people in their government" and which called for a dramatic rollback in the role of the federal government in American society (cited in Continetti 2006:8). Abramoff's chief political ally was Texas congressman Tom DeLay, the Republican majority whip and later majority leader, who was nicknamed "The Hammer" for his reputation for nailing down financial contributions for himself and his political allies. Matthew Continetti describes DeLay as a man "who viewed government as a business—one that maximized the advantages of business so that business would then donate to their political war chests" (2006:16).

Working with antitax activist and Gingrich protégé Grover

Norquist—who once said that he wanted to shrink the federal government to so small a size that it could be drowned in a bathtub—DeLay formed the **K Street Project**, named after the Washington, D.C., business corridor where some of the most powerful corporate lobbyists in the country have their offices. The goal of the K Street Project was nothing less than the wholesale partisan realignment of the lobbying industry with the Republican Party (Continetti 2006; Moyers 2006).

As DeLay and his political allies pressured lobbyists to abandon their ties to the Democratic Party, an orgy of political corruption ensued. But Abramoff was arguably the "poster child" for the scandal and the corrupt practice of lobbying in the United States. Most noteworthy was Abramoff's role in bilking millions of dollars from the nation's Native American Indian tribes, money that he claimed was being spent on lobbying to promote their interests in the casino industry. In addition to profiting himself, Abramoff persuaded the tribes to make large campaign contributions to his Republican allies. Then there was the case of the Marianna Islands, a territory of the United States, which was touted by DeLay as a paradise of "free market" capitalism. Garment factory owner Willie Tan courted DeLay and paid Abramoff millions of dollars to lobby on his behalf to seek political support to exempt the Mariannas from US immigration and labor laws, enabling Tan to subject his workers to some of the most exploitative conditions in the world, while at the same time labeling his products "Made in America." During this time, Abramoff had access to influential members of the George W. Bush administration, including the president himself (Continetti 2006; Moyers 2006).

While padding their campaign coffers, DeLay and his ilk, such as Congressman Bob Ney of Ohio,[10] were also traveling around the world at taxpayer expense or as guests of corporate lobbyists, flying on corporate jets, staying in luxury hotels, playing golf on lavish courses, and dining in expensive restaurants (Abramoff owned his own extravagant restaurant in Washington, D.C., where his political friends ate for free). During these junkets, they met with an amalgam of rather unsavory people, as Continetti describes: "African dictators. Islamic fanatics. Russians with ties to military intelligence. Israeli guerrillas. Small-time mobsters" (2006:88).

The scandal finally reached the light of day in 2005, and a slew of indictments and guilty pleas ensued. Abramoff pled guilty to several counts of fraud and related offenses and was sentenced to four years in prison. Meanwhile, DeLay was indicted for campaign law violations and decided against seeking reelection to Congress.[11] A score of other lobby-

Box 5.1 Murthaville

Jack Murtha had an illustrious career. A Marine Corps officer and the first Vietnam veteran to be elected to the US House of Representatives, he had stalwart military credentials. For this reason, the country took notice when he called for the immediate withdrawal of US troops from Iraq in 2005. Murtha served in the US Congress from 1974 until his death in 2010, but not without controversy, as some critics think that Murtha was "ethically challenged," a reputation he acquired after being named an "unindicted conspirator" in the cases of Congressmen Frank Thompson and John Murphy during the Operation ABSCAM scandal. Murtha provided testimony against the two congressmen, admitting that he had been approached about a bribery scheme. Although he had not accepted money, he was caught on videotape implying that he might be open to the possibility in the future (SourceWatch.org 2010a; Zengerle 2009).

Murtha served for many years on the House Appropriations Defense Subcommittee, as chair for several years and as its ranking Democrat for more than a decade. In that capacity, he steered federal defense dollars, as much as $2 billion over the years, to his home district in Johnstown, Pennsylvania, bolstering what was otherwise a decaying economy. In return, his benefactors contributed large sums of money to his campaign coffers. At first glance, there is nothing unusual about this, as most congressional representatives try as best they can to bring federal dollars—so-called **earmarks**—back to their home districts. "What Murtha [was] doing, everybody else is doing," says Melanie Sloan, the executive director of Citizens for Responsibility and Ethics. "It's just to such a higher degree that it becomes shocking" (quoted in Zengerle 2009:22). Some of Murtha's detractors would characterize him as an emboldened enabler of a system of "legalized corruption," a vivid illustration of why the US system of campaign financing needs reform. But, as Murtha said, "If I'm corrupt, it's because I take care of my district" (p. 22).

Nonetheless, some of Murtha's benefactors have tainted his legacy. Take Bill Kuchera, for example, a convicted marijuana dealer who is now a pillar of the Johnstown community, who has been under investigation for improperly using money awarded to his defense contracting company, Kuchera Defense Systems, for his own personal expenses. Kuchera is also suspected of receiving illegal kickbacks from Coherent Systems International, a subcontractor that "had partnered with [Kuchera Defense Systems] on a series of defense contracts worth more than $30 million" (Zengerle 2009:24).

Lobbyist Paul Magliocchetti, who worked with Murtha for 10 years as a staffer on the defense appropriations subcommittee, also has raised

continues

Box 5.1 continued

eyebrows for enriching his clients (and himself) from his association with Murtha. Concurrent Technologies, for instance, owes its very existence to Murtha, leveraging an initial contract that Murtha had arranged for metalworking research, worth $27 million over five years, into an ongoing multimillion-dollar business. Another Magliocchetti client, Windber Medical Center, was on the brink of closure before Murtha inserted $2.5 million into a 1998 defense appropriations bill to fund a heart disease research program for military personnel and their families, a program that funneled money to Windber as well as Walter Reed Army Hospital and Bethesda Naval Hospital. A year later, Murtha secured $7.5 million more for Windber to partner with Walter Reed on a breast cancer research program. Nick Jacobs, CEO of Windber, knew who was buttering his bread: "Do you think that if Mr. Murtha wasn't in office that all this stuff would be here?" he asked. "I don't think so" (quoted in Zengerle 2009:24). When asked what he thought the impact of Murtha's departure from Congress would mean, Jacobs said, "I think it will be worse than the Johnstown Flood," referring to three catastrophic floods that had devastated the area over the years (p. 25).

ists and Republican congressmen who were part of the Abramoff-DeLay network or who committed similar crimes of their own have also been convicted, fined, and/or sentenced to prison (Continetti 2006; Moyers 2006; Talking Points Memo 2007b; Wilber and Johnson 2008).

Profiting from War and Disaster

In his famous speech on the occasion of leaving office in January 1961, President Dwight Eisenhower warned the country of the consequences of the **military-industrial complex**: "In the councils of government, we must guard against the acquisition of unwarranted influence, whether sought or unsought, by the military-industrial complex." The same warning would be apropos for what Naomi Klein (2007) calls the disaster-capitalism complex: the scores of corporations conducting business with the US government that collectively reap billions of dollars through unethical and illegal practices such as fraudulent overcharging, the provision of shoddy products and services, outsourcing contracted work for profit, noncompetitive contracts, and open-ended contracts that allow companies to keep coming back to the government for more and more money (see Chapters 2 and 3). The point to be made here is that this is done with the complicity of public officials who have the responsibility of deciding who receives the government's business. According to Klein, the disaster-capitalism complex is "a full-fledged new economy . . . tasked with nothing less than building and running a privatized security state, both at home and abroad," funded by taxpayer dollars (p. 299).

September 11, 2001, Klein argues, "launched the disaster-capitalism bubble" (2007:299). As Roger Novak of Novak Biddle Venture Partners, a venture capital firm that invests in homeland security companies, noted, investors are "seeing how big the trough is and asking, How do I get a piece of that action?" (quoted in Klein 2007:299). Scott Shane and Ron Nixon observe that "[w]ithout a public debate or formal policy decision, contractors have become a virtual fourth branch of government," receiving hundreds of billions of dollars in federal contracts (about $400 billion in 2007, up from $207 billion in 2000) because of the market in homeland security, disaster relief, and the Iraq and Afghanistan wars (2007:1). Corporate contractors still manufacture military equipment, satellites, and the like, but they also deploy mercenary soldiers, fly pilotless spy aircraft, collect intelligence, prepare agency budgets, and even run the Federal Procurement Data System, the government's online database for tracking contracts, "despite regulations forbidding the outsourcing of 'inherently governmental' work" (2007:1; see also Scahill 2007; Shorrock 2008).

Shane and Nixon add that the explosion of the contracting component of government also raises questions about cost and accountability, as contracts are increasingly awarded without competitive bidding, and government agencies "are crippled in their ability to seek low prices," if they desired to do so, or "supervise contractors and intervene when work goes off course because the number of government workers overseeing contracts has remained level as spending has shot up." Indeed, nowadays "far more people work under contracts than are directly employed by the government" (2007:1).

Moreover, the companies that are awarded contracts are not necessarily the ones that do the best work. Rather, they are the ones that have lobbied the government and their political benefactors most successfully, spending millions of dollars on lobbyists and donations to political campaigns. Since 1995 the top 100 federal contractors, which earned nearly $300 billion from federal contracts in 2007 alone, have been cited for 676 cases of "misconduct" and paid fines of $26 billion to settle cases of fraud, waste, or abuse, an apparently small price to pay for doing government business, which accounts for 90 to 95 percent of the earnings of some companies (Scahill 2009b; Shane and Nixon 2007). According to Congressman Henry Waxman, "Billions are being squandered, and the taxpayer is being taken to the cleaners" (quoted in Shane and Nixon 2007:2).

In Chapter 2 we noted the phenomenon of the corporate-government "revolving door," whereby societal elites circulate in and out of the private and public sectors to ensure that government operates in corporations' best interests. But government service itself often becomes a springboard for private gain at the public spending trough. Take the post-mayoral career of Rudy Giuliani, for instance, who has parlayed his visibility as mayor of New York City at the time of the 9/11 attack into the launch of his Giuliani Partners consulting firm and Giuliani Capital Advisors investment banking firm, companies that aim to profit from the expanding market in homeland security and energy needs (Barrett and Collins 2006; Berman 2007).

In 2004, one of Giuliani's associates, Bernard Kerik, was President George W. Bush's initial choice to head the newly formed Department of Homeland Security (DHS). Kerik had begun his political career as Giuliani's driver and bodyguard during the 1993 mayoral campaign that brought Giuliani to power. Having only achieved the rank of third-grade detective, the lowest rank above a patrol officer, Kerik was appointed by the new mayor to a job in New York City's corrections department and then to the position of corrections commissioner. In 2000, Giuliani appointed Kerik to the position of police commissioner, a post he held for 16 months before joining Giuliani in his private business ventures. As a member of a federal panel that was supposed to advise the DHS on the purchase of security technology, Kerik was in a position to steer business to companies in which he had a financial interest (Barrett and Collins 2006).

In a short time, Kerik became a wealthy man promoting the wares of the security industry. His most lucrative source of income came from his service on the board of directors of Taser International, a manufacturer of stun guns, which earned Kerik $6.2 million in pretax income through stock options that he sold in 2004. His nomination to head the DHS, however, was derailed by allegations of corruption, and in 2007 he was indicted on an assortment of charges related to misusing the office of police commissioner to grant favors to business interests in exchange for financial remuneration and then lying about it to investigators.[12] He pled guilty to eight felony counts and was sentenced to four years in prison. Giuliani's judgment as he embarked on his (unsuccessful) 2008 bid for the Republican presidential nomination was called into question (Gearty and Mcshane 2008; Lipton 2004; Quaid 2007; *Wisconsin State Journal* 2007b).[13]

Larry Noble, director of the Center for Responsive Politics, has raised questions about whether the advice that "corporate-politicians" like Giuliani purport to give about public policy—whether in or out of office—"is in their own interests rather than the public interest" (quoted in Roche and Silverstein 2004:A8). In 2004, for example, Giuliani Partners signed a client, Pharmaceutical Research and Manufacturers of America (PhRMA), that was concerned about proposals to loosen government restrictions on the reimportation of prescription drugs that US companies sell to Canada and Europe, where national price controls reduce costs to consumers. As Wayne Barrett and Dan Collins (2006) report, the largest profits from drugs come from sales in the United States, where drug manufacturers charge whatever the market will bear.

> But American senior citizens had begun taking bus trips to Canada to buy their medication, and, in a far more ominous development for the drug companies, members of Congress were talking about making it legal to import cheaper prescription drugs from across the border. PhRMA wanted Giuliani Partners to prepare a report on the safety of these practices, and although it's possible no promises were made, there was a presumption that the report would find reimportation to be a bad and dangerous thing. (p. 306)

Indeed, this is precisely what Giuliani Partners found in a study that concluded: "As the nation tightens its borders against possible future terrorist attacks, it risks undermining security and safety by opening them to non-FDA approved prescription drugs" (cited in Barrett and Collins 2006:306).

The blurred boundaries between corporate and public interests were also noticeable in the years and months leading up to the Iraq War, which began in March 2003 following warnings from an amalgam of lobbyists, public relations specialists, and confidential advisers to senior federal officials about Iraqi dictator Saddam Hussein's capability and willingness to use weapons of mass destruction against the United States. These warnings, it turned out, were exaggerated if not patently false (see Chapter 6). The point to be made here is that some of the same people who pushed the nation into a preemptive war against Iraq have been making lots of money by lobbying for and/or employing themselves at companies pursuing "federal contracts and other financial opportunities in Iraq" (Roche and Silverstein 2004:A7).

R. James Woolsey, former director of the Central Intelligence Agency, is a prominent example of the phenomenon of mixing his "business interests with what he contends are the country's strategic interests"

(Roche and Silverstein 2004:A8). After leaving the CIA in 1995, Woolsey remained "a senior government advisor on intelligence and national security issues," and before the Iraq War he "was a founding member of the Committee for the Liberation of Iraq, an organization set up in 2002 at the request of the [Bush] White House to help build public backing" for its war plans. Woolsey also wrote about the "need for regime change and sat on the CIA advisory board and the Defense Policy Board, whose unpaid members . . . provided advice on Iraq and other matters to Defense Secretary Donald Rumsfeld."[14] At the same time, Woolsey was "a partner in a company that invests in firms that provide security and anti-terrorism services" and in the employ of two private companies that profited directly from government contracts in Iraq.

The invasion of Iraq was undertaken, in part, to secure oil reserves for US corporate interests. Indeed, US corporations were concerned that Saddam Hussein was prepared to divert upward of $38 billion in oil projects to non-US (especially European, Russian, and Chinese) firms. At a secret February 2001 meeting, which the public did not learn of until much later, senior executives of at least four of the largest oil companies—ExxonMobil, Conoco, Shell, and BP America—met with aides to Vice President Dick Cheney about this issue. As Mark LeVine reports, those in attendance were looking over

> a map of Iraq and an accompanying list of "Iraq oil foreign suitors."
> . . . The map erased all features of the country save the location of its
> main oil deposits, divided into nine exploration blocks. The accompa-
> nying list of suitors revealed that dozens of companies from 30 coun-
> tries—but not the United States—were either in discussions over or in
> direct negotiations [with Hussein] for rights to some of the best
> remaining oil fields on earth. (2005:5–6; see also Behan 2006)

After the invasion of Iraq and ensuing US occupation, former ambassador Paul Bremer was appointed by President Bush to head the Coalition Provisional Authority (CPA), the temporary US-run government of Iraq. Prior to this appointment, Bremer had founded Crisis Consulting Practices, a division of the insurance giant Marsh & McLennan, which specializes in helping multinational corporations prepare for, manage, and recover from crises ranging from terrorism and natural disasters to product recalls and class action lawsuits. Bremer soon announced that all of Iraq's 200 state-owned enterprises would be sold to private investors. Unlike the Marshall Plan that followed World War II, which infused US money into war-torn Germany to rebuild the German economy, the CPA aimed to divert the business of rebuilding Iraq to non-Iraqi companies. Consequently, Iraqis, for the most part, did not see the "corporate reconstruction" of Iraq as a godsend, but rather as a "modernized form of pillage" (Klein 2007:350; Palast 2007).

According to Klein's account, the reconstruction of Iraq administered by the CPA got under way with an initial outlay of "$38 billion from the US Congress, $15 billion from other countries and $20 billion from Iraq's own oil money" (2007:346). Not a single governmental function "was considered so 'core' that it could not be handed to a [private] contractor, preferably one who provided the Republican Party with financial contributions" (p. 348). "The Bush administration could easily have stipulated that any company receiving US tax dollars had to staff its projects with Iraqis. It could also have contracted for many jobs directly with Iraqi firms. Such simple, common-sense measures did not happen for years because they conflicted with the underlying strategy of turning Iraq" into a boondoggle for US corporations (p. 356).

> If within six months of the invasion, Iraqis had found themselves drinking clear water from Bechtel pipes, their homes illuminated by GE lights, their infirm treated in sanitary Parsons-built hospitals, their streets patrolled by competent DynCorp-trained police, many citizens (though not all) would probably have overcome their anger at being excluded from the reconstruction process. But none of this happened, and well before Iraqi resistance forces began systematically targeting reconstruction sites it was clear that . . . [the CPA operation] had been a disaster. (p. 356)

Working under contracts that guaranteed their costs and profits, indemnified under CPA provisions that barred prosecution under Iraqi law,[15] and freed of all regulations, "many foreign corporations did something entirely predictable: they scammed wildly. . . . The mismanagement continued for three and a half years until all the major US reconstruction contractors pulled out of Iraq, their billions spent, the bulk of the work still undone" (pp. 356–357).

Klein suggests that the conventional view of the corporate and government sectors as constituted by a revolving door of elites does not quite capture the phenomenon of "corporate-politicians" who continue to profit from their private-sector interests *while they are in public office*. The conventional view implies "that there is still a clear line between the state and the [disaster-capitalism] complex, when in fact that line disappeared long ago. The innovation of the Bush years lies not in how quickly politicians moved from one world to the other but in how many [felt] entitled to occupy both worlds simultaneously" (2007:315).

Dick Cheney is a prime example. After serving as secretary of defense during the administration of George H. W. Bush, Cheney became CEO of Halliburton, which, as noted in Chapter 3, engaged in some of the dubious business practices characteristic of other companies in the 1990s, such as overcharging for services and misrepresenting company profits. During the 2000s, according to the Department of Defense Contract Audit Agency, Halliburton subsidiary Kellogg Brown and Root, which has earned nearly $32 billion in government contracts since 2001, was responsible for "the vast majority" of war-zone fraud cases in Iraq and Afghanistan (quoted in Scahill 2009b:1).[16] While Cheney became a wealthy man during his tenure at Halliburton in the 1990s, he did not divest himself of all his financial ties when he assumed the vice presidency in 2001, earning millions in stock dividends and a deferred income of $211,000 annually. He therefore continued to benefit "from the stunning improvement in Halliburton's fortunes" due to a combination of soaring energy prices and federal war contracts, both of which flowed directly from Cheney's advocacy of war and other policies that have benefited the US energy industry (Klein 2007:313; see also Kennedy 2004; Rothe 2006).

The career of James Baker offers another variation of the phenomenon of the corporate-politician. Baker served as chief of staff to President Ronald Reagan and as secretary of treasury and secretary of state under President George H. W. Bush. Since leaving office, his corporate law firm, Baker Botts, has represented corporations like Halliburton as well as the royal family of Saudi Arabia. He is also a partner in the Carlyle Group, a multibillion-dollar investment firm that has holdings in defense-oriented businesses that profited immensely from the Iraq War (Klein 2007).

In 2003, President George W. Bush named Baker as a special envoy on Iraq's debt. As a representative of the United States, Baker was tasked with the job of persuading governments around the world to forgive 90 to 95 percent of Iraq's crushing debt in order to free up "resources that were desperately needed to meet Iraq's humanitarian crisis and to rebuild the country" (Klein 2007:318). At the same time, however, a consortium of companies, including the Carlyle Group, had offered to help Kuwait, one of Iraq's main creditors, to collect $27 billion that Iraq owed to them. In a business plan titled "Proposal to Assist the Government of Kuwait in Protecting and Realizing Claims Against Iraq," Baker is named 11 times, "making it clear that Kuwait would benefit from working with a company that employed the man in charge of erasing Iraq's debts" (Klein 2007: 318). The price for this political leverage was $1 billion, which Kuwait

Box 5.2 Hurricane Katrina and the Politics of Disaster Relief

In Chapter 4 we noted the ineffective response at all levels of government to Hurricane Katrina, which devastated the city of New Orleans in 2005. Local, state, and federal authorities had known about the city's vulnerabilities beforehand, but no preventative actions were taken. At the time of the crisis, President George W. Bush undermined his credibility by saying: "I don't think anybody anticipated the breach of the levees." And as federal relief to New Orleans was not only slow in coming but also grossly inadequate when it did come, his praise of Federal Emergency Management Agency (FEMA) director Michael Brown became a national joke: "Brownie, you're doing a heck of a job" (quoted in Blumenthal 2005b:2). A congressional report on the government's response that was released the next year criticized the "failure of leadership," the inability of various "government agencies to share critical information," and the "confusion over issues of responsibility" that made the natural disaster even worse (CNN.com 2006:1–2). More than a year after the hurricane had struck, daily power outages were still common, the sewage and water system was in disrepair, medical facilities were understaffed, and thousands of residents were living in FEMA-supplied travel trailers and mobile homes laced with formaldehyde (Farmer 2009; *New Republic* 2006; Spake 2007).

FEMA was established in 1979, and in its first few years of operation was known as a bumbling organization, a "dumping ground" for political cronies, according to one FEMA advisory board member (quoted in Blumenthal 2005b:3). Former South Carolina senator Fritz Hollings once called FEMA officials "the sorriest bunch of bureaucratic jackasses I've ever known" (quoted in Marek 2006:36). During President Bill Clinton's term of office, however, he appointed James Lee Witt to head the agency, the first director to have any prior experience in emergency management, and he elevated FEMA to cabinet status. Under Witt's leadership, FEMA earned a reputation for "setting high professional standards and efficiently dealing with disasters" (Blumenthal 2005b:3).

FEMA's success as a "showcase" federal agency made it an inviting target for the George W. Bush administration, which wanted to minimize the role of the federal government in the life of the nation. Bush appointed Joseph Allbaugh, his 2000 presidential campaign manager, to head the organization. According to Sidney Blumenthal's account:

> [Allbaugh] immediately began to dismantle the professional staff, privatize many functions and degrade its operation. In his testimony before the Senate, Allbaugh attacked the agency he headed as an example of unresponsive bureaucracy: "Many are

continues

Box 5.2 continued

concerned that federal disaster assistance may have evolved into both an oversized entitlement program and a disincentive to effective state and local risk management. Expectations of when the federal government should be involved and the degree of involvement may have ballooned beyond what is an appropriate level." (2005b:4)

After the terrorist attacks of September 11, 2001, FEMA lost its cabinet status and was placed under the auspices of the newly formed Department of Homeland Security. The large majority of its budget was diverted to local preparedness and first-responder grants to terrorism-related activities rather than to natural disaster and accident assistance, which most authorities thought was the greater need (Marek 2006).

Allbaugh stepped down in 2003 to start a lucrative business in corporate lobbying and federal contract procurement. He turned the reins of the agency over to Brown, his deputy and college roommate, who had been fired from his previous job as commissioner of the International Arabian Horse Association (Blumenthal 2005b; Klein 2007). Nonetheless, during the summer of 2004, when the state of Florida was hit with a series of powerful hurricanes, FEMA earned high marks for providing Floridians with much needed relief—in fact, perhaps more relief than was needed. It was an election year, and "[n]o expense was spared bringing relief to storm victims who just happened to live in the most important swing state in the country" (Boehlert 2005:1). Even Miami-Dade County, which suffered little or no hurricane damage, received $30 million in aid to help residents replace their televisions, computers, and appliances. Standing alongside Florida governor Jeb Bush, the president's brother, Brown bragged: "FEMA and the Department of Homeland Security are bringing literally thousands of assets to respond to [the hurricane]" (quoted in Boehlert 2005:2).

Hurricane Katrina was much more devastating than the ones that hit Florida, and the opportunity to profit from disaster relief much greater, as was the rapacity for greed. The no-bid contracts, aversion to hiring local people, and shoddy delivery of services that were apparent in Iraq were all apparent in the aftermath of Katrina. A congressional report published in 2006 found "significant overcharges, wasteful spending, or misman-agement" in portions of contracts collectively worth $8.75 billion (cited in Klein 2007:411; see also Fineman 2005; Yen 2007). Moreover, a year after the hurricane, it was reported that Mississippi governor Haley Barbour, former chairman of the national Republican Party, had managed to secure as much federal support for his state as had been secured for the state of Louisiana, "even though Louisiana suffered more than three times the number of seriously damaged homes and lost one more major city than its easterly neighbor" (*New Republic* 2006:7).

would have to invest with the Carlyle Group. According to Klein, "It was straight-up influence peddling: pay Baker's company to get protection from Baker." When the story of this crass conflict of interest broke, Carlyle was forced to back out of the consortium, "forfeiting its hope of landing the $1 billion" (2007:318). Baker, too, eventually cashed out his financial interest in Carlyle. In the meantime, the real damage had already been done: Baker had performed poorly as the US envoy, failing to secure the kind of debt forgiveness that he had been recruited to obtain.

Abuse of Power for Political Gain

In considering the abuse of power for political gain, we will begin with the infamous Watergate scandal that occurred during the Republican administration of Richard Nixon, and then turn to the presidency of Democrat Bill Clinton, including the dubious circumstances of the investigation that led to the impeachment of the president. We will also consider the corruption of the electoral process that brought George W. Bush to power and kept him in office for eight years. Finally, we will consider the US Attorneys scandal that occurred during the Bush presidency, which raises some troublesome issues about the politicization of the Department of Justice in the 2000s.

Watergate

The most infamous burglary in the history of the United States took place on the morning of June 17, 1972. Five men dressed in business suits entered the headquarters of the Democratic National Committee at the Watergate hotel and office complex in Washington, D.C. They were there to check on malfunctioning electronic surveillance equipment they had planted on an earlier trip in order to spy on the Democratic Party. This time they were discovered by the night watchman, who called the police. The burglars, it turned out, were under the employ of President Richard Nixon's reelection campaign, the Committee for the Reelection of the President, dubbed CREEP. Nixon assured the American public that the matter was under investigation by the proper authorities and that he knew nothing about what had transpired. Nixon did not anticipate, however, that two years later he would be forced to make public the transcripts of his tape-recorded White House conversations and admit that "portions of the tapes . . . are at variance with certain of my previous statements" (quoted in Miller 1974:29).

Even prior to the discovery of the tapes, journalists investigating the burglary—especially Bob Woodward and Carl Bernstein of the *Washington Post*—had made headway unraveling the case.[17] The press reported that a $25,000 check from Nixon's campaign fund had been deposited in the bank account of one of the Watergate burglars and that the White House had tried to involve the FBI and CIA in the concealment of evidence that linked CREEP officials to the crime (some of the burglars had previously worked for the CIA, and G. Gordon Liddy, who masterminded the burglary and planned other illegal acts, had been an FBI agent).[18] We also learned that Nixon's aides had ordered a burglary of the office of Defense Department analyst Daniel Ellsberg's psychiatrist in an effort to discredit Ellsberg. In 1971 Ellsberg had leaked classified documents known as the **Pentagon Papers** to the press, revealing how government officials—both Republicans and Democrats—had deceived Congress as well as the public about its rationale and plans to escalate the controversial Vietnam War (explored in Chapter 6) (Bernstein and Woodward 1974; deHaven-Smith 2010; Ellsberg 2002; Summers 2000).

The tapes were not discovered until after the Senate Select Committee on Presidential Campaign Activities began investigating the case in May 1973 and after White House presidential counsel John Dean had testified about the role he and others (including Nixon) had played in a cover-up (see Chapter 2). Both the Senate committee and the special prosecutor who had been appointed by the Department of Justice asked Nixon to turn over the tapes. The president refused and the dispute moved through the courts. Eventually, in July 1974, the US Supreme Court forced Nixon's hand. The excerpt from the tapes that proved most damaging at the time was of a conversation that took place just six days after the Watergate burglary between Nixon and his chief of staff, H. R. "Bob" Haldeman. In this conversation Nixon said:

> Now, on the investigation, . . . the Democratic break-in thing, we're back in the problem area because the FBI is not under control . . . because they've been able to trace the money . . . through the bank sources. . . . And . . . it goes in some directions we don't want it to go. [Former attorney general and current CREEP chairman John] Mitchell came up with yesterday, and . . . John Dean analyzed very carefully . . . and . . . concurs now with Mitchell's recommendation that the only way to solve this . . . is for us to have [deputy CIA director Vernon] Walters call [acting FBI director L. Patrick] Gray and just say "Stay to hell out of this, . . . we don't want you to go any further on it." (quoted in Miller 1974:26)

After transcripts of the tapes were released, the House Judiciary Committee recommended that Nixon be impeached for obstruction of justice, abuse of presidential powers, and illegal withholding of evidence from Congress. Nixon saw the handwriting on the wall—even Republican leaders encouraged him to step down—and he reluctantly resigned from office on August 9, 1974. Vice President Gerald Ford became president, and pardoned Nixon a month later for all federal crimes that Nixon *might* have committed and for which Nixon *might* have otherwise been prosecuted (Summers 2000).

It is interesting to note that Ford had become vice president because his predecessor in that office, Spiro Agnew, also had been forced to resign. In 1973, federal officials began investigating charges that Agnew, as Baltimore County executive and governor of Maryland, had accepted bribes from contractors (e.g., highway construction companies) to grant them government work. Apparently Agnew had continued to accept payments even while serving as vice president. Agnew pleaded "no contest" to charges of income tax evasion. He was fined $10,000 and sentenced to three years of unsupervised probation (Rosoff, Pontell, and Tillman 2007; Simon [1982] 2006; Summers 2000).

Although Agnew's crimes had nothing to do with the Watergate burglary and cover-up, the **Watergate scandal** has come to refer, as noted in Chapter 1, not just to a single burglary but to a larger cluster of crimes and abuses of governmental power, including other burglaries, illegal wiretappings, obstruction of justice, tax audits of political foes, dissemination of false and defamatory stories about Democratic rivals,[19] solicitation of campaign contributions in exchange for favors, and appropriation of campaign funds for private use (Dean 1976; deHaven-Smith 2010; Rosoff, Pontell, and Tillman 2007; Summers 2000). In the end, a number of White House and campaign aides served time in prison, with Liddy serving the longest sentence (52 months).[20] He went on to become a syndicated radio talk-show celebrity, proselytizing right-wing politics to his listening audience.

To be sure, abuses of presidential power both preceded and followed the Watergate affair, but what Watergate represents at its core is a profound disregard for the democratic process. Nixon had built his political career on attacking opponents for being soft on national security and soft on crime, and he had made many enemies along the way. He felt that he had been the victim of election shenanigans in Chicago, where there is evidence that Mayor Richard Daley helped rig the vote that delivered the state of Illinois to John Kennedy in the 1960 presidential election (Gumbel 2005).[21] And during the 1968 election campaign, which brought Nixon to power, President Lyndon Johnson had ordered the FBI to wiretap Nixon's plane (Gray 2008). Nixon felt entirely justified in using similar tactics against his political foes, and he encouraged and condoned a culture among his minions of doing whatever it took to advance their collective political power, even to the point of committing crimes. But the truth of the matter is that Nixon actually believed that he, as president, was above the law. As he told journalist David Frost in a 1977 interview, "When the president does it, that means that it is not illegal" (Dean 1976; deHaven-Smith 2010; Rosoff, Pontell, and Tillman 2007; Thomas 2005).

The Clinton Presidency

Richard Nixon was never formally impeached, but a quarter century later Bill Clinton was, for matters related to a sexual affair he had with White House intern Monica Lewinsky. Clinton was elected to the presidency in 1992 after serving as governor of Arkansas. During the presidential campaign, Clinton was under scrutiny for making several misleading (if not false) statements regarding his efforts to avoid military service during the Vietnam War, his smoking of marijuana while in college, his extramarital affair with Gennifer Flowers, and his dubious business associations with the "wheelers and dealers" of Arkansas (Conason and Lyons 2000; Hitchens 1999; Woodward 1999).

Whitewater was perhaps the first Clinton scandal to be given a name. In the late 1970s, Bill and Hillary Clinton became partners with James and Susan McDougal in a 230-acre Whitewater real estate development project that went bust. The McDougals were owners of the Madison Guaranty Savings and Loan in Arkansas. Madison Guaranty failed during the 1980s S&L debacle, leaving US taxpayers with a $60 million bailout bill (see Chapter 3).[22] The McDougals had engaged in several of the illegal financial schemes available to corrupt S&L operators, and after Clinton was elected president, they were convicted of several crimes. One scheme involved a fraudulent overvaluation of Madison Guaranty's real estate assets that was used by the McDougals to secure a $3 million government loan. Over a third of that money was lent to Jim Guy Tucker, Clinton's successor as governor of Arkansas, who used it to purchase a water and sewer utility. Susan McDougal served two years in prison for her involvement, James McDougal died in prison while serving a three-year term, and Tucker resigned from office and received four years of probation and eighteen months of home detention (Conason and Lyons 2000; Haddington 1996; Stewart 1996; Woodward 1999).

If money from the McDougals' illegal transactions had been used to repay Whitewater loans, the Clintons may have benefited indirectly. But according to James Stewart's account, "[t]he Clintons had virtually nothing to do with Whitewater and were simply 'passive' investors" (1996:447). Their only wrongdoings pertaining specifically to Whitewater involved overvaluing assets on financial disclosure forms and overestimating losses on their income tax returns, which amounted to a tax savings of less than $2,000 on overall losses of about $43,000 (Conason and Lyons 2000). While these were relatively minor infractions, the story of the Clintons' financial activities during the 1980s hardly portrays them in a flattering light. They took advantage of whatever opportunities they had "to make easy money, even when that meant accepting favors or special treatment from people in businesses regulated by the state" (Stewart 1996:445). The Clintons' behavior lent credence to accusations that they used their influence to thwart regulators investigating Madison Guaranty and to facilitate the McDougals' financial crimes.[23]

The Clintons managed to dodge the Whitewater bullet. More troublesome, however, was their pattern of withholding information and making misleading statements. Before coming to Washington, D.C., for instance, Hillary had worked for the Rose Law Firm (RLF) in Arkansas. The McDougals were among her clients. At first, Hillary claimed that her legal work for the McDougals had been minimal, and she denied knowing anything about their crimes. RLF records revealed, however, that she had billed the McDougals for over a dozen meetings or conversations. While there is no evidence that she did anything wrong, her lack of forthrightness left a contrary impression (Conason and Lyons 2000; Stewart 1996; Woodward 1999).

Throughout Clinton's presidency there were numerous occasions when his aides denied press reports or stonewalled official inquiries into their actions. In the so-called **Travelgate** scandal, staff members of the White House Travel Office were dismissed. Administration officials said they were ridding the office of corruption, but their plans to divert White House travel business to friends of the Clintons suggested another motive as well.[24] In **Filegate**, a White House aide was found collecting FBI files on hundreds of Republican Party officials in an effort that appeared aimed at finding information to discredit them. The aide was summarily dismissed. In **Fostergate**, a White House attorney removed documents from the office of White House lawyer Vince Foster, a former RLF attorney, after he committed suicide, leading to suspicions of devious motives. The right-wing press had a field day, circulating rumors that Foster (and others) had been murdered by assassins working on behalf of the Clintons (Conason and Lyons 2000; Froomkin 2000; Stewart 1996; Woodward 1999).

Webster Hubbell, another former RLF lawyer, had been made an associate attorney general in the Clinton administration's Department of Justice. He was forced to resign in the face of a criminal indictment for income tax evasion and mail fraud related to his practice of overbilling clients at the RLF. Hubbell received a prison sentence of nearly two years, but during an 18-month period following his resignation he received $500,000 in consulting fees from various Clinton associates. One $100,000 fee was paid by a subsidiary of the Lippo Group, an Indonesia-based conglomerate that was accused of illegally funneling foreign campaign contributions to the Democratic National Committee. Mochtar and James Riady, who had controlling interest in the Lippo Group, had banking interests in Arkansas that dated back to the early 1980s. One of Lippo's clients was the People's Republic of China. Although Clinton denied that he ever changed his policy position because of this association, he did reverse his campaign stance against open trade relations with China and approved the sale of vital missile technology to that nation (Stewart 1996; Woodward 1999).

Each of these episodes, taken in isolation, might appear relatively insignificant. But taken as a whole, they begin to add up. Moreover, the Clintons' strategy of first brushing aside accusations, then promising full disclosure while simultaneously frustrating every inquiry, did not serve the president well. According to Stewart, "It would have been relatively easy, early on, to disclose everything and correct the record. But as time passed, the Clintons' drop-by-drop concessions gave credence to their critics and undermined their integrity" (1996:432). And these critics were a determined lot. Hillary Clinton once commented that her husband had been the victim of a "vast right-wing conspiracy" determined to bring down his presidency. While her claims may have been exaggerated, there was a well-funded and concerted effort, abetted by Clinton's own reckless behavior, to do just that. As Joe Conason and Gene Lyons note in their revealing exposé, there was in fact "a loose cabal, if not quite a 'vast conspiracy,' involving longtime Clinton adversaries from Arkansas and elsewhere," an angry amalgam of defeated politicians, disappointed office seekers, right-wing conspiracy fanatics, and wealthy ideologues who thought that Clinton's policies would destroy the country (2000:xiv).[25] Add to the mix a bevy of scandal-mongering profiteers selling stories to the tabloids, and a complicit mainstream media looking for the next Watergate story, and you have a volatile mix of fact, speculation, and outright fiction.

The Republican majority in Congress was determined to pursue Clinton's alleged wrongdoings, and it authorized an investigation by the Office of Independent Councel, to be headed by Kenneth Starr, a highly partisan Republican attorney.[26] Starr had been a partner in the Kirkland & Ellis law firm, and continued to draw a million-dollar salary from this firm while serving at the Office of Independent Councel. Among Kirkland & Ellis's "biggest clients were tobacco and auto companies seeking to minimize government regulation and avoid lawsuits, as well as the Republican National Committee and a host of wealthy right-wing foundations" (Conason and Lyons 2000:134).

During his investigation, Starr had unlimited taxpayer money at his disposal, spending about $2.45 million alone on private investigators over a four-year period. When the investigation of Whitewater turned up empty, he turned his attention to Clinton's greatest vulnerability, his reputation for sexual infidelity, an opportunity that was afforded by a sexual harassment lawsuit that had been initiated against the president by Paula Jones, a clerical employee of the Arkansas Industrial Development Commission, in 1994. Starr embraced the case full throttle and began investigating Clinton's sexual predilections, a questionable deviation from the initial rationale for his investigation of Whitewater, for what had begun as an inquiry into financial wrongdoing turned into an inquiry into sexual behavior, and the lying about it under oath (Conason and Lyons 2000; Woodward 1999).

Jones's allegations against Clinton stemmed from a state-sponsored conference on "quality management" she had been helping to staff at the Excelsior Hotel in Little Rock, Arkansas, which Clinton was attending in May 1991 during the presidential campaign. She alleged that Clinton had spotted her in the hotel and wanted to meet her. A state trooper who was a member of the then-governor's security detail brought her up to Clinton's room. Although Jones had said nothing about it at the time, later she claimed that Clinton had made untoward sexual advances.[27] In going public with her story, Jones became a cause célèbre of the anti-Clinton movement and thousands of dollars came pouring into the Paula Jones Legal Fund (Conason and Lyons 2000; Woodward 1999).

After losing a court challenge to postpone the Jones lawsuit until after his presidency, Clinton was required to give a deposition. In that deposition he was asked about a consensual sexual relationship he had had with a young White House intern, Monica Lewinsky.[28] Under oath, in January 1998, Clinton denied the allegation regarding Lewinsky and then told the American public that he "did not have sexual relations with that woman." Seven months later, in the face of DNA evidence (traces of

Clinton's sperm) found on Lewinsky's dress, the president admitted that he had not told the full truth about the Lewinsky affair (he admitted that he had received oral sex, which in his view did not constitute sexual relations). Questions remained as to whether Clinton had committed perjury in the Jones deposition and in the subsequent testimony he gave before a grand jury, and as to whether he had encouraged Lewinsky to give false testimony as well (Conason and Lyons 2000; Woodward 1999).[29]

Starr issued a 473-page report that made the case for impeachment on grounds of perjury and obstruction of justice, but that also read like a salacious graphic novel. In December 1998, a majority of the House of Representatives passed two articles of impeachment against the president (for perjury and obstruction of justice), making Clinton the first *elected* president ever to be impeached.[30] In February 1999, however, Clinton was acquitted in the Senate, where the vote fell far short of the two-thirds majority needed to remove the president from office. Nevertheless, the Clinton presidency was severely damaged and Clinton's place in history indelibly tarnished (Conason and Lyons 2000; Woodward 1999).

The Disputed Election of 2000

During his drive to the presidency, George W. Bush—son of the former president and then-governor of Texas—dodged accusations that he had used drugs during his youth (he acknowledged he had been a heavy drinker) and that he had received political favors to enroll in the National Guard to avoid serving in the Vietnam War and had not fulfilled all of his obligations to report for duty. After being defeated in the February New Hampshire primary by decorated war veteran Senator John McCain, Bush knew he had to win the South Carolina primary or his candidacy would be in serious jeopardy (Ackerman 2004; Corn 2003).

South Carolina Bush supporters, whom the Bush campaign claimed were acting on their own, started spreading vicious rumors about McCain. They made phone calls posing as pollsters and distributed leaflets, e-mails, and faxes saying that McCain had been brainwashed during his captivity as a prisoner-of-war in Vietnam, that he had fathered a child with a black prostitute, and that he had infected his wife with venereal disease and was responsible for her addiction to drugs. Bush never spoke out against these cruel smears made on his behalf, and he won the primary (Corn 2003).[31]

The November 2000 election between Governor Bush and Vice President Al Gore came down to the wire. Both candidates needed to win Florida to give them enough Electoral College votes (270) to win the election. Before the Florida vote came in, Gore was leading Bush by an electoral margin of 267 to 246. Florida had 25 electoral votes, and Gore needed only 3 more to reach the 270 majority that would have given him the presidency. But in a winner-take-all system, a Bush victory in Florida would give him a 271-to-267 victory.

After the Florida polls closed, the media initially declared Gore the winner, based on information gathered from exit polls. Later that evening, however, the media followed the lead of Fox News Channel, a highly partisan conservative news network, and retracted its call for Gore and pronounced Bush the winner. Interestingly, the head of Fox's Election Night Decision Desk who made the call for Bush was none other than Bush's cousin John Ellis, a man whose impartiality many would question. At 2:16 A.M., after speaking to Jeb Bush, George's brother and governor of Florida, Ellis made the call, announcing to his colleagues at the Fox decision desk: "Jebbie says we got it!" (Moore 2008:36). Within minutes, the other networks followed suit, anointing George W. Bush as the next president of the United States. As it turned out, this projection was wrong; the race was, in fact, too close to call, and two hours later the networks retracted their projections. But David Moore argues that it is "difficult to overestimate the impact of the erroneous network call on the post-election political environment," because it created a public perception that Bush had won and that Gore was a "sore loser" who was attempting to reverse the outcome (2008:37; see also Boehlert 2000).

Although Gore had won the national popular vote by over half a million ballots, the official Florida vote count first placed Bush ahead by 1,784 ballots, just 0.03 percent of the 5.9 million recorded in the state. Under Florida law, if the vote margin is less than 0.05 percent, a mandatory recount is required. The initial recount was done inconsistently— some of the counties did not actually recount the ballots but merely rechecked the math from election night tabulations—but it reduced Bush's official margin of victory to just 327 votes (Corn 2003).

Meanwhile, reports of problems with Florida ballots surfaced that revealed ways in which the election may have been unfairly tipped to Bush over Gore. There was the case of the so-called butterfly ballot, for example, which had candidates Bush and Gore on the left side of the ballot and conservative Reform Party candidate Pat Buchanan on the right side. Evidence indicated that many (especially elderly) Democratic voters found the ballot confusing, leading them to vote for Buchanan, or for both Buchanan and Gore, when they intended to vote for Gore.

These "Democrats for Buchanan" ballots, which would have given Gore an estimated 6,000 to 9,000 additional votes, were forever lost to the vice president. And, as we shall see, there were other sources of lost votes that also might have won the election for Gore (Corn 2003; Dershowitz 2001; Palast 2003).

Given these problems, the Gore campaign requested an additional *hand recount* in four heavily Democratic counties—Miami-Dade, Broward, Palm Beach, and Volusia—as it was permitted by law to do. It was at this point that the nation was introduced to the problem of antiquated punchcard ballots, which require voters to push a stylus through a perforated hole to dislodge a chad, which might be left "hanging" or merely "dimpled." A punchcard system, which is less accurate than an optical-scan system, was used in about 60 percent of Florida precincts, including the four counties that were the target of the Gore recount request. Poor (particularly minority) residents were more likely to have voted with the antiquated technology and hence to have had their ballots discarded. These lost votes were referred to as "undervotes," in comparison to invalidated "overvotes," which included instances where a voter marked or punched a ballot and also specified the name of the *same* candidate in the space designated for "write-in" votes (Corn 2003; Dershowitz 2001; Lantigua 2001; Palast 2003).

Kathryn Harris, the Florida secretary of state, was in charge of supervising the state election process. In spite of the obvious conflict of interest, Harris was also cochair of the Bush campaign in Florida, where Bush's brother Jeb happened to be governor. As the hand recount was still ongoing, Harris predictably exercised her *discretionary* authority to bring the counting to an end within seven days of the election, as she was permitted (but not required) by law to do. Predictably as well, the Gore campaign filed a legal appeal to extend the recount deadline, while the Bush campaign appealed to stop it (Moore 2008; Silverman 2002).

As both sides jockeyed for position in the courts, the Gore team received a favorable decision from the Florida Supreme Court, which ruled that a hand recount of the *undervotes* for the entire state should be undertaken. This statewide recount was begun, but was soon stopped when the Florida court was reversed by the US Supreme Court. In a slim five-to-four decision in **Bush v. Gore,** the majority sided with the Bush team and decreed the election to be over. Thirty-six days after the initial ballots were cast, Harris certified that Bush had won by 537 votes.

Legal analyst Alan Dershowitz (2001), among others, has characterized the US Supreme Court's decision as a case of "supreme injustice." US Supreme Court justices are nominated by the president (and con-

firmed by the Senate) and nowadays are chosen as much for their ideological predilections as their legal expertise. The composition of the
2000 Court clearly favored the Republicans, and many think its decision
in *Bush v. Gore* was overtly political.

The basis of the Bush campaign's legal argument was that continuing the hand recount would have violated the Fourteenth Amendment of
the US Constitution, which says that a person may not be deprived of
"the equal protection of the laws." In what was arguably a partisan interpretation of this clause, the Court ruled that continuing the recount
would deprive Bush voters (but not Gore voters) of their right to equal
protection. The majority reasoned that since the rules governing the
hand recount varied from precinct to precinct—for instance, whether or
not both "hanging" chads and "dimpled" chads would be counted—the
recount would be unfair to those voters whose ballots had been counted
by machines before the recount had begun. But, as Dershowitz asks,
wouldn't voters whose ballots were *not properly counted* by machines
"suffer much more serious violations of their equal protection rights"
(2001:61)? Given the diversity of ballot designs and voting technologies
that existed throughout the state (and indeed the entire country), the logical extension of the Court's ruling would have been to invalidate the
entire presidential election. As Win McCormack suggests, the Court
"speciously ignored the fact that the Florida ballots, prior to any
recount, were *already* counted differently, and that the very purpose of
recounting was to correct for this discrepancy" (2001:32).

Moreover, the Court's legal logic was inconsistent with the majority
justices' own prior rulings. Previously, for example, the majority of
judges had ruled that claims about equal protection violations "should
be able to identify with some degree of specificity the alleged victim"
and also prove that the contested actions had a clear discriminatory purpose (Dershowitz 2001:77). The majority also had previously ruled that
the Court's function is to establish legal precedents, not to declare
unique dispositions. Yet in *Bush v. Gore* the majority wrote: "Our consideration is limited to the present circumstances, for the problem of
equal protection in election processes generally presents many complexities" (cited in Dershowitz 2001:81). In other words, as Dershowitz
pointedly notes: "In future election cases, don't try to hold the Court to
what it said in this case, because it decided this case not on general principles applicable to all cases, but on a principle that has never before
been recognized by any court and that will never again be recognized by
this court" (2001:81).

A year after the election, a consortium of eight media organizations completed an unofficial hand recount of the Florida vote. The consortium concluded that if only the admissible ballots of the four counties contested by Gore had been recounted, Bush would have won the election by about 225 to 400 votes. But if ballots for the entire state had been recounted, Gore would have won by about 40 to 400 votes (CNN.com 2001; Corn 2001, 2003; Fessenden and Broder 2001).

Journalists also uncovered additional controversies that had unfairly tipped the election to Bush and would have given Gore a larger margin of victory. Apparently, Florida election officials, under the direction of Secretary of State Harris, inappropriately did their best to deny former convicted felons from voting in the election altogether. Most states deny felons serving time in prison or on parole the right to vote, but all except 14 states restore that right upon completion of sentence. Florida is one that does not. In 2000 there were an estimated 50,000 to over 100,000 former felons who had moved to Florida from other states with their voting rights intact. According to Florida court rulings, these individuals have the right to vote in Florida elections. Nevertheless, the Governor's Office of Executive Clemency mailed these people a notice informing them that they were "required to make application for restoration of civil rights in the state of Florida," in other words, to ask Governor Jeb Bush for clemency in order to vote (cited in Palast 2003:40). Few of these individuals followed up on this "requirement"—a requirement that had been ruled null and void by the courts (Lantigua 2001; see also Hull 2006; Manza and Uggen 2005).

As Florida election officials tried to purge their voter registration lists of people they deemed ineligible to vote, thousands of eligible voters were mistakenly removed. Take the case of the so-called former felons from Texas. ChoicePoint, a private firm with close Republican ties, was hired by the state of Florida to provide the names of Texas ex-felons who had moved to Florida. As it turned out, *none* of the approximately 8,000 people who were identified and consequently scrubbed from the voter list had actually been convicted of felonies—they had been convicted of misdemeanors. The state also hired Database Technologies of Atlanta, since merged into ChoicePoint, to provide them with lists of ineligible voters who had moved to Florida from other states. As it turned out, the Database Technologies lists contained an error rate of 15 percent. And because African Americans experience higher rates of incarceration than other groups, the majority of people targeted by these purging efforts were black. Since African Americans vote overwhelmingly for Democratic candidates, these efforts significantly advantaged Bush (Lantigua 2001; Palast 2003).

Another problem that contributed to the skewed results involved the data criteria that were used to match people who appeared on the ex-felon lists compiled by Database Technologies and ChoicePoint, with people on the Florida voter lists. According to a vice president of ChoicePoint, Florida officials instructed the company to provide them with "more names than were actually verified as being a convicted felon" (quoted in Palast 2003:57). One way this was accomplished was to establish criteria that would identify a match even if only part of a name on the ex-felon list matched the name on the voting list. In one case, Reverend Willie David Whiting, a black pastor living in Florida, was confused with Willie J. Whiting, a former felon from Texas, and hence the pastor was denied the opportunity to vote. Florida resident Johnny Jackson Jr. was matched with Texas ex-felon John Fitzgerald Jackson. David Butler of Florida was matched with Ohio ex-felon David Butler Jr. Randall Higgenbotham of Florida was matched with ex-felon Sean Higgenbotham, also of Florida. There were innumerable mistaken matches like these, as well as many misdemeanor offenders who were mistakenly identified as felons, as in the Texas ChoicePoint list. On top of all this, African American residents of Leon County "complained of a Florida Highway Patrol checkpoint on a road leading to a polling place . . . [that] amounted to harassment of black voters" (Lantigua 2001:17). If these types of problems had not occurred, Gore might have received more than 30,000 additional votes (Palast 2003).

The US Attorneys Scandal

On December 7, 2006, David Iglesias was one of seven US Attorneys around the country who were asked by Mike Battle, the director of the Executive Office for US Attorneys of the Department of Justice, to resign. An internal DOJ memo titled "Plan for Replacing Certain United States Attorneys," which had been sent to key DOJ and White House officials, gave Battle a script he was to follow when notifying the seven individuals: "The Administration is grateful for your service . . . but has determined to give someone else the opportunity in your district . . . for the final two years of the Administration. We will work with you to make sure there is a smooth transition, but intend to have a new . . . Attorney in place by January 31, 2007" (cited in Iglesias 2009:112). It is not unusual for a new president to replace US Attorneys when he first takes office. Both President Bill Clinton and President George W. Bush did this. What is unusual is the dismissal of a large number in the middle of a term. Moreover, Iglesias and the other attorneys who were fired

Box 5.3 Computerized Voting: Dilemmas of Digital Democracy

Although the 2000 Florida election debacle was marked by the question of antiquated voter technology, it also raised a concern about computerized voting. In Volusia County, for example, the electronic tabulator erroneously subtracted 16,022 votes from Gore's total just minutes before the networks called the election for Bush. Although this mistake was discovered and corrected, CBS later admitted that it had been "critical" in the network's election-night decision. Investigators traced the mistake to a second memory card on a system provided by Global Elections Systems that had been improperly, and suspiciously, uploaded. According to Talbot Ireland, a master programmer for Global Elections Systems, "There is always the possibility that the 'second memory card' or 'second upload' came from an unauthorized source" (quoted in Kennedy 2008:66; see also Ardizzone, Michaels, and Cohen 2006).

There is evidence from other elections since, including the 2004 presidential election, that the integrity of US democracy is threatened by computer technology, and touch-screen voting machines (without paper records) have already produced some rather curious results. For instance, in the 2002 senatorial election in Georgia, which involved decorated war veteran Max Cleland, the Democratic incumbent, and Saxby Chambliss, the Republican challenger, preelection polls showed Cleland ahead by 5 percentage points; and in the gubernatorial race, Democratic incumbent Roy Barnes was ahead of Republican challenger Sonny Perdue by 11 points. On election day, however, Chambliss won with 53 percent of the vote, and Purdue won with 51 percent (Kennedy 2008).

The computerized voting in the Georgia election was run by Diebold Inc., one of the major electronic voting-machine companies in the United States, and one also known to have ties to the Republican Party. Prior to the election, the president of Diebold's election unit, Bob Urosevich, arrived in Georgia from Diebold headquarters in Texas to personally distribute a software "patch" that was supposed to correct glitches in the computer program. According to Chris Hood, a consultant who worked for Diebold in Georgia, "Diebold employees altered software in some 5,000 machines in DeKalb and Fulton counties—the state's largest Democratic strongholds" (quoted in Kennedy 2008:64). It is possible, Hood suggests, that a hidden program on a memory card could have adjusted the votes to a preferred result. But without a paper record that could verify the results in a recount, there is no way of knowing whether or not the machines in Georgia were rigged. As Avi Rubin, a specialist on electronic-voting security observes, "With electronic machines, you can commit wholesale fraud with a single alteration of software. . . . There are a million little tricks you can build into the software that allow you to do whatever you want" (quoted in *Rolling Stone* 2006:54).

Anecdotal accounts of the 2004 presidential election also indicate several cases where votes intended for Democratic candidate Senator John Kerry were recorded for President Bush, votes for Democratic constituencies were undercounted, or Bush was given extra votes (Kennedy 2008; A.

continues

Box 5.3 continued

Miller 2005; M. Miller 2005; Palast 2007). These are not insignificant matters, especially in the state of Ohio, where the entire national election came down to Bush's victory by an official margin of less than 119,000 votes out of more than 5.7 million votes cast statewide. Questions about the validity of the outcome in Ohio have been fueled by a report of a Republican fundraising letter sent by Walden O'Dell, CEO of Diebold, prior to the election, indicating that he was "committed to helping Ohio deliver its electoral votes to the president" (cited in Smyth 2003). Bob Fitrakis offers the following examples, some of which were purportedly corrected and some not, that may have affected the outcome in Ohio:

> In various polling stations in Democrat-rich inner city precincts in Youngstown and Columbus, voters who pushed touch screens for Kerry saw Bush's name light up. . . . A voting machine in Mahoning County recorded a negative 25 million votes for Kerry. . . . In Gahanna Ward 1B, at a fundamentalist church, a so-called "electronic transfer glitch" gave Bush 4,258 votes when only 638 people had actually voted. . . . In Miami County, at 1:43 A.M. the morning after Election Day, with the county's central tabulator reporting 100 percent of the vote, 19,000 more votes mysteriously arrived; 13,000 were for Bush at the same percentage as prior to the additional votes, a virtual statistical impossibility. In Cleveland, large, entirely implausible vote totals turned up for obscure third party candidates in traditional Democratic African-American wards. Vote counts in neighboring wards showed virtually no votes for those candidates, with 90 percent going instead for Kerry. (2008:192–193)

Moreover, James Blackwell, the Republican secretary of state in Ohio, made numerous decisions designed to suppress the African American vote, such as allocating too few voting machines per capita in large urban areas, which led to long lines and waiting periods of up to 5 hours, and in some places up to 10 hours; many people grew impatient and left without voting (A. Miller 2005). None of these problems occurred in Republican-leaning districts. Thus, an investigation into voting irregularities in Ohio headed by Democratic congressman John Conyers concluded:

> The role of voting machines and computers in our election represents an increasingly serious issue in our democracy. Our concerns are exacerbated by the fact that there are few companies who manufacture and operate voting machines, and they tend to be controlled by executives who donate largely, if not exclusively, to the Republican Party and Republican candidates. Issues such as the need for verifiable paper trails and greater accountability all warrant further investigation and possible legislation. (cited in A. Miller 2005:60)

(nine were also fired in 2005–2006) were all Bush appointees (Iglesias 2009; Media Matters for America 2007).

According to Iglesias (2009), the Bush White House and key congressional Republicans were unhappy with the attorneys' record of prosecuting cases of Democratic political corruption and alleged voter fraud that they believed benefited Democratic candidates. At the time of their dismissals, three of the fired attorneys were also conducting corruption probes of Republicans. Key Republicans made inquiries into ongoing investigations, asking for information that was required by law to remain confidential. Iglesias's jurisdiction covered the state of New Mexico, and he received such inquiries from Senator Pete Domenici and Congresswoman Heather Wilson. In one phone call from Domenici, the senator asked whether an ongoing corruption inquiry of a Democratic candidate would lead to an indictment before the November 2006 congressional election, in time to help the Republican win. Domenici was displeased when Iglesias refused to cooperate with his desired timeline (Eggen 2007; Goldstein 2007; Iglesias 2009; Talking Points Memo 2007a).

Whereas Democrats tend to worry about voter *access,* such as increasing the participation of low-turnout constituencies like minorities and college students, Republicans worry about voter *fraud,* such as registration of people who lack proper proof of identity or who do not have citizenship status.[32] But more than fraud is at issue, as indicated by what Iglesias describes as the "reprehensible" practice of **caging,** whereby political operatives target a particular group whose vote they want to suppress (2009:83). Congressman John Conyers's investigation of the 2004 presidential election in Ohio, for instance, uncovered a case of caging by the Ohio Republican Party, which "sent registered letters to newly registered voters in minority and urban areas," who are more likely to vote Democratic, "and then sought to challenge 35,000 individuals who refused to sign for the letter or whose mail otherwise came back as undeliverable" when they showed up at the polls to vote (A. Miller 2005:32–33; see Box 5.3). Iglesias also cites the example of voter registration applications being "sent to a predominately black college during the summer months. When absent students failed to fill out the forms and these were returned as undeliverable, effective challenges to residency could [later] be mounted" (2009:83).

Iglesias thinks that the Bush administration officials involved in the attorney dismissals thought that he and others would "simply slink into our respective corners to lick our wounds" and go quietly away (2009:114–115). But this was not the case. The firings became a national scandal and led to a congressional inquiry, which also revealed the politicized hiring practices of the Bush DOJ, whereby attorneys were hired on the basis of political and ideological criteria, not legal experience or expertise. For example, those whose professional résumés indicated affiliations with conservative political or religious organizations were given preference over those who had affiliations with civil rights or human rights groups that were deemed too liberal. A report by the Office of the Inspector General and the Office of Professional Responsibility found that the biased hiring practices were in violation of civil service laws and could expose the government to civil lawsuits (Johnson 2009; Lichtblau 2008).

One of the most questionable aspects of the US Attorneys scandal was the overzealous prosecution of former Alabama governor Don Siegelman. Siegelman was a popular Democrat in a largely Republican state, the only person in Alabama history to serve in all four of the state's top statewide elected offices: governor, lieutenant governor, attorney general, and secretary of state. Because of his electoral success, he had become a thorn in the side of the Republican Party (Alexandrovna 2008).

Siegelman was defeated in his bid for reelection in 2002 by Republican challenger Bob Riley after a curious set of events. On election night, Baldwin County first reported results that put Siegelman ahead by about 19,000 votes, giving him a 3,120-vote victory margin out of about 1,364,600 votes cast statewide. However, sometime in the middle of the night, Baldwin County conducted a recount, and the next morning reported that Siegleman had actually received less than 13,000 votes, making Riley the winner. Suspiciously, the recount was conducted with only Republican county officers and election supervisors present. Nonetheless, Republican attorney general Bill Pryor certified the recounted vote totals and awarded the governorship to Riley (Alexandrovna 2008; Gundlach 2008; Wilson 2007).

Pryor, who was elected attorney general in 1998, had been at odds with Siegelman as early as 1997, when Lieutenant-Governor Siegelman had criticized Pryor for his close ties to the tobacco industry. Pryor also had close ties to Karl Rove, George W. Bush's chief political adviser, and Leura Canary, the US Attorney for the Middle District of Alabama, whose husband is a close friend of Rove. Almost as soon as she was appointed by President Bush as US Attorney in 2001, Canary began investigating Siegelman for his alleged involvement in a case of Medicaid fraud, which the presiding judge summarily dismissed for lack of evidence in May 2004 (Alexandrovna 2008; Wilson 2007).

Seventeen months later, after Siegelman expressed his intention to run for governor again in 2006, new charges were brought against him, this time for allegedly receiving a bribe from Richard Scrushy, the founder and former CEO of HealthSouth Corporation, in exchange for an appointment to a state hospital regulatory board, a post Scrushy had held under three previous Republican governors. According to the indictment, Scrushy had agreed to donate $500,000 to help "pay off a debt incurred by a non-profit foundation set up by Siegelman and others to promote" a state lottery fund for universal education in Alabama (Alexandrovna 2008:79; Wilson 2007).

The case was assigned to Judge Mark Fuller, who had been appointed to a federal judgeship in 2002 after serving as district attorney in Alabama.[33] When the jurors could not initially reach a unanimous verdict, Fuller told them that he had "a lifetime appointment" and could wait as long as it took (quoted in Wilson 2007:4). Siegelman was subsequently convicted and Fuller sentenced him to seven years and four months in prison; and in an unusual move, Fuller would not allow Siegelman to remain free while he appealed his case (Alexandrovna 2008; Wilson 2007).

Siegelman and his attorneys, as well as reporters in the media, have raised questions about the jury's impartiality, offering evidence that e-mails were exchanged between jurors, that some jurors were reading online news coverage of the case, and that one or more jurors had repeated contacts with the prosecution's legal team during the trial. In March 2008, after being incarcerated for nine months, a US appellate court approved Siegelman's release from prison while he appeals. The following year the court struck down some (but not most) of the charges and ordered a new sentencing hearing. The case is ongoing at the time of this writing (Alexandrovna 2008; Johnson 2009; Wilson 2007; Zagorin 2008).

Summary

In this chapter we shifted our attention from corporate crime to government crime, beginning with the problem of political corruption, which we defined as a form of government malfeasance undertaken by public officials and politicians for direct personal gain. This gain may be both financial and political—that is, it may involve the misuse of public office to accumulate personal wealth as well as to acquire, maintain, and exercise political power. These two domains of corruption—*financially remunerative corruption* and *abuse of power for political gain*—often overlap and mutually reinforce each other.

Regarding financially remunerative corruption, we reviewed notable cases at the local, state, and federal levels of government, as well as the K Street Project lobbying scandal and the problem of corruption in the corporate-government nexus of the disaster-capitalism complex. Turning to the abuse of power for political gain, we examined the infamous Watergate scandal, the Clinton presidency, the disputed presidential election of 2000, and the US Attorneys scandal of the George W. Bush administration.

Notes

1. Tammany Hall, originally founded as the Tammany Society in 1789, was the name of the Democratic political machine in New York City.

2. Harry Daughtery, Harding's attorney general, was also tried (but acquitted) for another corruption scandal related to the bootlegging of alcohol; and Harding's Veteran Bureau director, Charles Forbes, was convicted of embezzlement and served two years in prison (Noggle 1965).

3. The rabbis were laundering money made from selling fake Gucci and Prada bags in a network that stretched from the United States to Israel and Switzerland, and they were even selling kidneys bought from vulnerable people to sell to doctors in Israel (CNN.com 2009; Halbfinger 2009).

4. Barack Obama did not leave Illinois untouched by political scandal because of his association with Antoin "Tony" Rezko, a Chicago "fixer" extraordinaire. Rezko, who had been involved in fundraising for politicians from both political parties since the 1980s (he had raised more than $1 million for Blagojevich) and who had served on several state boards, was indicted in 2006 and later convicted for using his influence to extort money from investment firms wanting to do business with the state. Prior to his presidential campaign, Obama had been the beneficiary of some of Rezko's fundraising largesse, and had even bought some real estate from him. But there is no evidence that Obama did anything untoward with respect to his relationship with Rezko (McClelland 2008).

5. These data are from a study conducted by the *Corporate Crime Reporter* (2007), which ranked the following states as having the highest per capita rates of corruption: (1) Louisiana, (2) Mississippi, (3) Kentucky, (4) Alabama, (5) Ohio, (6) Illinois, (7) Pennsylvania, (8) Florida, (9) New Jersey, and (10) New York.

6. During the famed days of Mayor Richard J. Daley's Democratic political machine in Chicago, which lasted from 1955 to 1976, "city workers had to kick back about 5 percent of their salaries to the political organization that guaranteed their jobs" (Weisberg 2008:2). Weisberg notes that Illinois corruption has been the province not just of Chicago Democrats but also of suburban Republicans.

7. Edwards's son was also convicted and sentenced to seven years in prison (Rosoff, Pontell, and Tillman 2007).

8. Operation ABSCAM raised the issue of entrapment, which is a potential defense to criminal liability. However, a successful entrapment defense must

show that the defendant had no predisposition to commit a crime—that is, the government's actions were such as to have caused a normally law-abiding person to commit a crime that he or she was not predisposed to commit.

9. In Chapter 1 we also noted the Sewergate scandal, which occurred during the Reagan administration.

10. Ney was convicted on charges of corruption and sentenced to 30 months in prison (Schmidt and Grimaldi 2007).

11. DeLay was accused of funneling $500,000 in corporate campaign contributions through his political action committee to Republican candidates in the 2002 election, which is explicitly prohibited under Texas law, and was convicted in November 2010 on charges of money laundering.

12. For a broader consideration of police corruption, see Barker and Carter 1999, Berger, Free, and Searles 2009, and Rosoff, Pontell, and Tillman 2007.

13. The media often gave Guiliani high marks for New York City's response to 9/11. But Wayne Barrett and Dan Collins (2006) suggest that the decisions he made prior to the terrorist attacks actually made the disaster worse—for example, his decision to locate the city's Emergency Operations Center in one of the World Trade Center buildings, even though the World Trade Center had already been the site of a terrorist bombing in 1993 that left six people dead and more than a thousand injured. Consequently, on 9/11 the Emergency Operations Center was inoperative, contributing to the failure of key responding agencies to communicate with one another. And irrespective of the location, a study conducted by the National Institute of Standards and Technology found that "New York City did not have a formalized Incident Command System that encompassed citywide emergency response operations" (cited in Barrett and Collins 2006:40). Barrett and Collins argue that Guiliani's post-9/11 effort to don the mantle of terrorism expert is based on a "grand illusion" (see also Griffin 2008).

14. For other examples of former (and sometimes current) governmental officials giving policy advice that advanced their commercial interests, see Hersh 2004, Klein 2007, and Roche and Silverstein 2004.

15. In 2006 a federal jury in Virginia found the Custer Battles security firm guilty of fraud for its actions in Iraq. But the judge nullified the verdict, accepting Custer Battles's and the Bush administration's claim that US contractors working in Iraq under the CPA were indemnified under US law as well (Klein 2007).

16. Halliburton sold its stake in Kellogg Brown and Root for a gain of $933 million in 2007 (Bloomberg News 2007).

17. One of Woodward and Bernstein's key informants, who gave them "off the record" information that guided their investigation, was known as "Deep Throat." For over three decades the journalists protected his identity. In 2005, just before he died, Mark Felt decided to reveal himself. Felt had been the associate director of the FBI at the time (Thomas 2005).

18. The FBI and CIA, as noted in Chapters 1 and 2, also were involved in activities they did not want disclosed to the American public (see also Chapter 6). For his part, Liddy, along with other White House personnel such as former CIA agent Howard Hunt and lawyer Charles Colson, had seriously contemplated some rather nefarious schemes that, though they were not carried out, are

indicative of the "anything goes" mind-set that pervaded the Nixon administration. These included plans to disrupt the 1972 Democratic National Convention and lure convention delegates into uncompromising positions with prostitutes, kidnap radical leaders who planned an antiwar demonstration at the 1972 Republican National Convention, set a fire at the Brookings Institution to create a diversion so that they could steal documents, and even assassinate investigative journalist Jack Anderson (Bernstein and Woodward 1974; Dean 1976; deHaven-Smith 2010; Summers 2000).

19. There is evidence that Democratic candidates who might have made a stronger challenge to Nixon's reelection chances were harmed by these efforts, which focused on Senators Edward Kennedy, Edmund Muskie, and Henry Jackson. Nixon eventually ran against Senator George McGovern, whom he defeated in a landslide (Gumbel 2005; Summers 2000).

20. See Beck 1982 for the cast of characters and the sentences they received.

21. Nixon also believed that he had been the victim of election shenanigans in Texas, the home state of Senator Lyndon Johnson, Kennedy's running mate (Greenberg 2000). See Gumbel (2005) for a historical review of corrupted elections in the United States.

22. Compared to the losses on Neil Bush's Silverado savings and loan (about $1 billion), $60 million was a relatively small amount (see Chapter 3, note 6).

23. Clinton's political foes *falsely* claimed that while he was governor he had pressured David Hale, a municipal judge and corrupt businessman, to make an illicit $300,000 loan from Hale's Capital Management firm to the McDougals, and that money from Madison Guaranty had been diverted to a Clinton campaign fund. Hale made these allegations in the face of a criminal indictment, hoping to exchange information about Clinton for leniency (Conason and Lyons 2000).

24. Largely unreported in the press were the allegations of mismanagement of funds and other malfeasance by Travel Office director Billy Hale. Hale was tried but found not guilty of charges that he funneled $50,000 of Travel Office funds into his personal account (Conason and Lyons 2000).

25. Most notably, wealthy right-wing ideologue Richard Mellon Scaife, whose self-professed mission was "to discredit and if possible destroy Bill Clinton," funded the so-called Arkansas Project, providing the *American Spectator* magazine with some $2.4 million over a four-year period in an "attempt to gather intelligence leading to the political ruin of the president" (Conason and Lyons 2000:108, 111).

26. Prior to Starr's appointment, a special prosecutor appointed by Attorney General Janet Reno had been assigned to look into the case. After a five-month investigation, Robert Fiske, a moderate Republican attorney with a record of successful prosecution of "several highly sensitive white-collar and organized-crime cases," had cleared Clinton of any wrongdoing (Conason and Lyons 2000:119). Fiske's findings, however, only infuriated congressional Republicans, who then authorized an investigation of their own.

Toward the end of his investigation, Starr announced his intention to accept a position as the first dean of the newly created School of Public Policy at

Pepperdine University (Conason and Lyons 2000). When the press revealed that the school had been established through a $1.35 million grant from Richard Mellon Scaife (see note 25 in this chapter), the apparent conflict of interest forced Starr to decline the position. Later, in 2004, he became dean of the Pepperdine School of Law.

27. Those who knew her described Jones "as an unreliable, self-dramatizing person who had made a pest of herself hanging around the reception desk outside the governor's office, prattling about Clinton's sex appeal like a starstruck teenager" (Conason and Lyons 2000:126).

28. That relationship itself could be considered sexual harassment if harassment is construed to refer to sex with a subordinate under one's employ, even if the sex was consensually accepted, encouraged, or even initiated by the employee.

29. While the impeachment process was unfolding, the trial judge in the Jones lawsuit ruled that Jones had not shown she had suffered any damages, even if the sexual harassment had occurred, and dismissed the case. Jones appealed the decision but then agreed to accept an $850,000 out-of-court settlement (without an apology or admission of culpability from Clinton) in exchange for dropping her appeal (Conason and Lyons 2000).

30. Andrew Johnson, who became president after the assassination of Abraham Lincoln, was the only other president to be impeached. Like Clinton, Johnson was acquitted.

31. McCain, of course, denounced these tactics, but during his own bid for the presidency in 2008, his campaign waged a similar (though unsuccessful) scurrilous campaign against Senator Barack Obama, accusing him, among other things, of being anti-American and cavorting with terrorists (Berman 2008; Schell 2008).

32. Much of the Republicans' ire about voter fraud has been directed at the Association of Community Organizations of Reform (ACORN), which has been involved in voter registration drives around the country. Critics of ACORN believe that the organization has been systematically registering ineligible voters. But the evidence for this rests on a few cases of lower-level ACORN employees submitting fraudulent registrant names (employees were paid for every voter they registered). When ACORN administrators discovered the fraud, these registrant names were reported to election authorities, as required by law, and eliminated from the voter list, and the offending employees were fired (de Vogue 2008; Iglesias 2009).

33. Gary McAliley, Fuller's replacement as district attorney, later accused Fuller of defrauding the Alabama retirement system by spiking salaries when he served as district attorney (Alexandrovna 2008).

6

State Crimes
of Foreign Policy

JOHN FOSTER DULLES (1888–1959) WAS A QUINTESSENTIAL member of the power elite in the United States. His grandfather and namesake, John Watson Dulles, was a lawyer-diplomat who negotiated international treaties and loans to foreign governments, undertook diplomatic missions for US presidents, and served as secretary of state under President Benjamin Harrison. John Foster Dulles attended law school at George Washington University and took a position with the prestigious law firm Sullivan & Cromwell, where his client list was "nothing less than a guide to the biggest multinational corporations of early–twentieth century America" (Kinser 2006:13). Until the mid-1930s, Dulles had a law office in Nazi Germany and was a public supporter of Adolf Hitler.[1] Following World War II, he helped negotiate international treaties and was appointed by President Dwight Eisenhower as secretary of state, a position he held from 1953 to 1959.

As a man of deep Christian faith, Dulles was staunchly anti-Communist, and with the dawn of the Cold War he advocated an uncompromising attitude toward the Soviet Union, resolutely opposing economic and cultural exchanges with any country under Communist rule and promising to "'roll back' Communism by securing the 'liberation' of nations that had fallen to its 'despotism and godless terrorism'" (Kinser 2006:117). The methodology of this foreign policy was first and foremost financial and diplomatic. Ruling elites in foreign countries would be kept in power as long as they were hospitable to US interests. The "carrot" comprised foreign loans, economic aid, and bribery. The "stick" comprised military intervention and regime change (Kramer and Michalowski 2005; Moyers 1988; Perkins 2004).[2]

Dulles's posture invoked a Darwinian struggle of survival of the fittest, where in a dangerous world filled with ruthless enemies, one must employ all means necessary in order to survive. As noted in Chapter 2, a report prepared for the White House by a commission headed by former president Herbert Hoover during Dulles's term as secretary of state, set forth the policy bluntly: "If the United States is to survive . . . [w]e must learn to subvert, sabotage and destroy our enemies by more clever, more sophisticated, more effective methods than those used against us" (cited in Moyers 1988:42).

Arguably the first shot in this Machiavellian game of world affairs was fired in Iran in 1953, when the Central Intelligence Agency fomented and funded a successful coup d'état that resulted in the overthrow of the democratically elected government headed by Prime Minister Mohammad Mossadegh, who was once dubbed by *Time* magazine as the "Iranian George Washington" (Kinser 2006). Under Mossadegh's leadership, the Iranians had decided to nationalize the oil industry, which was controlled by the British. **Nationalization** refers to the process whereby a government assumes control and/or redistributes ownership of a nation's industries or natural resources, with the purported intent of benefiting the entire nation rather than foreign corporate interests. This process may (but not always) involve compensation to corporations for the appropriation of their businesses.

Mossadegh intended to compensate the Anglo-Iranian Oil Company, a corporation owned principally by the British, which "had held a monopoly on the extraction, refining, and sale of Iranian oil" since 1901 (Kinser 2006:117). During that time, less than 16 percent of the company's profits were paid to Iran, a practice Mossadegh intended to change. Dulles was concerned that this policy did not bode well for US oil interests in the region. To further that end, he decided to employ the CIA, an offshoot of the Office of Strategic Services, which had been formed during World War II. Established by the **National Security Act** of 1947, the CIA was authorized to gather intelligence about perceived foreign threats to national security and also to engage in covert activities to oppose such threats. During the administration of President Harry Truman, the CIA had been deployed to support anti-Communist political parties in Europe. Never before, however, had it been used to overthrow a government. Fortuitously for Dulles, it just so happened that his younger brother Allen was director of the CIA, making for seamless deployment of the CIA in Iran in what was dubbed **Operation Ajax** (Kinser 2006; Moyers 1988).

The method of regime change in Operation Ajax employed both propaganda and violence. Journalists, publishers, Islamic clergy, and other opinion leaders were bribed to create a climate of public hostility and distrust toward Mossadegh and his government. Demonstrators were paid to flood the streets of the capital, Tehran, where they converged on parliament to demand Mossadegh's ouster. Gangs of street thugs started riots as the city descended into violence. According to the plan, order would be restored by bringing the country back under the control of its ruling monarch, Mohammed Reza Pahlavi, the Shah of Iran, whose influence had been dramatically curtailed under Mossadegh. The Shah's subsequent rule, which lasted for a quarter century, was a brutal dictatorship, until he too was overthrown, this time by an anti-American Islamic revolution led by Ayatollah Ruhollah Khomeini in 1979 (Kinser 2006; Moyers 1988; Simon [1982] 2006).

The consequences of US interference in the affairs of a country like Iran are aptly noted by constitutional law professor Edwin Firmage: "You create in that state sufficient forces of unrest that don't have stability. You create a nation who hates you enormously, who views you as a devil, an evil force. . . . And those chickens come home to roost" (quoted in Moyers 1988:39). As one Iranian diplomat observed 50 years after the Iranian coup: "The 1953 coup and its consequences [were] the starting point for the political alignments in today's Middle East and inner Asia. With hindsight, can anyone say that the Islamic Revolution of 1979 was inevitable? Or did it only become so once the [democratic] aspirations of the Iranian people were temporarily expunged in 1953?" (quoted in Kinser 2006:203).

The actions of the US government in Iran and other countries that are described in this chapter fall under the rubric of **state crimes**, which we have characterized as illegal acts of political repression, whether violent or nonviolent, aimed at maintaining social order or fomenting disorder, as the case may be (see Chapter 2). State crimes may entail the violation of US law, international law, or the law of the affected nation (or, if we were to adopt a broader definition of crime, analogous social injuries). In the area of foreign policy, criminologists have characterized state crimes that occur at the nexus of corporate and government power as part of the US "imperial project" of keeping foreign markets open to US commerce at all costs (Kramer and Michalowski 2005:454). In this chapter, we will consider US actions to overthrow foreign governments—from Latin America in the 1950s through the invasion of Iraq in the 2000s. We will also consider the state practice of torture—from the Cold War through the contemporary War on Terror—as a tool of political repression.

Overthrowing Foreign Governments

We begin with an overview of US actions in three Latin American countries—Guatemala, Cuba, and Chile—from the 1950s to the 1970s. We then consider events that led to the Vietnam War, which cover the same three decades, as well as the Iran-Contra scandal of the 1980s.

Latin America, 1950s–1970s

A year after the Iranian coup, in **Operation Success**, the CIA also engineered the overthrow of Jacob Arbenz, the democratically elected president of Guatemala. Arbenz had embarked on an ambitious reform program to redistribute land to the impoverished peasantry (less than 3 percent of the landowners controlled more than 70 percent of the land). This action was a direct challenge to the United Fruit Company, a US corporation, which owned about one-fifth of Guatemala's arable land, less than 15 percent of which it cultivated. The United Fruit Company persuaded the US government that it could not let Arbenz's reforms stand (Kinser 2006; Moyers 1988; Simon [1982] 2006).[3] Decades later, in 1999, President Bill Clinton apologized to a group of civic leaders in Guatemala City: "It is important that I state clearly that support for military forces and intelligence units which engaged in violence and widespread repression was wrong, and the United States must not repeat that mistake again" (quoted in Kinser 2006:207).

Clinton's belated apology was fitting, but Guatemala did not exhaust the violence unleashed by past US interventions in Latin America and elsewhere. In the Watergate tapes, for example, President Richard Nixon had expressed concern that an investigation of his administration might disclose to the public "the whole **Bay of Pigs** thing . . . which would be very unfortunate . . . for [the] CIA and this country" (quoted in Miller 1974:27). It appears that the five Watergate burglars were former CIA operatives, four of whom were Cuban exiles who years earlier had been involved in a US campaign to overthrow Cuban dictator Fidel Castro. One component of this effort was an invasion that was to take place at the Bay of Pigs on the south coast of Cuba.[4]

In 1959 Castro had taken power after leading a successful revolution against his dictatorial predecessor, Fulgencio Batista. As Batista had been an ally of the United States, Castro turned to the Soviet Union for military and economic aid and proceeded to nationalize US businesses in Cuba. Of course, economic and political elites in the United States deemed Castro's program of nationalization harmful to US interests (Douglass 2008; Kinser 2006; Summers 2000; Waldron and Hartmann 2005).

Nixon, who was vice president at the time of the Cuban Revolution, had been one of the main strategists behind a plan to deploy about 1,500 CIA-trained Cuban exiles, with support of US ground troops and planes, to invade the Bay of Pigs and overthrow the Castro government. When Nixon lost the 1960 presidential election to John Kennedy, the Kennedy administration inherited the anti-Cuban operation. Kennedy reluctantly approved a revised plan that would not involve direct intervention of US troops, expecting that the Cuban people would join with the invaders in overthrowing the Castro regime. Only supportive air strikes would be forthcoming, provided the invaders could secure a beachhead from which to launch the operation. The invasion took place in April 1961, about three months after Kennedy took office. When Castro's forces launched a successful counteroffensive, the invaders were pinned down at the beach. The CIA and US military thought that Kennedy would relent and fully commit US troops and planes. But Kennedy, concerned about a confrontation with the Soviet Union, did not; and the invaders were left defenseless and forced to surrender (Douglass 2008; Summers 2000; Talbot 2007; Waldron and Hartmann 2005).

Chile was another Latin American democracy that was dismantled by the US government in that era. In the late 1960s, the CIA and private US corporations funneled millions of dollars into Chile to try to block the election of presidential candidate Salvadore Allende, who had been campaigning on a platform of nationalizing foreign industries. Central to this effort was International Telephone and Telegraph, which feared losing its dominance over Chile's burgeoning communications business, and Kennecott Copper Construction and Anaconda Copper Mining Company, the "twin titans" of the global copper industry (Kinser 2006:174; Rosoff, Pontell, and Tillman 2007).[5]

After Allende was elected in 1970, the US government tried to destabilize the Chilean economy, withholding supplies necessary for Chilean industries, pressuring world financial institutions to deny Chile loans, and organizing an international boycott of Chilean products. The CIA supported military leaders who opposed Allende and encouraged them to assassinate General René Schneider, a prominent military figure who "fiercely opposed any military interference in politics" (Kinser 2006:182). General Schneider was killed in 1970, and three years later the Allende government was overthrown and Allende was killed too. Thousands of pro-Allende Chileans were arrested, tortured, murdered, and/or exiled under the dictatorship of General Augusto Pinochet, who came into power after the coup. A similar story has been repeated elsewhere in Latin America and other developing countries: military dictators backed by the US government have ruled through fear, intimidation, and brutality; and government "death squads," some financed or trained by the CIA, have kidnapped, tortured, and murdered those who threatened their regimes (Klein 2007; McCoy 2005; Simon [1982] 2006; Summers 2000).

The Vietnam War

For the most part, at the time, Americans remained uninformed or aloof of the events described thus far in this chapter.[6] In Vietnam, however, the United States was rocked to its foundation. Vietnam, a French colony since the nineteenth century, had been occupied by the Japanese during World War II. After Japan surrendered in 1945, popular Vietnam leader Ho Chi Minh declared his country's independence in a speech "before a large crowd in the northern city of Hanoi . . . that any American would have found familiar" (Kinser 2006:150): "All men are created equal. They are endowed by their creator with certain inalienable rights. Among these are life, liberty, and the pursuit of happiness" (quoted on p. 150).

Although the French, with the United States' backing, were determined to resume their control after World War II, Vietnamese guerrilla fighters forced them to capitulate. When the French ended their rule over Vietnam in a muted ceremony in October 1954, few anticipated the conflict that would ensue. By international agreement, the country was to be divided between North Vietnam and South Vietnam for two years, at which time an election would be held to choose the leader of a united country. By all accounts, Ho was expected to win that election (Ehrlich and Goldsmith 2009; Kinser 2006).

An independent Vietnam was not a prospect the United States could easily abide, especially because Ho was an avowed Communist. To counter Ho's leadership in North Vietnam, the United States installed Ngo Dinh Diem, a devout Catholic and staunch anti-Communist, as prime minister of South Vietnam. When Diem and the United States refused to hold the promised 1956 election, tensions between the South and North mounted. In 1960, the North Vietnamese known as the Vietcong launched a guerrilla military campaign aimed at "the elimination of the US imperialists and the Ngo Dinh Diem clique" (quoted in Kinser 2006:154).

Diem was an unpopular leader, even in South Vietnam. As a member of a religious group that represented only 10 percent of the country, he lacked a natural following; and his regime was known for cronyism and corruption. He survived two early coup attempts only with the help of

CIA money used to bribe dissident leaders, and his increasing reliance on US support only further undermined his popularity (Kinser 2006).

During the Kennedy administration, from 1961 to 1963, US troops under the guise of military "advisers" launched ground and air attacks against the Vietcong, which also cost the lives of 108 Americans. But with the Vietcong establishing control of 20 percent of South Vietnam, the United States faced a decision: Should it draw down the number of troops and withdraw, or should it further escalate its military involvement? The United States, as we now know, chose escalation (Kinser 2006).

Back in Washington, D.C., some officials in the Kennedy administration advocated overthrowing the unpopular Diem and replacing him with a more effective military leader: General Duong Van Minh. That view prevailed, in spite of Kennedy's reservations. The coup went forward, and Diem was ousted and killed. But General Minh only held power for three months before he, too, was overthrown in another coup, which was followed by a succession of military strongmen who ruled South Vietnam by force while the United States sent in more troops— more than 500,000 by the mid-1960s—in a war that lasted until 1975. More than 58,000 US troops lost their lives in that conflict; the Vietnamese lost more than 1 million (Douglass 2008; Kinser 2006; Talbot 2007).

A key event in the escalation of the Vietnam War, which the Vietnamese call the American War, was the passage of the **Gulf of Tonkin Resolution** in the summer of 1964, which gave President Lyndon Johnson congressional authorization to commence open warfare against North Vietnam. President Kennedy, before his assassination in November 1963, had been reluctant to escalate the war (Kinser 2006; Douglass 2008; Talbot 2007). President Johnson, on the other hand, was not. He firmly believed in the **domino theory** of Communist aggression; if the Communists were allowed to take over the South, he thought, they would soon push the war to "the beaches of Waikiki" (quoted in Kinser 2006:155).

Prior to the passage of the Gulf of Tonkin Resolution, the US Navy had been deploying destroyers on intelligence-gathering missions off the coast of Vietnam in the Gulf of Tonkin, outside of international waters. These operations were conducted in conjunction with secretive "undeclared" US and South Vietnamese military strikes against the North Vietnamese in the area. On August 2, 1964, a North Vietnamese patrol consisting of three Soviet-built motor torpedo boats confronted the USS *Maddox,* a destroyer that had been part of these operations, in international waters. As the United States dispatched the USS *Turner Joy*

destroyer and fighter jets to the area, the captain of the *Maddox* instructed his gun crews to fire three warning shots if the North Vietnamese
came within 10,000 yards of the ship. When the warning shots were
fired, the North Vietnamese launched three torpedoes, which missed
their mark, but the North Vietnamese did hit the *Maddox* with a round of
deck guns. The *Maddox* and fighter jets then turned back the North
Vietnamese boats, "damaging two and leaving one dead in the water"
(Hickman 2010:2; Marolda 2010).

Two days later, with the *Maddox* and *Turner Joy* still cruising the
area, the *Maddox* picked up a series of radar and sonar signals that suggested another attack. The ship took some evasive maneuvers and fired on
the radar targets. When the *Maddox* captain reported the incident to the
top command, he noted that no actual visual sightings of the North
Vietnamese had been made and that the signals the *Maddox* had received
might have been caused by the turbulent weather conditions in the area. In
fact, the purported attack was a false alarm; no second attack had taken
place. Nonetheless, the propaganda value of the mythical attack was
immense, enabling President Johnson to garner congressional and public
support for passage of the Gulf of Tonkin Resolution and thus launching a
new phase in this long and costly US war (Cohen and Solomon 1994;
Ehrlich and Goldsmith 2009; Hickman 2010; Marolda 2010).[7]

The Iran-Contra Scandal

In the aftermath of Watergate, the US Congress began investigating the
operations of the CIA and set up mechanisms that allowed for greater
congressional oversight of the organization.[8] President Jimmy Carter
(1977–1981) appointed Admiral Stansfield Turner to direct the agency;
and when Turner reduced the agency's covert operation section from
1,200 to 400 agents, many in the CIA were quite obviously displeased.
They did not consider themselves dispensable. Better to have their old
boss, George H. W. Bush—who had served as CIA director for the year
prior to Carter's taking office—back at the helm. The election of
President Ronald Reagan and Vice President George Bush in November
1980 was welcomed by most everyone in the CIA (Chambliss 1988;
Mayer 2009).

The most significant cluster of crimes that occurred during the
Reagan administration became known as the **Iran-Contra scandal**. The
two elements of this scandal—the Iran component and the Contra component—initially represented two independent foreign policy operations. Iran, as noted earlier, experienced an Islamic revolution that

Box 6.1 The Kennedy Assassination

In this and the preceding chapter, we have reviewed attempts by political officials and the US government to subvert the democratic process, even to the extent of working to overthrow democratically elected governments of foreign countries. These events are facts of the historical record. There are other events, however, that remain more opaque, more of a mystery, and attempts to "connect the dots" are often disparagingly dismissed as the ravings of crank "conspiracy theorists" (deHaven-Smith 2010).

Bill Moyers, a respected journalist, is no crank, and he notes that the actions of the US government—its clandestine operations at home and abroad—are made "more chilling" by the November 22, 1963, assassination of President John Kennedy in Dallas, Texas (1988:44). No event in American history has been more shrouded in myth and conjecture than the assassination of the thirty-fifth president of the United States. The **Warren Commission**, appointed by President Lyndon Johnson and headed by US Supreme Court justice Earl Warren, concluded in 1963 that assassin Lee Harvey Oswald had acted alone. Oswald, a former Marine who became involved in US intelligence, is believed by some to have been a Soviet defector, by others to have been a double agent. He lived only two days from the time he was arrested until he was shot by Jack Ruby, a night-club owner, while he was being transferred from the city jail to the county jail.

Lamar Waldron and Thom Hartmann (2005, 2008) are among those who believe that Oswald, who moved in the circles of the shadowy US government, was a patsy for an assassination plot involving organized crime, a view that finds support in a 1979 investigation by the House Select Committee on Assassinations (Blakey and Billing 1981). Waldron and Hartmann muster substantially more evidence than was available to the assassinations committee (including interviews with key players and previously classified information), evidence that implicates Mafia bosses Santo Trafficante, Johnny Rosselli, and especially Carlos Marcello, the godfather of New Orleans, who controlled criminal operations in Louisiana and Texas. These men, among other criminal associates, were furious with the president and his brother Robert Kennedy, both of whom had been investigating organized crime even before coming to the White House, John as senator and Robert as a senatorial aid. When President Kennedy appointed his brother as attorney general, the organized crime bosses had reason to be concerned. In fact, in 1961, Robert Kennedy had succeeded in deporting Marcello, who was born in Tunisia, to Central America. Marcello managed to reenter the United States, but he was under prosecution by the Justice Department at the time of the assassina-

continues

FURTHER EXPLORATION

Box 6.1 continued

tion. Waldron and Hartmann note as well that Jack Ruby had ties to organized crime. They muster evidence to show that he was tasked with the job of eliminating Oswald, who had professed his innocence, so he could not reveal what he knew.

When Nixon feared that an investigation of Watergate might lead to disclosure of "the whole Bay of Pigs thing" (discussed elsewhere in this chapter), he might also have been thinking of the CIA plots to assassinate Fidel Castro, some of which were coordinated with organized crime. Organized crime bosses did not like Castro any more than did the US government, because the Cuban dictator had been closing down their casino gambling operations in Havana, where they had flourished prior to the Cuban Revolution. Waldron and Hartmann (2005, 2008) argue that the organized crime bosses, having penetrated the US intelligence apparatus, were also in a position to know about John and Robert Kennedy's secretive plan for a second invasion attempt of Cuba in December 1963. The authors offer evidence of a cover-up that withheld information from the Warren Commission in order to conceal this plan, noting that Robert Kennedy, who also was assassinated under suspicious circumstances in 1968, was involved in this cover-up too.

To be sure, the Warren Commission's account, which posits Oswald as the lone assassin, has its staunch defenders (Bugliosi 2007; Posner 1994), but much to their chagrin, national polls consistently find that 70–80 percent of Americans have doubts about that version of events (Bugliosi 2007). At a minimum, it is clear that the Warren Commission did not investigate all leads. And so suspicions linger and accusations persist, as Moyers notes, intimating "a dark, unsolved conspiracy behind [Kennedy's] murder. You can dismiss them, as many of us do, but since we know now what our secret government planned for [others], the possibility remains: once we decide that anything goes, anything can come home to haunt us" (1988:44).

replaced the regime that had been installed and supported by the United States back in 1953. In November 1979, anti-American forces seized the US embassy in Tehran, taking over 50 hostages, who were not released until just after Reagan was inaugurated in January 1981.

The hostage crisis had been a major problem for the Carter administration. Had Carter been able to pull an "October surprise" just before the election, he would have had a better chance of winning. Former Carter administration official Gary Sick (1991), among others, believes a deal may have been struck between the Reagan-Bush campaign and representatives of the Iranian government to delay the release of the hostages. There is evidence that William Casey, the Reagan-Bush campaign director who later headed the CIA, had met with Iranian arms dealers who had contacts in the Iranian government. Some also allege that the Reagan-Bush campaign had informants within the US military-intelligence community who provided information about US aircraft movements related to the hostage crisis. And some believe that someone associated with the Reagan-Bush camp stole briefing papers from President Carter's reelection campaign before the October presidential debates. While such charges have never been proven, the history of Watergate and other clandestine actions of the US government makes these allegations entirely plausible to more than a few people knowledgeable about that era. If true, they "would be tantamount to treason" (Hagan 1997:74; see also deHaven-Smith 2010; Simon 2006).

During the early years of the Reagan administration, Iranian forces bombed US (and French) embassies in the Middle East. Over 200 US troops stationed in Beirut, Lebanon, were killed in their barracks during a suicide bombing. More hostages were taken, including William Buckley, the CIA's chief of station in Beirut. The US government's official policy, the public was told, was not to negotiate with terrorists. It was also a violation of the **US Arms Export Control Act** to sell arms to countries (like Iran) that supported terrorism. But negotiate with Iran the United States did; it also sold arms (missiles and missile parts) to Iran, at first through Israel but later directly. In the process, arms-merchant middlemen such as retired US Air Force general Richard Secord and Iranian-born businessman Albert Hakim (now a US citizen) grew rich. Following the arms sales, hostages were not always released; and when they were, more were taken. Perhaps the official policy of not negotiating with terrorists was the right stance after all. But there was money to be made, and the Reagan administration needed it (Brinkley and Engelberg 1988).

This brings us to the Contra part of the Iran-Contra scandal. Like Iran, the Central American country of Nicaragua experienced a revolution in the late 1970s that the US government opposed. Dictator Anastasio Somoza, an ally of the United States, was removed from power, and the Sandinista National Liberation Front took control of the government. The Sandinistas turned to Cuba and the Soviet Union for economic and military aid. The Reagan administration, which believed the Sandinistas were fomenting revolution elsewhere in Latin America, found this unacceptable (Kinser 2006; Moyers 1988; Simon 2006).

The Contras, the armed Nicaraguan opponents of the Sandinista regime, did not have popular support in their country. They were essentially a creation of the CIA, which was now headed by Casey. Without the CIA and the money and training it supplied, there would have been no Contras. Although Reagan often compared the Contras to the "founding fathers" of the United States, they included former military officers of the Somoza regime as well as men who condoned terrorism, accepted money from drug traffickers, and even trafficked in drugs themselves (see Box 6.2).

In the aftermath of the Vietnam War, the American public did not have the stomach for such a controversial foreign policy campaign, especially if it threatened to involve US troops. And the CIA-Contra operation did not get good publicity, as Nicaraguan harbors had been mined and oil facilities burned, and innocent people were being terrorized and killed. Excerpts of a CIA pamphlet on guerrilla warfare that the Contras had been reading were reported in the press: "It is possible to neutralize carefully selected and planned targets, such as court judges [and] security officials. . . . Professional criminals should be hired to [take] . . . demonstrators to a confrontation with the authorities to bring about uprisings and shootings that will . . . create a martyr" (cited in Alpern 1984:30).

During the early 1980s, the US Congress, which has constitutional power over governmental appropriations, vacillated in its support of the Contras, approving funds, taking them away, approving them again. But in a definitive legislative statement, the **Boland Amendment**, Congress proclaimed:

> During fiscal year 1985, no funds available to the Central Intelligence Agency, the Department of Defense, or any other agency or entity of the United States involved in intelligence activities may be obligated or expended for the purpose of which would have the effect of supporting, directly or indirectly, military or paramilitary operations in Nicaragua by any nation, group, organization, movement or individuals. (cited in Brinkley and Engelberg 1988:414)

President Reagan signed the Boland Amendment into law in October 1984, creating a perplexing problem for his administration: How would it maintain the Contras when it was *illegal* to do so? What followed was nothing short of an assault on the US Constitution. As Senator John Kerry said, the administration was "willing to literally put the Constitution at risk because they believed somehow there was a higher order of things, that the ends do in fact justify . . . the means. That's the most . . . totalitarian doctrine I've ever heard of" (quoted in Moyers 1988:28).

The task of supporting the Contras was given to the National Security Council, a White House advisory board headed by Robert McFarland. According to McFarland, Reagan instructed him to find a way to keep the Contras' "body and soul together" (quoted in Brinkley and Engelberg 1988:12). McFarland assigned a US Marine lieutenant-colonel, Oliver North, the job of working out the details and being the White House liaison to the Contras. North and associates raised millions of dollars from private groups and individuals in the United States and from allies such as the governments of Saudi Arabia, Taiwan, and Brunei. Central American countries such as Costa Rica, El Salvador, Guatemala, and Honduras were pressured or cajoled (with a promise of military aid) to allow their territories to be used as bases for the Contra resupply operation. At the request of CIA director Casey, North worked with Secord and Hakim to create a private (profit-making) organization, which they called **The Enterprise**, to coordinate the operation. Senator Daniel Inouye described The Enterprise as "a shadowy government with its own air force, its own navy, its own fundraising mechanism, and the ability to pursue its own ideas of the national interest, free from all checks and balances and free from the law itself" (quoted in Moyers 1988:24). The link between the Iran and Contra initiatives was forged as profits from the Iranian arms sales were diverted through The Enterprise to the Contras. This became, according to North, "an attractive incentive" to continue to sell arms to Iran (quoted in Brinkley and Engelberg 1988:16). Moreover, Casey envisioned The Enterprise as a permanent "off-the-shelf" entity with the stand-alone capacity to conduct covert operations beyond the purview of Congress.

The secrecy surrounding these operations began to crumble in October 1986, halfway through President Reagan's second term, when a Contra resupply plane linked to the CIA was shot down over Nicaragua. The story was covered worldwide. And in November a Lebanese magazine disclosed the arms sales to Iran. Reagan and other White House officials first denied the stories but soon decided they would have to cut their losses, concede that some improper conduct had occurred, and develop a cover story to protect the president. In the meantime, North and his secretary frantically destroyed as many incriminating documents and memorandums as possible. But they did not get everything.

The cover story cast North in the role of a renegade, a well-intentioned soldier who had gone too far. North, however, was not about to take all of the blame. When he was granted immunity to testify before the (televised) joint House and Senate hearing, which began in May 1987, he became a media sensation. He was "a defiant hero, an obedient soldier, a blameless scapegoat whose conduct had been dictated or approved by his superiors" (Rosoff, Pontell, and Tillman 2007:394). "This nation," North said, "cannot abide the communization of Central America. We cannot have Soviet bases on the mainland of this hemisphere" (quoted in Moyers 1988:28).

During the Watergate scandal, it had taken two years to develop evidence that linked Nixon to criminal activities. Just over two years after the Iran-Contra scandal broke, Reagan's term expired. It was only later that the American public learned the full extent of Reagan's complicity, but by then any question of impeachment was moot. Several members of The Enterprise and a number of Reagan administration officials, however, pled guilty or were convicted of crimes.[9] The sentences overall were less severe than the sentences given to the Watergate defendants. All but one received only probation or fines. Admiral John Poindexter, who had succeeded McFarland as National Security Council adviser, received a six-month prison term, but his conviction was overturned on appeal. Like North, he had been granted immunity for his congressional testimony. Thus, said the US Supreme Court, his right to a fair trial had been compromised. North had his three felony counts reversed on appeal as well. He pronounced himself "totally exonerated," became a highly paid luminary on the lecture circuit, and was Virginia's Republican nominee for the US Senate in 1994 (Rosoff, Pontell, and Tillman 2007:395). He lost the election and joined the ranks (along with G. Gordon Liddy) of right-wing media pundits.

Iraqgate

Since August 1990, when Iraqi dictator Saddam Hussein invaded the country of Kuwait, which precipitated the 1991 Gulf War, US policies vis-à-vis Iraq have been in the news. And even prior to the controversial US invasion of Iraq in March 2003 and the ensuing US occupation of that country, scandal had marked the relationship between the United States and this now-notorious Middle East nation. Although no single name has been given to these events, we will collectively refer to them here, in the tradition of Watergate, as **Iraqgate**.

The BNL Scandal

When the Iran-Contra story first broke, then–vice president George H. W. Bush claimed that he was out of the policymaking loop. Later he would say that he knew nothing of the details. Bush was in fact a major player in Iran-Contra, although the public did not realize this until after he became president in 1989. As vice president, Bush had spoken out in cabinet meetings in favor of both the Iran and Contra operations, and had participated in discussions about potential illegalities. He had even helped arrange an apparent "quid pro quo" deal (something done in return for something else) with Honduran president Roberto Suazo Cordova, promising to deliver over $110 million in economic and military aid in exchange for support of the Contras (Hagan 1997; Moyers 1990).

The evidence regarding Bush's involvement began to mount during the 1992 presidential campaign. It was not just Iran-Contra, however, that dogged the Bush administration. From 1980 to 1988, Iran and Iraq had been at war with each other. This may explain why the Reagan-Bush administration wanted to supply Iran with arms. But the United States was supporting Hussein and Iraq, too, perhaps because it seemed better to have these two countries fighting each other than causing problems for America.[10] After the end of the Iran-Iraq War, the Bush administration mistakenly calculated that Iraq was now the key to establishing stability in the Middle East, and the administration continued to provide Hussein military aid. When Hussein invaded Kuwait in 1990, however, Bush felt compelled to take military action. Many gave Bush high marks for leading an international coalition to a decisive victory in the 1991 Gulf War, forcing Iraqi troops out of Kuwait.[11] Yet few at the time knew the full extent of Bush's prior support of Hussein.

The first of a series of scandals involving Iraq did not surface until 1992, as Bush's reelection campaign was getting under way. The Atlanta branch of the Banca Nazionale del Lavoro (BNL), headquartered in Rome, had provided Hussein with several billion dollars in loans, guaranteed in part by the US government. The BNL claimed that the loans had been made for grain sales but that Hussein had deceived them and used the money to build up his military (including nuclear) capabilities. This was just a cover story. In reality the loans had been approved by the Bush administration with full knowledge of Hussein's intentions. The scheme, which was in violation of the US Arms Export Control Act, had apparently been arranged because the administration assumed that Congress would not support a policy of military aid to Iraq. It was Iran-Contra politics all over again (Friedman 1993; Hagan 1997; Simon 2002).

The Bush administration attempted to delay an official investigation of BNL as well as an inquiry into an Iraqi firm that was skimming money from the (bogus) grain program. Administration officials (including officials from the CIA) lied to Congress and submitted altered docu-

Box 6.2 CIA Complicity in Drug Trafficking During the Cold War

During the Cold War, which lasted until the dissolution of the Soviet Union in 1991, the CIA cooperated with drug traffickers who assisted the United States in military and covert operations against Communist-aligned insurgents and governments around the world. This alliance with drug criminals immunized traffickers from law enforcement investigation and prosecution and contributed to the contraband that was imported into the United States, with devastating consequences for many communities.

CIA complicity in the global drug trade seems to have begun in the 1950s when the agency collaborated with Corsican criminal syndicates in Marseilles, France, to curtail Communist influence on the city's docks at a time when the Corsicans were becoming the leading supplier of heroin to the United States. During that decade, the CIA also supplied anti-Communist forces in Burma with arms and air logistics, which they used to build a burgeoning trade in opium (McCoy 2003).

One of the most well-known cases of CIA complicity occurred during the Vietnam War, when the agency enlisted the support of General Vang Pao, the leader of an army of Hmong tribesmen in Laos whose primary cash-crop business was opium. Vang Pao operated a laboratory for the conversion of opium to heroin at its Long Cheng headquarters in northern Laos; and the agency permitted him to use its airline, Air America, to transport drugs. Some of the profits from the Southeast Asian drug trade were allegedly laundered through the Nugan Hand Bank, an Australian institution that had a branch in Thailand. Several CIA officials, including former agency director William Colby, had close ties with this bank, and Drug Enforcement Administration (DEA) agents reported that their investigation into this drug network had been blocked by the CIA (Chambliss 1988; McCoy 2003).

During the 1980s, the same pattern of complicity and interference in DEA investigations played out as a byproduct of the CIA's support of Afghan guerrillas who were resisting the Soviet Union's invasion of their country, as well as the agency's involvement with Contra insurgents who were working with the United States to overthrow the Sandinista government of Nicaragua. In the latter case, CIA cargo planes and airstrips that were used for the illegal transport of arms to the Contras were exploited by traffickers to smuggle drugs from Latin America into the United States. Proceeds from the drug trade were also used by the Contras to fund the anti-Sandinista military campaign. This CIA complicity, which was investigated in the mid-1980s by the Senate Subcommittee on Terrorism, Narcotics, and International Operations, headed by John Kerry, included tolerance of drug trafficking by Panamanian dictator Manuel Noriega, who was also a paid CIA asset, and by the notorious Colombian Medellín cartel. One drug trafficker, John Hull, a rancher from the United States living in Costa Rica, was a CIA agent (or asset) who operated half a dozen airstrips protected by the agency that were off

continues

Box 6.2 continued

limits to local police and customs officials (Chambliss 1988; Kinser 2006; McCoy 2003; Scott and Marshall 1991).

Perhaps the most controversial allegation of CIA involvement in Latin American drug trafficking was advanced by reporter Gary Webb in an investigative series published in the *San Jose Mercury News* in 1996. Webb exposed a connection between the Contra drug network and Danilo Blandon, a former Nicaraguan official who lived in California. Webb claimed that the Contra-Blandon connection was a significant part of the low-cost crack cocaine market that emerged in some African American communities in the 1980s. Blandon allegedly supplied "Freeway Rick" Ross, an African American drug dealer in Los Angeles, with tons of cocaine, which Ross converted to crack to build a burgeoning drug business that spread throughout California and the Midwest. Webb further alleged that the CIA had provided the Blandon-Ross network with immunity from investigation and prosecution by local law enforcement, the DEA, and US Customs during the time of the anti-Sandinista operation. In the late 1980s, after the operation had ended, Blandon and Ross lost their protection and were prosecuted. While Ross received a 10-year sentence, the US Justice Department arranged to free Blandon and repatriate him to Central America (McCoy 2003).

Webb's exposé outraged African Americans, some of whom accused the CIA of willfully attempting to inundate their communities with drugs. When then–CIA director John Deutch denied any agency complicity, over 2,000 protestors marched in the streets of Los Angeles demanding an official investigation. Maxine Waters, a Los Angeles congresswoman and leader of the Congressional Black Caucus, also wrote a letter to the US attorney general charging that the city she represented may have been introduced to crack cocaine because of the actions of US government officials. At this point, President Bill Clinton instructed Deutch to attend a public meeting in Los Angeles, where he faced some 800 angry residents and promised a full investigation of the story that had appeared in the *Mercury News* (McCoy 2003).

Subsequently, a CIA investigation was launched under the direction of Inspector General Frederick Hitz. Seventeen investigators conducted 365 interviews and examined 250,000 pages of documents over a period of about a year and a half and published a two-volume report. When Hitz formally presented the report to Congress in 1998, he said he had found no evidence that the CIA as an organization or anyone in its employ had been involved in trafficking that brought drugs into the United States. Hitz was parsing words, however, because he admitted that there were in fact instances in which the CIA had not terminated relationships with individuals who were alleged to be involved in drug trafficking, nor had the agency made any effort to investigate such allegations. Hitz also told Congress that at the start of the Contra operation in 1982, the CIA had reached an understanding with US attorney general William French Smith that drug-trafficking violations by "nonemployee" assets would not be reported to law enforcement authorities (McCoy 2003).

ments to conceal their activities. But the cover-up began to unravel, in large part due to the relentless reporting of conservative syndicated columnist William Safire (e.g., 1992a, 1992b). A month before the November election against Arkansas governor Bill Clinton, Bush appeared on *Larry King Live* and said he had been an innocent dupe. That was the best spin he could put on the affair.

Bush lost the election, but before leaving office he pardoned a number of individuals associated with the earlier Iran-Contra scandal. Congressional Democrats lost any motivation to pursue the defeated ex-president. Safire (1993) reported that the Clinton administration agreed to forgo investigation of Iraqgate if Bush refrained from criticizing the new president during his first year in office. US taxpayers were left to pay some $2 billion of Hussein's defaulted loans. This was, of course, not the end of the story of controversial US actions toward Iraq.

The Emergence of Al-Qaida

Since the 1970s, US citizens overseas have been targets of terrorism resulting from conflicts abroad, but the 1993 bombing of the World Trade Center in New York City demonstrated for the first time to Americans that terrorism could happen at home, on their own soil. The explosion, which left six people dead and more than a thousand injured, shattered Americans' sense of security. The World Trade Center bombing, part of a failed plot to bomb other targets as well, was the act of Islamic extremists working under the leadership of Shaikh Omar Abdul Rahman, a man with a checkered past. Rahman had been expelled from Egypt for being part of a conspiracy in the 1981 assassination of Egyptian president Anwar Sadat, who had entered into a landmark peace accord with Israel. Although Rahman was on the US State Department's list of undesirables, he had been given a CIA visa to enter the country. Rahman had been working with the CIA, which had been financing and training Afghan rebels who were resisting the Soviet Union's military occupation of Afghanistan from 1979 to 1989. Apparently it did not occur to the CIA that Rahman might try to target the United States. Rahman received a life sentence for his role in the bombing conspiracy. The other conspirators were given sentences ranging from 25 years to life (Kinser 2006; White 2003; Wright 2006).

At the time, few Americans had ever heard of Osama bin Laden or the terrorist organization **Al-Qaida** ("The Base"). Bin Laden, an exiled Saudi Arabian millionaire who had gone to Afghanistan to fight the Soviets, is suspected of financing the 1993 World Trade Center bombing. He is also believed to be responsible for the August 1998 bombings of the US embassies in Kenya and Tanzania (which killed 12 Americans and nearly 300 Africans), the October 2000 bombing of the USS *Cole* during its docking in a Yemen harbor (which killed 17 sailors), and the infamous September 11, 2001, attacks (which killed over 3,000 people) (Dreyfuss 2005; Martin 2003; Sperry 2003; Wright 2006).

Al-Qaida, formed in the chaotic aftermath of the Afghan anti-Soviet resistance, recruited "Afghan Arab" veterans who had fought against the Soviets, and who, at a minimum, were sheltered by the Taliban, a fundamentalist Islamic military regime, which took control of most of the country in the latter half of the 1990s. Although the US government never recognized the Taliban as the legitimate government of Afghanistan, in the years prior to 9/11 the US State Department and some US oil companies were courting and negotiating with representatives of the regime, hoping to ensure their cooperation in the development of oil and gas pipelines in the region that would link energy reserves in the Caspian Sea to markets throughout Asia (Brisard and Dasquié 2002; Dreyfuss 2005; Martin 2003; Sperry 2003).

After the 9/11 attack, the George W. Bush administration succeeded in putting together an international coalition to topple the Taliban in Afghanistan, but also began plans to launch a preemptive war against Saddam Hussein without this cooperation, and in the face of much international opposition (Clarke 2004; Isikoff and Corn 2006; Rich 2006; Suskind 2006). This war, which some criminologists and legal analysts believe was a violation of international law, was begun in March 2003.[12] It arguably diverted valuable resources from the Afghanistan campaign and enabled bin Laden to reconstitute his base of operations on the Pakistan side of the Afghanistan-Pakistan border (Bergen 2007; Clarke 2004; Hersh 2004; Ricks 2006).

Weapons of Mass Destruction

The prelude to the Iraq War, even before 9/11, was the desire of **neoconservative** policymakers to advance a post–Cold War vision of the United States as having the prerogative to engage in unilateral military action to protect its vital interests, including access to raw materials such as Middle Eastern oil, around the globe. The term *neoconservatism* entails a political ideology that promotes the unilateral use of US military power to advance US interests. It equates global capitalist markets with "freedom," even when that freedom, as we have seen, needs to be imposed and maintained through military force against a resistant populace (Dean 2006; Klein 2007; Kramer and Michalowski 2005; O'Huallachain and Sharpe 2005).[13]

In 1992, in the wake of the dissolution of the Soviet Union, aides to then–secretary of defense Dick Cheney prepared a neoconservative document titled "Defense Planning Guidance," which "depicted a world dominated by the United States, which would maintain its superpower status through a combination of positive guidance and overwhelming military might" (Armstrong 2002:78). The first objective of US defense policy, according to the guidance document, should be to prevent the reemergence of a new rival to US dominance. To achieve this goal, it also advocated the use of preemptive military force, or **preventive war** (Kramer and Michalowski 2005).

The core ideas of the defense guidance document were later endorsed in a report titled "Rebuilding America's Defenses: Strategy, Forces, and Resources for a New Century," which was issued by the neoconservative think tank **Project for a New American Century**, the members of which included advisers who would play central roles in the administration of George W. Bush. Early in the Bush administration, months before 9/11, regime change in Iraq and US designs on Iraqi oil were never far from view (Behan 2006; Clarke 2004; see Chapter 5).[14] The Project for a New American Century recognized, however, that it would be difficult to garner public support for this foreign policy agenda without a "catalyzing event" comparable to Pearl Harbor (quoted in Kramer and Michalowski 2005:459; see also Altheide and Grimes 2005; Armstrong 2002; Ricks 2006).

That catalyzing event, as we now know, was 9/11. Within hours after the 9/11 attack, Secretary of Defense Donald Rumsfeld was asking his aides to devise plans to strike Iraq, even though there was no evidence linking Saddam Hussein to that event (Clarke 2004; Roberts 2002). To justify these plans, the Bush administration not only implicated Saddam Hussein in the attacks, but also claimed that he possessed weapons of mass destruction (WMD)—biological, chemical, and especially nuclear weapons—that posed an imminent threat to the security of the United States. These claims, we later learned, were based on misleading if not fraudulent evidence, with the administration fully aware of intelligence that contraindicated their assertions. In the administration's view, however, even if there was only a "one percent chance" that Iraq had WMD, the preventive war was justified (Clarke 2004; Isikoff and Corn 2006; Rich 2006; Ricks 2006; Suskind 2006).[15]

The media, for the most part, capitulated to the administration's claims about Hussein. *New York Times* journalist Judith Miller was especially noteworthy for her articles that cited anti-Hussein Iraqi defectors testifying about Hussein's WMD capabilities. Vice President Cheney

Box 6.3 September 11, 2001

In the year following the 9/11 attack, top White House national security adviser and future secretary of state Condoleezza Rice made several public statements in which she claimed that no one in the George W. Bush administration had ever conceived of the possibility of terrorists flying planes into buildings on US soil. When asked by a reporter whether the 9/11 attack represented an intelligence failure, Rice replied: "I don't think anyone in the administration could have predicted that these people would take an airplane and slam it into the World Trade Center, take another one and slam it into the Pentagon—that they would try to use an airplane as a missile" (quoted in Shenon 2008:238). Later, Rice would have trouble explaining why the contents of a President's Daily Brief titled "Bin Laden Determined to Strike in the US" and delivered to the president a month prior to the 9/11 attack, had not alerted the administration to the threat, because the brief included a reference to the hijacking of planes and "scores of ongoing FBI investigations of Al Qaeda threats, as well as reports of recent efforts by terrorist groups to carry out surveillance of the New York skyline" (Shenon 2008:238; see also Graham 2004; Hersh 2004; Mayer 2009).

Moreover, the White House's chief terrorist adviser, Richard Clarke (2004), had been trying to alert the Bush administration from the moment it took office that Al-Qaida should receive prioritized attention. But the administration was too worried about renegade states such as Iraq to heed Clarke's (and others') warnings. Former acting FBI director Thomas Pickard reported that prior to 9/11, Attorney General John Ashcroft told him: "I don't want to hear about Al Qaeda anymore. . . . There's nothing I can do about that" (quoted in Shenon 2008:247). Both the CIA and the FBI, perhaps for lack of administration support, failed to connect the dots and fully investigate leads regarding Al-Qaida operatives within the United States, including those who were learning how to fly (but not land) planes. In a revealing exposé, Senator Bob Graham (2004) documented a dozen instances in which the 9/11 plot could have been discovered and potentially foiled (see also Bamford 2008; Farmer 2009; Ridgeway 2005; Shenon 2008).

Although the Bush administration initially resisted the establishment of an official commission to investigate 9/11, it eventually relented to public pressure, especially from the families of 9/11 victims. The information the bipartisan **9/11 Commission** had at its disposal was very controlled, however. The White House appointed Phillip Zelikow, a confidant of Rice and author of a national security strategy paper justifying preventive war, as executive director of the commission. Zelikow saw to it that the commission's work would not jeopardize US ties to Saudi

continues

Box 6.3 continued

Arabia; hence investigation of Saudi "spies," as Graham (2004) called them, who may have provided financial and logistical support to at least two of the 9/11 hijackers, was thwarted. The CIA could be blamed for its mistakes, but above all Rice and other high-ranking officials, including the president and vice president, were to be protected from culpability. Zelikow also tried to use the commission to air evidence regarding the alleged ties between Iraq and Al-Qaida (Griffin 2004; Mayer 2009; Shenon 2008; Woodward 2006).

David Ray Griffin (2008), a leading critic of the 9/11 Commission, outlines 25 unanswered questions or internal contradictions regarding the official version of the events, questions that others have raised as well (Ahmed 2005; Farmer 2009; Hersh 2004; Ridgeway 2005). Regarding the events that transpired on 9/11, government officials offered testimony that they knew (or should have known) to be untrue, and then had to change their stories. Among other things, critics point to the paralysis of US aviation security and military defense systems that led to a failure to shoot down the hijacked planes before they crashed into the buildings (see Chapter 4). According to John Farmer, a senior counsel to the 9/11 Commission, the official version has given the American public false assurance that masks "the fundamental disconnects that existed that day: between and among agencies; between the bureaucracy within agencies and the agencies' departmental leadership; and also between the different agencies and the national leadership" (2009:289).

then cited the *New York Times* in his statements to the press as an authoritative source supporting the administration's justification for launching the preventive war (Altheide and Grimes 2005; Isikoff and Corn 2006; Rich 2006; Ricks 2006).

The clandestine background to Miller's reporting and Cheney's remarks, however, was that the Iraqi defectors were part of a propaganda campaign organized for the purpose of **strategic disinformation**— that is, the intentional dissemination of false information to achieve political goals (Altheide and Grimes 2005; Judis 2002).[16] Indeed, the Iraqi defectors belonged to a group led by Ahmad Chalabi, the **Iraqi National Congress**, which was funded by the CIA and Pentagon and used to "sell" the war to the American people (Bamford 2005; Isikoff and Corn 2006; Rich 2006; Ricks 2006). John Rendon, a public relations specialist for the Rendon Group, was hired to organize and disseminate these stories to the press. Rendon described his role this way: "I am an information warrior and a perception manager . . . a person who uses communication to meet public-policy or corporate-policy objectives" (quoted in Bamford 2005:3).

Two years into the war, we also learned from the leak of the infamous **Downing Street memo** written by Sir Richard Dearlove, the head of British foreign intelligence, to Prime Minister Tony Blair in July 2002, as well as from other sources, that intelligence in the White House had been "fixed around the policy" and that high-ranking US officials had intentionally ignored CIA warnings that their allegations regarding Iraq's WMD could not be substantiated by the weight of the available intelligence (cited in Pincus 2005:A18). (Downing Street is the location of the residence and official offices of the prime minister.) In other words, there was no genuine effort to find out whether the concerns about Iraq were in fact true—for instance, by giving United Nations WMD inspectors a chance to make a determination—before US troops were committed to battle (Isikoff and Corn 2006; Rich 2006; Ricks 2006; Suskind 2006).

A month after the invasion, after the Hussein regime had been toppled, President Bush decided to celebrate the apparent victory with a photo op, becoming the first sitting president to land by jet on the deck of an aircraft carrier, the USS *Abraham Lincoln,* which was stationed 30 miles off the coast of California. Bush exited the plane decked in full flight gear and then delivered a speech under a banner that declared "Mission Accomplished," announcing that "major combat operations in Iraq have ended" (CNN.com 2003). At that time, Bush and his minions had not anticipated the insurgency that would take the United States into its longest war since Vietnam, one that will cost as much as $3 trillion and has taken the lives of about 4,400 US troops and wounded thousands of others, to say nothing of other nations' troops, members of the press, and of course the many Iraqis themselves who have met a similar fate.[17]

In the fall of 2003, as casualties on all sides were mounting, a team of about 1,400 weapons inspectors called the **Iraq Survey Group**, a joint venture of the CIA and Defense Intelligence Agency, reported that no WMD could be found in Iraq. One vial of 10-year-old botulinum was discovered in an Iraqi scientist's home, and this was touted by administration officials as verification of Iraq's biological weapons program. But this particular strain of botulinum, called *clostridinum botulinum okra B,* is the type used in Botox as a medical treatment for muscle spasms and spasticity and as a cosmetic treatment for wrinkles. This strain of botulinum can cause deadly food poisoning but is not very dangerous if inhaled. Moreover, the Iraq Survey Group found no evidence that Iraq had succeeded in weaponizing this material (Drogin 2003; Lumpkin 2003; Rich 2006; Woodward 2006).

The Iraq Survey Group did find evidence, on the other hand, that Hussein had reconstituted Iraq's missile program, which would have enabled him to project missiles beyond the 90-mile limit that had been imposed by United Nations resolutions, and that Hussein had never stopped trying to procure "raw materials, equipment, spare parts, and expertise overseas" for this program (Drogin 2003:26). This is an entirely different matter, however, than suggesting that Iraq had a WMD program that constituted an imminent threat requiring an immediate preventive war to stop it. Moreover, the Iraq Survey Group concluded that the Gulf War and subsequent United Nations inspections had destroyed Iraq's WMD program, that Hussein had not tried to rebuild it, and that ongoing aggressive inspections might have been a suitable alternative to war (Kramer and Michalowski 2005; Priest and Pincus 2004; Rich 2006; Woodward 2006).[18]

The Mushroom Cloud

Arguably the US administration's most compelling argument for preventive war was the claim that Hussein had not only WMD, but also nuclear weapons that he was capable of launching against the United States. Administration officials, including the president and vice president, repeatedly said that the United States could not afford to wait for a "smoking gun" that could come in the form of a "mushroom cloud" (Hersh 2004; Ricks 2006). Although this claim was not supported by the evidence, it was a powerful claim nonetheless. Take the case of Dick Armey, the influential Republican majority leader of the House of Representatives. Armey reports that he was at first skeptical about the rationale for war, until Vice President Cheney persuaded him that Hussein would "in the not-too-distant future . . . acquire nuclear weapons." According to Armey, Cheney also told him that Hussein's ability to miniaturize WMD, including nuclear weapons, had been "substantially refined since the first Gulf War" and that Iraq was "developing packages that could be moved even by ground personnel." Armey, of course, found this "suitcase nuke scenario" frightening. Cheney also told Armey that Al-Qaida was in fact "working with Saddam Hussein and members of his family" and that Iraq now had a "portable . . . delivery system in their relationship" with the terrorist organization. "I was trying to be respectful," Armey recalled, "without being openly cynical. I had to sort of take the vice president's word. . . . Because what do I know? I assumed that what he's telling me is verifiable intel" (quoted in Gelman 2008:216–218).

What Cheney told Armey, however, was not verifiable; it was just a theory. And Armey left the meeting with the feeling that he had been "bullshitted" by Cheney: "I reckon that's about as plain spoken as I can put it," he said (quoted in Gelman 2008:219). Nevertheless, faced with emphatic administration assurances, as well as a crescendo of public pronouncements, Armey lost faith in his own doubts and supported the administration's call for a congressional authorization for war. Later, when he discovered that he had been right to doubt the administration's case for war, Armey wondered: "Did Dick Cheney . . . purposely tell me things he knew to be untrue? I will go so far as to say I seriously feel that may be the case. . . . Had I known or believed then what I believe I know now, I would have publicly opposed this resolution right to the bitter end, and I believe I might have stopped it from happening, and I believe I'd have done a better service to my country had I done so" (quoted on pp. 221–222).

After the invasion was already under way, particular controversy arose over President Bush's January 2003 State of the Union speech, which had preceded the attack. Bush told the world that "the British government has learned that Saddam Hussein recently sought significant quantities of uranium from Africa," suggesting that Iraq had reconstituted its nuclear weapons program (quoted in *New Republic* 2003:8). At the time of the speech, however, White House officials knew full well that this claim had been disputed by their intelligence sources. Indeed, the CIA had previously dispatched former ambassador Joseph Wilson to Niger, the alleged source of the uranium, to investigate this claim. Wilson had concluded, as he later wrote in a scathing *New York Times* op-ed piece published in July 2003, that it had not taken him long to determine "that the information was erroneous" and "that it was highly doubtful that any such transaction had ever taken place" (quoted in Kerr 2003:A9). Wilson also noted that Vice President Cheney's office had been specifically informed of his findings by the CIA and that these findings had been discounted in order to legitimize the administration's efforts to skew intelligence so as to justify its desire for preventive war. Moreover, we later learned that documents alleging the Niger-uranium connection had come from Italian intelligence sources and had been forged, apparently with the knowledge of high-ranking administration officials, as part of the organized campaign to garner public support for the war (Giraldi 2005; Isikoff and Corn 2006; Rich 2006; Wilson 2005).

If the president had purposely deceived Congress, it would have constituted a crime and an impeachable offense. But the only aspect of the Niger case that resulted in criminal prosecution was related to an article written by conservative political columnist Robert Novak a week after Wilson's op-ed piece was published. Novak reported that a White House official had informed him that Valerie Plame, the wife of Ambassador Wilson, was a CIA operative. Novak's outing of Plame, who had worked undercover for three decades and was, ironically, a specialist in WMD, destroyed her career and endangered her contacts overseas. While Novak's right to publish the information he received is protected by the First Amendment, the initial disclosure itself constitutes a felony that is punishable by up to 10 years in prison. Wilson believes that the leak of his wife's name was intended to stifle complaints from knowledgeable persons inside the government who knew that the administration had misrepresented intelligence about the threat posed by Iraq (Isikoff and Corn 2006; Rich 2006; Wilson 2005).

When news of this scandal, dubbed **Plamegate**, surfaced, President Bush said in no uncertain terms that he would do everything in his power to get to the bottom of it and that anyone in his administration who was responsible would be summarily dismissed. A special prosecutor, Patrick Fitzgerald, was appointed by the Justice Department to investigate the case. The investigation dragged on past the November 2004 presidential election, in which Bush won reelection in a controversial vote that came down to the state of Ohio, reminiscent of Florida in the 2000 election (see Chapter 5). Finally, in October 2005, Fitzgerald announced that he would seek an indictment against only one individual, I. Lewis "Scooter" Libby, not on charges related to the leak itself, but for obstruction of justice, perjury, and making false statements about the leak. Libby was Vice President Cheney's top aide, and Fitzgerald found compelling evidence that other White House officials, including Cheney and Bush's top political adviser, Karl Rove, had been directly or indirectly involved.[19] Libby was eventually convicted and sentenced to a prison term of two and a half years, a $250,000 fine, and two years of probation. President Bush, however, immediately commuted the prison sentence, leaving Libby to face only the fine and probation. No one else, contrary to Bush's initial tough stance, was held responsible for the crime (Corn 2007; Hutcheson 2007; Isikoff and Corn 2006; Rich 2006).

The Question of Torture

In the spring of 2004, reports of widespread abuse, humiliation, and outright torture of Iraqi prisoners held by US intelligence operatives, military personnel, and private contractors in the **Abu Ghraib** prison out-side of Baghdad hit the news.[20] Some of the interrogators had taken pho-tos of abused and beaten prisoners and disseminated them on the Internet for all the world to see, undermining the credibility of the United States. Some of the photos showed naked prisoners being forced to feign homosexual acts and form a pile of naked bodies as smiling interrogators looked on. Others showed prisoners in stress positions with electrical wires attached to their bodies and growling dogs standing by. Later we learned that these practices were not unique to Abu Ghraib but also occurred at US facilities in Afghanistan, Guantánamo, Cuba,[21] and other sites around the world. Although the administration blamed these practices on maverick interrogators who had gone too far, and some lower-level personnel were punished, we later learned that these practices had been systematically sanctioned by high-ranking officials—including Secretary of Defense Rumsfeld, Vice President Cheney, and President Bush himself. Moreover, little useful intelligence was gath-ered from these interrogations, and the large majority of Iraqis and other Muslims who were victimized by these practices were completely inno-cent bystanders to the malaise that has become the Middle East (Hersh 2004; Lithwick 2008; Mayer 2009; McCoy 2006).

What happened at Abu Ghraib and other US sites, as we shall see, did not take place in a historical vacuum. These practices were, in fact, an outgrowth of a long-standing US torture regime begun in the after-math of World War II in the early days of the Cold War.

Emergence of the US Torture Regime

In the last half of the twentieth century, according to historian Alfred McCoy (2006), the United States exhibited a contradictory attitude toward torture.[22] On the one hand, the United States was a leader in the international movement for human rights, opposing torture before the United Nations and other international forums, and signing treaties that banned it, such as the **Geneva Conventions**.[23] At the same time, howev-er, the newly formed CIA ignored these same humanitarian precepts, propagating the practice of torture throughout the globe. The rationale, as noted earlier, was the belief that the United States was facing an unscrupulous enemy in the form of Communism and the Soviet Union.

In its early years, the CIA commissioned a review of Nazi interroga-tion techniques, including hypnosis, drugs, electroshock, and psy-chosurgery, and then began a program of extreme cognitive experimen-tation on witting and unwitting subjects, the latter including military personnel and hospital patients, without their consent. From 1950 to

1963 the CIA spent about $25 million, a rather large sum of money at the time, to research the effects of various techniques, enlisting the assistance of 185 nongovernmental researchers at 80 institutions, including 45 universities and 12 hospitals.[24] Through trial and error, in collaboration with non-agency researchers, the CIA slowly identified what would become the hallmarks of a modern psychological paradigm of **"no touch" torture** aimed, according to one CIA report, at "inducing regression of the personality to whatever earlier and weaker level is required for the dissolution of resistance and the inculcation of dependence" (cited in McCoy 2006:51).[25] The report noted that all interrogation techniques, whether physical or psychological, "are essentially ways of speeding up the process of regression" until the assault on the target's identity becomes "mentally intolerable" and the target complies with their captor's wishes (p. 51). Research had found that sensory deprivation, for example, which could be achieved through protracted isolation, was especially effective at inducing a psychological breakdown equivalent to acute psychosis in as little as two days.[26]

Self-inflicted pain, a technique learned from the Communists, was another method of "no touch" torture adapted by the CIA. A seminal agency study of Communist interrogation methods in the mid-1950s reported that simply forcing subjects to stand for 18 to 24 hours could cause "excruciating pain," as ankles double in size, blisters erupt and ooze "watery serum," heart rates soar, kidneys shut down, and delusions set in—outcomes that the CIA described as "nonviolent" (cited in McCoy 2006:46). The technique of forcing prisoners into stress positions such as **wall-standing** was also adopted, whereby subjects were made to stand spread-eagled against a wall, with fingers high above their head against the wall, legs spread apart and feet back, "causing them to stand on their toes with the weight of the body mainly on the fingers" (p. 55). These "self-inflicted" techniques were designed to make a person "feel responsible for their own suffering, thus inducing them to alleviate their agony by capitulating to the power of their interrogators" (p. 52). Other "no touch" torture methods included sleep deprivation, subjection to extremely loud noise and extreme heat and cold, sexual humiliation, and denial of food, beverage, and toileting privileges. **Water-boarding**, in which water is poured down a prisoner's throat to induce a sense of drowning, also became part of the CIA's torture regime. As we shall see, however, a problem with these techniques, besides their moral reprehensibility, is that they may elicit compliant behavior without eliciting accurate information, as subjects will tell interrogators whatever they want to hear in order to alleviate their suffering.

Exporting Torture

For three decades of the Cold War, from the 1960s through the 1980s, the CIA propagated its torture regime throughout the globe, first through undercover "police-training programs in Asia and Latin America and later collaborating with Army teams that advised local counterinsurgency forces" (McCoy 2006:60). For a dozen years, from 1962 to 1974, the CIA deployed "police advisers" who trained more than 1 million officers in 47 nations, including 85,000 in South Vietnam and 100,000 in Brazil.

Once a torture regime is unleashed, it becomes hard to control. It typically spreads from a limited number of high-valued targets to include countless innocent people. It also quickly moves by degrees beyond the original "no touch" techniques to harsher physical methods, as it did during the Vietnam War through the murderous **Phoenix program**, which was aimed at destroying the Vietcong revolutionary underground. Specially trained South Vietnamese counterinsurgency teams called provisional reconnaissance units, often under the direct supervision of the CIA, tortured and summarily executed prisoners, without trial or due process of law. The torture techniques practiced by the reconnaissance units included electroshock to men's testicles and women's vaginas. One US military intelligence officer witnessed "the insertion of a six-inch dowel into the ear canal" of one of his detainees and "the tapping through the brain until he died" (quoted in McCoy 2006:67). Overall, an estimated 41,000 Vietcong were killed through the Phoenix program (Hersh 2004; Mayer 2009; McCoy 2006).

The Phoenix program, according to McCoy, became a "seminal experience" for the entire US intelligence community, serving as a model for later counterinsurgency training in Latin America (2006:71). In the mid-1960s, for instance, US Army Intelligence launched **Project X**, which, according to a confidential Pentagon memo, was designed "to develop an exportable foreign intelligence package to provide counterinsurgency techniques learned in Vietnam to Latin American countries" (cited on p. 71). A manual produced for this program that was used at the Army Intelligence School provided training in the "use of sodiopentathol compound in interrogation, abduction of family members to influence the adversary, [and] prioritization of adversary personalities for abduction, exile, physical beatings and execution" (cited on p. 71). For the next quarter century, the US Army propagated these tactics— through direct training and dissemination of manuals—to the militaries of at least 10 Latin American countries.[27]

In the late 1970s, the CIA imported Argentine officers trained in the United States to assist local interrogators in Honduras. One officer, Sergeant Florencio Caballero, recalled the focus on "no touch" psychological methods, as he learned "to study the fears and weaknesses of a prisoner. Make him stand up, don't let him sleep, keep him naked and isolated, put rats and cockroaches in his cell, give him bad food, serve him dead animals, throw cold water on him, change the temperature" (quoted in McCoy 2006:95). Ines Murillo, who was tortured by Caballero's unit, described her 80 days of torture in 1983, when she was stripped naked and subjected to repeated electrical shocks. She was also given raw dead birds and rats for food, had freezing water thrown on her naked body every half hour for extended periods of time, and was denied sleep and made to stand for hours without being allowed to urinate.

In the United States, public disclosure of scenarios like these provoked congressional inquiries in the 1980s. International outrage, as well, led the United Nations to adopt the **Convention Against Torture**, which defined the practice broadly as "any act by which severe pain or suffering, whether physical or mental, is intentionally inflicted on a person for such purpose as obtaining from him or a third person information or a confession" (cited in McCoy 2006:100). The convention was approved by a unanimous United Nations vote. President Ronald Reagan sent it to Congress for approval in 1988 along with a ringing endorsement of the desire of the United States "to bring an end to the abhorrent practice of torture" (quoted on p. 100). At the same time, the Reagan administration proposed 19 reservations that stalled congressional ratification for the next six years. The main focus of the reservations concerned the issue of psychological torture. The administration thought that the definition of "mental pain" in the Convention Against Torture was too vague. To correct this problem, the State Department drafted a four-part diplomatic exception for US approval, defining psychological torture as limited to "prolonged mental harm" caused by "(1) the intentional infliction or threatened infliction of severe physical pain or suffering; (2) the administration . . . of mind-altering substances . . . ; (3) the threat of imminent death; or (4) the threat that another person will imminently be subjected to death . . . or other procedures calculated to disrupt profoundly the sense of personality" (cited on p. 100). In essence, the administration's exception was designed to protect the US "no touch" torture paradigm from international sanction, affirming only the United Nations ban on physical methods.

In 1992, however, US Army Intelligence revised its interrogation field manual for the post–Cold War era to more fully comply with the

Geneva Conventions and evolving international standards, banning not only conventional physical torture such as beatings and electroshock, but also prolonged stress positions, food deprivation, sleep deprivation, and mock executions. While violations of these guidelines could be prosecuted as crimes under the Uniform Code of Military Justice, the Army manual also categorically stated that torture was not only immoral but ineffective as well, yielding "unreliable results [that] may damage subsequent collection efforts, and . . . [inducing] the source to say what he thinks the interrogator wants to hear" (cited in McCoy 2006:102).[28] Moreover, the revised manual stated: "Revelation of use of torture by US personnel will bring discredit upon the US and its armed forces while undermining domestic and international support of the war effort. . . . [K]nowing that the enemy has abused US and allied PWs [prisoners of war] does not justify using methods of interrogation specifically prohibited" (cited on p. 102).

The Contemporary War on Terror

In September 2002, Cofer Black, the CIA's counterterrorism chief, told Congress: "All you need to know . . . is that there was a 'before 9/11' and there was an 'after 9/11.' After 9/11, the gloves came off" (quoted in McCoy 2006:119). Indeed, the contemporary **War on Terror** against radical Islamic fundamentalism, epitomized by the murderous practices of Al-Qaida, had replaced the Cold War as the dominant foreign policy paradigm of our era. Iraq, as we have suggested, was not a central battleground of this war until the US invasion. The Bush administration had not anticipated the insurgency that would ensue, and it was desperate for intelligence information that would help repel it (Cole and Lobel 2007; Crotty 2004; Hersh 2004; McCoy 2006).

In implementing torture as part of the War on Terror, the Bush administration reversed the limited restrictions that had been imposed during the Reagan administration to comply with international agreements. One mechanism of this reversal was the development of a legal framework that restricted US obligations to the Geneva Conventions and other international treaties, as well as obligations to the codes of the United States itself, to *state* actors rather than to *nonstate* actors such as Al-Qaida, which were not, in the Bush administration's view, subject to the protections afforded to conventional prisoners of war. In legal memorandums written by White House and Justice Department lawyers, the administration argued that neither Al-Qaida nor the Taliban were subject to US or international law. Secretary of Defense Rumsfeld concurred with this interpretation, arguing that "the current war on terrorism is not a conflict envisioned by the framers of the Geneva Convention" (quoted in McCoy 2006:115). President Bush agreed: "I don't care what the international lawyers say, we are going to kick some ass" (quoted on p. 113).

In conjunction with the CIA and other intelligence agencies, Rumsfeld launched a highly classified program that gave "prior authorization for kidnapping, assassination, and torture" of high-valued targets (McCoy 2006:116). The program included the practice of **extraordinary rendition**, whereby suspects were sent to countries like Egypt and Syria for torture by agents of foreign governments. The question that remained, however, concerned the level of pain and suffering that US personnel were allowed to inflict. In an important legal memorandum, assistant attorney general Jay Bybee, aided by his deputy John Yoo and vice presidential counsel David Addington, answered this question, defining the parameters of permissible actions to include anything other than physical pain that was the "equivalent in intensity to the pain accompanying serious physical injury, such as organ failure, impairment of bodily function, or even death" (cited on p. 121).[29] Moreover, Bybee asserted, any attempt to limit the commander in chief's power to order interrogations of this nature would constitute "an unconstitutional infringement of the President's authority to conduct war" (cited on p. 122; see also Cole and Lobel 2007; Hersh 2004; Mayer 2009).

When the Abu Ghraib prison scandal broke in spring 2004, Bush administration officials were forced to condemn the actions of a few "bad apples," while also denying that they had approved the "no touch" interrogation techniques, which, at the same time, they denied as constituting torture. President Bush epitomized this double speak when he remarked: "[T]his country does not believe in torture. We do believe in protecting ourselves" (quoted in McCoy 2006:177). Later, John Yoo, now a law professor at the University of California, Berkeley, would ask, "Why is it so hard for people to understand that there is a category of behavior not covered by the legal system?" (quoted on p. 161).

By the end of December 2004, the media reported on several FBI e-mails from Guantánamo that disputed the official denials about torture. One bureau agent had written the FBI director an "urgent report," complaining that prisoners were being subjected to "strangulation, beatings, placement of lit cigarettes into the detainee's ear openings and unauthorized interrogation" (cited in McCoy 2006:158). Another agent reported: "I entered interview rooms to find a detainee chained hand and foot in a fetal position to the floor with no chair, food or water. Most times they had urinated or defecated on themselves and had been left there for 18 to 24 hours" (cited on p. 158). Other agents reported that these coercive techniques were producing no intelligence of value while also compromising their own noncoercive approach. One senior agent noted that "every time the FBI established a rapport with a detainee, the military would step in and the detainee would stop being cooperative" (cited on p. 159).

McCoy thinks that the American people need to disabuse themselves of the notion that the interrogation techniques practiced at Abu Ghraib, Guantánamo, and elsewhere are a thing of the past. Probably the greatest sin committed by the few "bad apples" who were prosecuted was that they had allowed themselves to be photographed.[30] But McCoy does ask us to consider the practical value of torture and its broader consequences for the United States and the world. The methods employed during the Afghanistan and Iraq campaigns, as we have suggested, produced little useful intelligence. At best, they yielded no more information than standard techniques of building rapport through protracted noncoercive questioning that the FBI has successfully perfected over the years. Thus the "ends justify the means" argument remains unpersuasive to those who are knowledgeable about interrogations. Former FBI agent Dan Coleman, who worked closely with the CIA on counterterrorism cases and was the first FBI case agent to be assigned to Osama bin Laden in the mid-1990s, was appalled by these methods. "Have any of these guys ever tried to talk to someone who's been deprived of his clothes?" he asked. "He's going to be ashamed and humiliated, and cold. He'll tell you anything you want to hear to get his clothes back. There's no value in it. . . . Brutalization doesn't work. We know that. Besides, you lose your soul" (quoted in McCoy 2006:203).[31]

But what about the case of the so-called ticking time bomb, in which there is an imminent threat of a WMD attack that could possibly maim and kill thousands of people? In McCoy's view, this fanciful scenario rests on certain assumptions that are largely fictional:

> It assumes an improbable, even impossible, cluster of variables that runs something like this. First, the FBI or CIA captures a terrorist. Second, the capture takes place at the precise moment between plot's launch and bomb's burst. Third, the interrogators somehow have sufficiently detailed knowledge of the plot to know they must interrogate this very person and do it now. . . . Fourth, these same officers who have sufficient intelligence to know all about this specific terrorist and his ticking bomb are, for some unexplained reason, missing just a few critical details that only torture can divulge. . . . Such an extraordinary string of circumstances probably never has and never will occur. (2006:192)

McCoy also notes that torture undermines US democracy and the foundational ideals of American society:

> [A] nation that sanctions torture in defiance of its democratic principles pays a terrible price. For nearly two millennia, the practice has been identified with tyrants and empires. For the past two centuries, its repudiation has been synonymous with the humanist ideals of the Enlightenment and democracy. When any modern state tortures even a few victims, the stigma compromises its majesty and corrupts its integrity. Its officials must spin an ever more complex web of lies that, in the end, weakens the bonds of trust and the rule of law that are the sine qua non of a democracy. . . . Torture is evil, pure and simple. (pp. 3, 14)

Summary

In this chapter we considered US government actions that are indicative of the problem of state crime, which we defined as illegal acts of political repression, violent or nonviolent, aimed at maintaining social order or fomenting disorder. State crime may entail the violation of US law, international law, or the law of the affected nation. In the area of foreign policy, we explored state crimes that occur at the nexus of corporate and government power that aim to keep foreign markets open to US commerce at all costs.

We considered US actions in Iran in the 1950s and in Latin America in the 1950s–1970s, the Vietnam War and the Iran-Contra scandal, as well as the scandals that have marked US policies vis-à-vis Iraq (collectively called Iraqgate), most notably the actions that occurred during the administration of George W. Bush. Finally, we examined the state practice of torture as a tool of political repression, looking at the emergence of the US torture regime at the outset of the Cold War, its exportation abroad, and its use in the contemporary War on Terror.

Notes

1. For a review of US elite and corporate ties to Nazi Germany, see Berger 2002, Black 2009, Higham 1983, Matthews 2006, and Poole 1997.

2. John Perkins, in his provocative book *Confessions of an Economic Hit Man*, documents his experience as one of

> an elite group of men and women who utilize international financial organizations to foment conditions that make other nations subservient to . . . our biggest corporations, our government, and our banks. . . .

These take the form of loans to develop infrastructure—electric generating plants, highways, ports, airports, or industrial parks. A condition of such loans is that engineering and construction companies from [the United States] must build all these projects. . . . [T]he recipient country is required to pay it all back, principal plus interest. . . . [But] the loans are so large that the debtor is forced to default on its payments after a few years. When this happens, . . . we demand our pound of flesh. This often includes one or more of the following: control over United Nations votes, the installation of military bases, or access to precious resources such as oil. (2004:xx)

If these economic methods fail to induce compliance, Perkins adds, then the clandestine services are sent in and "heads of state are overthrown or die in violent 'accidents.'" If these clandestine methods in turn fail, then "young Americans are sent in to kill and die" (p. xxv).

3. The United Fruit Company subsequently sold some of its holdings to Del Monte (Kinser 2006).

4. Stephen Kinser (2006) notes the impact of the Guatemala experience on the attitudes of Latin American revolutionaries such as Che Guevara and Fidel Castro.

5. Chile was the world's leading producer of copper (Kinser 2006).

6. For discussions of US interventions in other countries, see Kinser 2006, McCoy 2006, Perkins 2004, Rosoff, Pontell, and Tillman 2007, and Waldron and Hartmann 2005.

7. The war also expanded into Laos, Thailand, and Cambodia.

8. The Senate investigation was headed by Senator Frank Church and the House investigation by Representative Otis Pike (Mayer 2009; Waldron and Hartmann 2005). It also included an inquiry into the FBI (see Chapter 2).

9. Casey, the man who probably knew the most about what had transpired, died in 1987.

10. In 1987, when Hussein was still an ally of the United States, the Iraqi dictator dropped conventional bombs, napalm, and poisonous gas on thousands of Kurds in northern Iraq (Von Zielbauer 2006).

11. On July 25, 1990, eight days prior to Hussein's invasion of Kuwait, Hussein met with the US ambassador to Iraq, April Glaspie, who told him: "We have no opinion on . . . your border disagreement with Kuwait." Glaspie said this statement, as reported in the media, was taken out of context and that she also told Hussein "that we would insist on settlements being made in a nonviolent manner, not by threats, not by intimidation, and certainly not by aggression" (cited in Kouba 2008). During the Gulf War, some of Bush's advisers encouraged him to continue on to Baghdad to try to remove Hussein from power. Bush, as we know, decided against this, fearing that the United States would become involved in a military quagmire (Ricks 2006).

12. For analyses of the doctrine of preventive war and the relevant body of international law, see Cole and Lobel 2007, Kramer and Michalowski 2005, Mayer 2009, and O'Huallachain and Sharpe 2005.

13. Neoconservatives were critical of foreign policy "realists," including those who had been part of the George H. W. Bush administration. Realists advocated a policy of containment against Iraq through diplomatic pressure,

ongoing weapons inspections, economic sanctions, and limited air strikes that posed little risk of US casualties. Reports indicate that Bush Sr. felt that the invasion his son undertook in Iraq was unwise; and Brent Scowcroft, Bush Sr.'s close friend and former national security adviser, wrote an op-ed piece in the *Wall Street Journal* in August 2002 opposing it. Although the Clinton administration had also been committed to regime change in Iraq, it was opposed to military intervention without United Nations authorization (Dean 2006; Kramer and Michalowski 2005; Ricks 2006).

Among George W. Bush's own advisers, Secretary of State Colin Powell was the most prominent representative of the realist school, but even he dropped his reservations and lent his credibility to the call for war. Later, Colonel Lawrence Wilkerson, Powell's former chief of staff, was highly critical of what he called the "oval office cabal" composed of Vice President Dick Cheney, Secretary of Defense Donald Rumsfeld, and National Security Adviser Condoleezza Rice in misdirecting US policy toward Iraq. White House advisers Paul Wolfowitz and Richard Perle were also forceful and influential advocates for war. Arguably, without the support of British prime minister Tony Blair, it would have been much more difficult for the Bush administration to go forward with its plans. The compliance of CIA director George Tenet, who told the president what he wanted to hear, was also significant. Tenet misrepresented the complexities of the intelligence available to him when he told Bush that the evidence regarding WMD was a "slam dunk" (Dean 2006; Lobe 2005; Ricks 2006; Suskind 2006; Woodward 2006).

14. Recall that Cheney had met with senior oil company executives to discuss the prospects of oil drilling in Iraq (see Chapter 5).

15. Cheney is purported to have first used the phrase "one percent chance" in relationship to the possibility that Pakistani scientists were helping Al-Qaida develop a nuclear weapon. "If there's a one percent chance," Cheney said, "we have to treat it as a certainty in terms of our response. . . . It's not about our analysis, or finding a preponderance of evidence. It's about our response" (quoted in Suskind 2006:62). According to Ron Suskind, who dubs this the "one percent doctrine," this claim "divided what had largely been indivisible in the conduct of American foreign policy: analysis and action. Justified or not, fact-based or not, 'our response' is what matters. As to 'evidence,' the bar was set so low that the word itself almost didn't apply" (2006:62). Suskind notes how one administration official told him that "guys like me live 'in what we call the reality-based community,'" which [the official] defined as people who 'believe that solutions emerge from your judicious study of discernible reality. . . . That's not the way the world really works anymore. . . . We're an empire now, and when we act, we create our own reality'" (2004:9).

16. In February 2002, as John Judis reports, the *New York Times* exposed a Pentagon plan to launch a new Office of Strategic Influence that would "provide news items, possibly even false ones, to foreign media organizations." The brouhaha over this led the Pentagon to abandon the new office, but Secretary of Defense Rumsfeld said, "You can have the name, but I'm going to keep doing every single thing that needs to be done—and I have" (cited in Judis 2002:12).

17. In the run-up to the Iraq War, the Bush administration estimated that it would cost $50–60 billion, some of which would be paid by other countries and Iraqi oil revenue. This was a gross underestimation. In contrast, economists

Joseph Stiglitz and Linda Bilmes (2008) estimate that when all is said and done, taking into account the cost of medical and disability care for injured war veterans, the cost of the war could exceed $3 trillion. Richard Clarke adds that the administration, most notably Secretary of Defense Rumsfeld, "ignored professional military advice and sent too few troops to Iraq to protect our forces" and secure the peace (2004:xvi; see also Ricks 2006).

18. David Kay, one of the world's leading weapons inspectors, was assigned to head the Iraq Survey Group. Kay soon discovered that some of the key prewar intelligence had been bogus. After the initial phase of the survey group was concluded, Kay resigned in frustration, saying, "We were almost all wrong, and I certainly include myself. . . . I don't think they [WMD] existed" (quoted in Woodward 2006:277–278). Kay believes that the CIA had actually been deceived by Hussein, who wanted the world to believe he had WMD when, in fact, he did not. The final report of the Iraq Survey Group, under the direction of Charles Duelfer, was issued in September 2004, confirming the initial findings (Priest and Pincus 2004; Ricks 2006; Woodward 2006).

19. In retrospect, Bush's press secretary, Scott McClellan, believes that Rove intentionally deceived him about what he knew about the leak, causing McClellan to misinform the public. McClellan also says that Bush backed up Rove's denials. "Karl didn't do it," Bush had said. "He told me he didn't do it" (quoted in McClellan 2008:183).

20. In the summer of 2010, the muckraking Internet website WikiLeaks released government documents about the war in Afghanistan that provide "evidence of widespread US killings of Afghan civilians and attempts to cover up killings, and . . . portray unaccountable Special Operations forces as roaming the country hunting people. . . . They describe incidents of mass outrage sparked by the killing of civilians and confirm that the United States is funding both sides of the war through bribes paid to the Taliban and other resistance forces" (Scahill 2010:8).

21. In 1903 the United States obtained a 99-year lease of Guantánamo Bay from the Cuban government, which was later extended indefinitely (Posner 2010).

22. Most of this section derives from McCoy 2006, but see also Cole and Lobel 2007, Hersh 2004, Kinser 2006, and Mayer 2009.

23. The first international Geneva Convention regarding treatment of prisoners of war predates World War II, but a stronger set of guidelines was established in 1949 in response to the abusive practices of the Germans and Japanese. Under the George W. Bush administration, the United States became the first country to authorize violations of the conventions. For more on the Geneva Conventions and other international law on torture, see Cole and Lobel 2007, Hersh 2004, and Mayer 2009.

24. At the end of World War II, the CIA recruited Nazi scientists, including Kurt Plotner, who had tested mescaline on Jewish prisoners. After the war, the agency commenced a review of Nazi-inspired drug experiments and began testing LSD (lysergic acid diethylamide) and THC (tetrahydrocannabinol, or cannabis, found in marijuana) for use in interrogation of suspected spies and double agents. The most notorious of these experimental programs was called MK-Ultra (McCoy 2006).

25. McCoy (2006) notes that Stanley Milgram's famous experiments on

obedience were funded, at least in part, through the Office of Naval Research (although it is not clear whether the money came from the CIA). Milgram set up an experiment whereby subjects were asked to administer electroshocks to a colleague of the experimenter, which, if real, would have been extremely painful if not fatal. The large majority of subjects complied. The upshot of the experiment was that ordinary people could be induced to commit torture if given the proper training and authorization.

In another well-known study of that era (not implicated in the CIA torture program), Philip Zimbardo conducted a two-week simulation of the prison experience using college students. Subjects were divided into prisoners and guards. Prisoners were forced to give up personal effects and wear hospital gowns and stocking caps over their heads to simulate shaved heads. Guards were given uniforms, clubs, and silver sunglasses to prevent eye contact; and they were instructed to address prisoners by number only, while prisoners were told to address guards as "Mr. Correction Officer." Otherwise, prisoners were forbidden to engage in unauthorized talking or use the bathroom without permission, and when they first entered the "prison" they were required to go through a humiliating "strip down" and shower. The experiment had to be canceled after six days because the level of brutality among some of the guards escalated. Guards devised their own punishments: confinement to solitary cells, orders to clean toilets with bare hands, withdrawing bathroom privileges (forcing prisoners to use buckets in their cells, which were not emptied), and denying prisoners food. After the Abu Ghraib scandal surfaced, Zimbardo (2007) published a book, *The Lucifer Effect: Understanding How Good People Turn Evil*, relating his classic research to what had transpired.

26. It may be easier to recover from physical torture than from psychological torture, as the psychological damage from these techniques may be irreparable.

27. The US Army's School of the Americas, initially based in Panama but later moved to the United States, also taught these methods to hundreds of Latin American officers. In the Philippines as well, from 1972 to 1986, torture was a key element of President Ferdinand Marcos's US-backed dictatorial rule. As Filipino interrogators "probed human consciousness in the ad hoc laboratory of thousands of torture sessions, . . . [they also] discovered the capacity of sexual humiliation to damage" the human psyche (McCoy 2006:75).

28. At the end of the Cold War, the United States resumed its role as an active participant in the international human rights movement, passing the Protection for Victims of Torture Act, which allowed civil lawsuits in US courts against foreign perpetrators who enter US jurisdiction. Congress also amended the federal criminal code to make torture a crime punishable by 20 years in prison. Both measures, however, maintained the Reagan exceptions to torture (McCoy 2006).

29. Bush administration officials tried to make a distinction between "enhanced interrogation" and torture, with "no touch" torture and water-boarding among the practices included in the former. Scott Horton (2007) credits the Nazis with being the first to make this distinction. The German phrase *"verschärfte vernehmung,"* meaning enhanced or intensive interrogation, was a Gestapo invention used to describe methods such as stress positions, sleep dep-

rivation, and hypothermia. After World War II, the United States prosecuted the perpetrators for war crimes, even though the victims, who were part of the Norwegian insurgency against the German occupation, were not official prisoners of war. In their defense, the Nazis argued, as did the Bush administration, that this put the victims outside the boundaries of international legal protection. McCoy (2006) adds that Bybee's definition of torture, which breached US military and international guidelines, put US personnel who followed it in legal jeopardy.

30. Nine US Army soldiers were court-martialed and convicted (Follman and Clark-Flory 2006).

31. McCoy notes that torture also has a pernicious effect on the torturer, as it unleashes "an unfathomable capacity for cruelty as well as seductive illusions of omnipotence. . . . [I]ts perpetrators remain wedded to its use, refusing to acknowledge evidence of its limited utility and high political cost" (2006:13–14; see also Zimbardo 2007).

7

Prevention and Control of White-Collar Crime

ERNEST FITZGERALD WAS HIRED BY THE DEPARTMENT OF Defense in 1965 after working for more than a dozen years in the private sector as a quality-control engineer and cost analyst. As a management systems deputy in the Office of the Assistant Secretary of the Air Force for Financial Management and Comptroller, Fitzgerald took his job seriously. Early in his career, according to Myron Peretz Glazer and Penina Migdal Glazer's account, Fitzgerald had been told that

> civilian and military officials in the Pentagon wanted defense contractors to earn high profits. These would not only ensure attractive opportunities for retired officials but also create a long-term relationship with a favored list of large corporations that employed experienced lobbyists to assist in obtaining congressional approval for large military budgets. Overlooking excessive costs and even concealing faulty equipment may have been acceptable to many high officials in the Defense Department; but for some federal employees, this cozy relationship between government and industry was a serious ethical breach and a massive waste of government funds. (1989:22)

Fitzgerald was one employee who refused to go along with a system he thought was corrupt. He started writing internal memos alerting his superiors to $2.3 billion in cost overruns related to the construction of C-5A aircraft that Lockheed corporation had been contracted to build. Fitzgerald was not alone in suspecting that Lockheed "had initially submitted an unrealistically low bid to get the contract," under the assumption that the Air Force would cover their extensive overruns as it had done in the past, especially because "the civilian undersecretary in charge of the operation had come from the aircraft industry and was sympathetic to their business needs" (Glazer and Glazer 1989:22; see also Fitzgerald 1972).

Fitzgerald was vocal in his advocacy of a "more efficient and cost-effective method of evaluating contractor performance," but his superiors told him that "cost overruns were anticipated and actually built into the contracts" (Glazer and Glazer 1989:22). In 1968 he was invited to testify before the Senate Subcommittee on Economy in Government, headed by Senator William Proxmire, a longtime foe of government waste, who had been investigating the C-5A project. Fitzgerald was advised by his superiors not to disclose what he knew about inaccurate reports that the Pentagon had submitted to Congress, but as Fitzgerald said: "When I was asked by Senator Proxmire to confirm his estimate of [the] C-5A cost increase, I committed truth" (quoted in Glazer and Glazer 1989:23).

Employees like Fitzgerald who publicly disclose unethical or illegal practices that take place in the organizations in which they work are known as **whistle-blowers**.[1] Roberta Johnson defines whistle-blowing in terms of four component parts:

> (1) An individual acts with the intention of making information public; (2) the information is conveyed to parties outside the organization, who make it public and a part of the public record; (3) the information has to do with possible or actual nontrivial wrongdoing in an organization; and (4) the person exposing the agency is not a journalist or ordinary citizen, but a member or former member of the organization. (2003:3–4)

Whistle-blowing is a risky business, however. For his courageous stance, Fitzgerald lost his job. He continued to fight the system, however, and was instrumental in the passage of federal legislation in the late 1970s to protect whistle-blowers against retaliation by their organizational superiors. Since then, the federal government and many states have passed additional legislation, but these laws are unevenly enforced, especially when "retaliation" is difficult to prove. Moreover, employees who might be in a position to know about organizational wrongdoing often have previously signed nondisclosure agreements, and they thus make themselves vulnerable to lawsuits and loss of compensation if they violate these contracts. Whistle-blowers are also subject to public "character assassination" by the people whom the whistle-blower is exposing and hence risk tarnishing their reputations and future job prospects. And if they steal or disclose internal organizational documents, they may be subject to criminal prosecution (Johnson 2003).

Although corporate and governmental whistle-blowers have and

will continue to be an important source of public disclosure of the pernicious impact of white-collar crime on American society, they are merely
stopgap measures. The question remains: Can anything be done to more
effectively prevent and control the malfeasance of privileged criminals?

— Grades

Promoting Ethical Conduct   *— Attendance records*

The moral tone of a society, as noted in the opening chapter of this
book, is set by those at the top. "Criminal propensities," as Gabriel
Tarde observed, "travel down and outward—from the powerful to the
powerless" (Beirne and Messerschmidt 1995:367). In writing about the
white-collar "criminaloid," Edward Ross expected their crimes to flour-
ish "until the growth of morality overtakes the growth of opportunities
to prey" ([1907] 1977:36; see Box 1.1). Thus a reasonable first step in
dealing with white-collar crime is to raise public awareness about it,
since apathy toward white-collar crime, as David Friedrichs suggests, is
arguably "more widespread than it is for conventional crimes, especially
when people do not consider themselves to be affected by it," or when
they oppose government regulation or dispute that such actions, which
may be associated with productive outcomes or political policies they
favor, need concern us at all (2007:308).

For those who accept the proposition of this book, including the
broadened definition of white-collar crime embodied in the "analogous
social injuries" concept (see Chapter 1), the educational arena is
arguably an appropriate place to initiate a critique of white-collar crime.
But even at the college level, criminal justice curriculums do not generally provide sufficient attention to this subject; and although most business schools teach something about business ethics, studies find that
"any improvements in students' ethical awareness or reasoning" as a
result of these courses are short-lived (Friedrichs 2007:309). Clearly,
ethics courses that "promote values that put integrity and concern with
the well-being of others ahead of personal or corporate enrichment and
advantage" will not be effective if the rest of the business curriculum
promotes "a mindset where attention to the bottom line trumps all other
considerations" (Friedrichs 2007:310). Thus Robert Prentice (2002) suggests that teaching business law, and the consequence of noncompliance
to law, may be more effective than teaching ethics.

Nowadays it has become increasingly common for corporations to
have an organizational code of ethics that encourages employees not
simply to make decisions that benefit the company, but to make deci-

sions that are consistent with a "broader social responsibility to promote society's well-being" (Friedrichs 2007:310). Most often, however, these codes are implemented to mitigate top management's responsibility for company transgressions or as "window dressing" intended for public relations (Toffler 2003). As long as top management continues to send a message that "heads will roll" unless the company grows a certain percentage in the next year or makes a certain profit, then "you're going to have people shipping inferior goods, juggling the books, bribing when they have to, [and] trampling workers beneath them" (Wilkes 1989:E24). Recall the top-management official cited earlier who said, "Business executives . . . have no right to wrap themselves in the mantle of moral philosophers and judges—especially to the detriment of the interests of their shareholders whose money they are using" (Silk and Vogel 1976:229; see Chapter 2).

Under these circumstances, potential whistle-blowers like Ernest Fitzgerald will continue to face ethical dilemmas. They must sacrifice the social value placed on loyalty to the organization in which they are a member, often incurring the wrath of coworkers, for a higher fidelity to other constituencies, including the society at large. Cynthia Ossias experienced these dilemmas as a senior staff attorney in the Legal Division of the California State Department of Insurance when she "came forward with information about secret arrangements" between Chuck Quakenbush, the elected insurance commissioner, and six insurance companies, related to more than 600,000 claims that customers had filed after the 6.7-magnitude earthquake that hit the San Fernando Valley in southern California in 1994 (Johnson 2003).

After the earthquake, when policyholders experienced problems receiving settlements from insurers, they turned to California's Department of Insurance for help if these claims were improperly denied. The insurance industry in California had already been under the gun for improper denial of claims from two earthquakes and a major fire that had hit the state in the previous few years. Quakenbush, who had rewritten regulatory guidelines to redefine insurance companies (not California residents) as the department's "customers," promised the companies lower penalties for future improprieties if they contributed "money for consumer aid and earthquake damage research" (Johnson 2003:41). Quakenbush proceeded to rake in millions of dollars from the companies, which he misappropriated for personal use: his reelection campaign, public service spots in which he was featured, consulting fees to a key adviser, and even a football camp attended by his sons.

As senior staff counsel, Ossias was in a position to learn of these transgressions. The payments *avoided* by the insurers were estimated to be as much as $3.7 billion, and only a fraction of the $12.5 million that was collected by the Department of Insurance actually went to the people of California.[2] After Ossias was discovered to have leaked internal department documents to the press that exposed the scandal, Quakenbush called in the California Highway Patrol to investigate her, and put her on administrative leave. In coming forward, Ossias risked criminal prosecution as well as the loss of her job and law license. She also felt that her "loyalties were at war . . . loyalty to my boss, loyalty to my agency, loyalty to the public and loyalty to the rules of professional conduct." In the end, Ossias felt "morally compelled to act. . . . I work with dedicated public servants. There are . . . [people] in every state agency who want to do the right thing for the citizens for whom they work" (quoted in Johnson 2003:45–46).

Some whistle-blowers aim not only to stop current practices but also to change social policy. Johnson (2003) calls these whistle-blowers "policy entrepreneurs," noting Hugh Kaufman as a commendable example. Kaufman, who served under Rita Lavelle in the Hazardous Waste Site Control Division of the Environmental Protection Agency during the Reagan administration, helped expose the cronyism and conflicts of interest that led to the Sewergate scandal of the 1980s (see Chapter 1).[3] He gave frequent media interviews and made several appearances before congressional committees, charging "the Reagan EPA with jeopardizing the public's health by failing to enforce hazardous-waste and toxic-chemical laws, arranging 'sweetheart deals' with polluters, and allowing partisan politics to affect enforcement of environmental laws." For his actions, Kaufman experienced reprisals: "his workload was increased with what he termed 'meaningless paperwork,' and he was harassed and investigated" by as many as 15 EPA employees who were assigned "to find grounds to dismiss and/or intimidate" him (Johnson 2003:56–57). But Kaufman was careful to coordinate his whistle-blowing with sympathetic congressmen and succeeded in deflecting the attacks against himself. His efforts forced Lavelle's dismissal (and eventual conviction for perjury) as well as the resignation of EPA director Anne Gorsuch, and led to greater public awareness and congressional oversight of the hazardous waste cleanup program and a moderation of Reagan's antiregulatory environmental policies.

Regulatory Reform

Previously we noted how the relatively "high level of consensus on the desirability of government regulation" of the economy began to erode in the late 1970s, especially among Republicans (Friedrichs 2007:256; see Chapter 1). The major thrust of federal regulatory policy from the Republican administration of Ronald Reagan to the Republican administration of George W. Bush has been to thwart proregulatory reform. Even the Democratic administration of Bill Clinton, which did pursue some significant antitrust cases and was more favorable toward environmental regulation, was generally supportive of corporate consolidation and the deregulation of financial markets (see Chapter 3).

Advocates of deregulation believe that the capitalist marketplace is capable of policing itself. This belief takes the form of policy in the approach of **self-regulation**, or voluntary compliance, which is based on the dubious assumption that if companies are allowed to monitor their own activities, they will report and remedy their own problems, or that the "invisible hand" of the market will somehow weed out unscrupulous competitors (Friedrichs 2007; Kennedy 2004). Nobel Prize–winning economist Joseph Stiglitz finds this ideology of laissez-faire capitalism, what he calls **market fundamentalism**—the belief that "unfettered markets by themselves can ensure prosperity and growth"—anachronistic; and he thinks that the notion of self-regulation is an oxymoron (2010:xiii). One basic flaw of market fundamentalism, he notes, is the problem of "externalities," whereby the economic and physical costs of production or financial transactions are passed on to other parties, as in the case of the recent financial crisis or the Deepwater Horizon oil spill (see Chapters 3 and 4). It is ironic, Stiglitz observes, that a "country in which socialism is often treated as an anathema has socialized risk" to compensate for the externalities of private profit-making (p. 16). There is really no such thing as a "free" market. Time and time again, deregulation has proven that it does not work.

Still, some people think that the danger of regulatory overreach causes more problems than it solves, and that it deters productive activities more than it deters prohibited ones. John Braithwaite (1982), for one, favors a policy of **enforced self-regulation**. As a practical matter, he thinks, government does not have the capacity to effectively supervise the vast array of economic activity in complex capitalist societies. Instead, why not encourage the development of personnel within corporations who "are concerned with responsible, ethical behavior and the long-term reputation" of the companies (Friedrichs 2007:319)? In Braithwaite's approach, a "corporate compliance director" would have the function of reporting to the "relevant regulatory agency and would be criminally liable for failing to do so" (2007:319; see also Ayres and Braithwaite 1992).

Even within regulatory agencies themselves, there is a tension between a *compliance* approach and a *deterrence* approach, with the former emphasizing persuasion and cooperation and the latter prosecution and punishment (Braithwaite, Grabosky, and Walker 1987). Regulatory agencies vary along these lines, with most personnel leaning toward compliance, thinking of themselves "less as a police force and more as government agents who seek to gain voluntary compliance with regulatory standards. . . . Informality and bargaining—and a norm of accommodation—take precedence over the strict implementation of legal rules" (Friedrichs 2007:259). It is not clear how much the commitment to accommodation is a function of necessity, as regulatory agencies are generally understaffed and underfunded, more so during some administrations than others. Moreover, the monetary fines levied against law violators are often too small to deter the misconduct. There is also the problem of regulatory capture, whereby agencies align themselves with the corporate "interests they are supposed to regulate and business influence grows until agencies defend the regulated business's interests instead of the public interest" (Neuman 2005:472–473). Clearly, regulatory agencies need to be administered and staffed by those who have the broader public interest at heart, but the "revolving door" of personnel who circulate in and out of the private and public sectors often creates conflicts of interest and a "fox guarding the henhouse" approach that thwarts effective regulatory control (see Chapters 1 and 2).

Daniel Faber (2008), a staunch proponent of environmental regulation, advocates what he calls the **precautionary principle**, whereby the burden of proof regarding the safety of a potentially harmful environmental practice should be placed on the industry, not the public. He contrasts this with a **risk assessment** approach that governs most environmental regulation, whereby agencies evaluate the costs and benefits of a particular economic activity and arrive at an "acceptable" level of public exposure to harm that is applied as a general standard to the industry. Faber also notes the environmental racism involved in placing the externalities of industrial production on poor and minority communities in the United States and developing countries abroad (see Chapter 4). As long as this inequity is maintained, the more privileged publics in developed countries will likely demand little in the way of precautions. Citizens will complain about lax regulations after the fact, as they did after the Deepwater Horizon spill, but all too many voters will continue to be seduced by the call to unburden corporations from the heavy hand of government.

On the financial front, even as "the ideology of deregulation has been exposed as a failure, the banks and their political allies are still invoking the bogeyman of big government to fight financial reform"—for example, by opposing the creation of "a strong Consumer Financial Protection Agency, dedicated to oversight of systematic risk, and new requirements to move derivatives onto exchanges and central clearing-houses" where regulators and investors can monitor the market (Johnson and Kwak 2010:A4–A5). Republican political consultant Frank Luntz "clearly spelled out the strategy to demonize" the reforms proposed by the administration of Barack Obama "by branding it as more bureaucracy, bailouts, and special interest loopholes" (Johnson and Kwak 2010:A5). But Stiglitz argues that "America's financial markets [have] failed to perform their essential societal functions of managing risk, allocating capital, and mobilizing savings while keeping transaction costs low. Instead, they [have] created risk, misallocated capital, and encouraged excessive indebtedness while imposing high transaction costs" (2010:7). Elizabeth Warren, a strong advocate of consumer protection, adds: "Today, nearly every product sold in America has passed basic safety standards well in advance of being put on store shelves" (2010:A6). Why should our financial products be any different?

> While manufacturers have developed iPods and flat-screen televisions, the financial industry has perfected the art of offering mortgages, credit cards, and check overdraft loans laden with hidden terms that obscure price and risk. Good products are mixed with dangerous products, and consumers are left on their own to sort out which is which. The consequences can be disastrous. More than half of the families that ended up with high-priced, high-risk . . . mortgages would have qualified for safer, cheaper . . . loans. . . . Study after study shows that credit products are deliberately designed to obscure costs and to trick consumers. The average credit-card contract is dizzying. Credit-card contracts that were a little over a page long in 1980 have ballooned to an unreadable 30 pages. Lenders advertise a single interest rate on the front of their direct-mail envelopes while burying costly details and hidden fees deep in the contract. Faced with impenetrable legalese and deliberate obfuscation, consumers can't compare offers or make clear-eyed choices about borrowing. Creditors can hire an army of lawyers and MBAs to design their programs, but families' time and expertise have not expanded to meet the demands of a changing credit marketplace. As a result, consumers sign on to credit products focused on only one or two features—nominal interest rates or free gifts—in the hope that the fine print will not bite them. (p. A6)

The Obama administration also floated a plan to regulate financial institutions that are "too big to fail," subjecting the larger, interconnected institutions that are capable of toppling the entire economy to stricter regulatory scrutiny and requiring them to "hold more assets and more cash as cushions against a downturn. They also would have to anticipate their own demise, drafting detailed descriptions of how they could be dismantled quickly without causing damaging repercussions" (Kuhnhenn 2009:A11). Not surprisingly, this plan was vehemently opposed by the corporations (and their political allies) that would be subjected to these controls.

Criminal and Civil Sanctions

Among those who side with the need for regulation, the advocates of deterrence believe that compliance mechanisms have proven ineffective and that credible criminal and civil sanctions must be utilized to achieve effective prevention and control of white-collar crime. Recall that, technically speaking, *criminal law* defines harmful conduct as a public matter and mandates the intervention of law enforcement authorities, while *civil law* defines harm as a private matter to be settled by individuals (and their attorneys) as private parties in the courts (see Chapter 1). One key difference between criminal and civil approaches, therefore, is that the cost of criminal prosecution is socialized and borne by the government, while the cost of civil litigation is privatized and borne by the plaintiff, who, if unsuccessful, risks payment of filing costs and attorney fees, unless they have a fee agreement to compensate their attorneys only if they win the case (Cullen et al. 2006; Swigert and Farrell 1980–1981).[4]

Another fundamental difference between the criminal approach and the civil approach is that the primary function of the former is intended to be *reductive*—that is, through the imposition of punishment, the behavior can be deterred; while the latter is intended to be *distributive*—that is, through compensation to the plaintiff, the cost of the transgression is transferred from the victim to the perpetrator (Cullen et al. 2006; Stone 1975).[5] In theory, both the reductive and distributive functions of the law could be served by either criminal or civil sanctions. But few jurisdictions provide compensation for victims in criminal cases; and although **punitive damages** in civil cases, when available, allow for the assessment of additional monetary penalties above and beyond compensatory payments, hence serving "the quasi-criminal function of deterrence, . . . [such] damages are imposed less frequently than compensatory damages" (Cullen et al. 2006:201).

Those who advocate the criminal prosecution of white-collar crime tend to emphasize the greater stigma that is attached to criminal sanctions, making it a more effective means of social control. As Michael Consentino, the Indiana prosecutor in the Ford Pinto reckless homicide trial, said: "criminal prosecution truly serves as the sole opportunity for the people of Indiana to express their outrage, to punish the defendant for the death[s] of these girls and to deter this defendant and others from like recklessness in the future" (quoted in Cullen et al. 2006:203; see Chapter 4).[6] Francis Cullen and colleagues underscore this view when they write: "Hauling a corporate offender into court makes it explicit just where the boundary line is drawn between acceptable and unacceptable conduct in business. . . . It sends a message that the system is fair and that no one, even powerful corporate executives, is above the law" (2006:348).

In deciding to pursue criminal prosecution, a decision has to be made as to whether to prosecute individuals within the corporation, the corporation itself, or both. In the Film Recovery Systems case involving the death of an employee, three FRS officials and the company itself were prosecuted (see Chapter 4). In the Pinto case, Consentino decided to forgo prosecution of individual executives and focus exclusively on the corporation. He reasoned that establishing the culpability of individuals in such a complex organization as Ford Motor Company would be too difficult; and he doubted that the state of Michigan, where the company was based, would comply with an extradition request to try the executives in another state (Cullen et al. 2006).

The issue of individual versus organizational prosecutions in white-collar crime cases also raises a broader conceptual issue regarding culpability. In her study of the *Challenger* space shuttle disaster, for instance, Diane Vaughan (2005) argued that individuals embedded in organizational environments in which risk-taking is normalized—the normalization of deviance—are not amoral calculators and do not generally have guilty intentions (see Box 2.3). Also recall how Dennis Gioia, who worked as Ford Motor Company's field recall coordinator during the Pinto controversy, felt "no strong obligation to recall" the vehicle and saw "no strong ethical overtones to the case whatsoever" ([1992] 1996:54; see Chapter 2). On the other hand, recall, too, the comments of Roger Boisjoly, a senior scientist on the scene during the *Challenger* disaster, who said: "One of the most pernicious problems of modern times is the almost universally held belief that the individual is powerless . . . within . . . large organizations. The end result can be a cancerous attitude that . . . metastasizes into decisions and acts of life-threatening responsibility" (Boisjoly, Curtis, and Mellican [1989]

1992:130–131; see Box 2.3).[7] Be that as it may, John Braithwaite and Brent Fisse argue that organizational outcomes "are more than the products of individual actions. . . . We routinely hold organizations responsible for a decision when and because that decision instantiates an organizational policy and instantiates an organizational decision-making process that the organization has chosen for itself" (1995:437, 441).[8]

If a prosecutor decides to pursue a white-collar case in criminal court, absent a plea agreement, he or she will need to establish guilt "beyond a reasonable doubt" at trial. One advantage of the civil approach is that the level of proof that is required—such as a "preponderance of the evidence" or a "greater weight of the evidence"—is less stringent.[9] Moreover, if successful, the amount of money awarded to plaintiffs may be far greater than the amount from fines assessed in criminal cases (which go into the government's coffers), especially if punitive damages are available.[10]

The Pinto case, on the other hand, suggests that the stigma associated with criminal prosecution may be of greater concern to corporations than civil litigation. It is noteworthy that Ford Motor Company spent far more money in attorney and other legal fees in its defense than it would have paid if it had simply pled guilty and paid the maximum fine of $30,000. Ford executives were concerned that a criminal conviction would tarnish not only their personal reputations, but also the company's reputation, which, they feared, could have an adverse impact on the Ford brand and the sales of their entire fleet of vehicles. They also were worried that the negative publicity associated with a conviction would lead the federal government to promulgate more rigorous safety standards that would hurt their profit margins (Cullen et al. 2006; Fisse and Braithwaite 1983).

As a practical matter, however, smaller companies are more likely to be criminally prosecuted than larger companies; and subordinate managers are more likely to be prosecuted than higher-level executives (Cohen 1989; Friedrichs 2007). In a nationwide survey of local prosecutors, Michael Benson and Francis Cullen (1998) found that corporate prosecutions were more likely in communities with lower rates of violent street crime and stronger and more diversified economies. They surmise that when citizens feel safe from street crime, they are more likely to demand protection from other harms; and in more prosperous communities, there are more resources available for white-collar prosecutions and citizens feel less vulnerable to the job losses they think may follow.[11]

Moreover, as already suggested, the legal system has been rather forgiving of white-collar offenders, for when they are prosecuted and convicted they receive less serious penalties than do other types of offenders (see Chapters 1 and 2). John Braithwaite and Gilbert Geis (1982) argue that sanctions for corporate crime would be more effective if they included provisions for publicizing corporate wrongdoers and their misdeeds (e.g., in television spots), hence increasing a company's exposure to negative publicity that could impact sales. Others advocate a system of corporate probation, whereby a company found guilty of a serious crime would be placed under the supervision of a probation officer or management specialist who has expertise in the field. Or, public representatives with their own staffs could be added to corporate boards of directors to monitor corporations and investigate complaints. Certainly, law-violating corporations should not be allowed to receive government contracts. These are some of the measures criminologists have offered for dealing with corporate crime (Coleman 2006; DeKeseredy and Schwartz 1996; Fisse and Braithwaite 1983; Friedrichs 2007).

Political and Media Reform

Friedrichs (2007) points to one of the paradoxes facing efforts to prevent and control white-collar crime: that although we depend on the government to promulgate and implement policies, the government and its personnel, as well as politicians generally, are often the source of criminality and malfeasance, too. Take the case of Daniel Ellsberg, who leaked the infamous "Pentagon Papers" to the press, revealing how government officials had deceived Congress as well as the public about their rationale and plans to escalate the controversial Vietnam War (see Chapter 5). Ellsberg was a Defense Department analyst who was part of a research team commissioned in 1967 by Secretary of Defense Robert McNamara, who had become "increasingly skeptical about the possibility of winning" the war (Glazer and Glazer 1989:32; Morris 2004).[12] Ellsberg was privy to classified government documents that indicated grave doubts about the viability of the corrupt South Vietnamese government the United States was supporting, and about how the United States had deliberately provoked the Vietcong and North Vietnamese into taking belligerent action (see Chapter 6). The documents suggested that the war was not winnable and that the primary reason the United States was staying the course was to "save American face" (Ehrlich and Goldsmith 2009; Ellsberg 2002; Glazer and Glazer 1989).

Glazer and Glazer describe the path Ellsberg took in becoming one of the most famous whistle-blowers in US history:

Box 7.1 Promoting Workplace Democracy

Among the panoply of solutions to the unchecked power of corporations in American society, some look to ways to make the workplace more democratic. **Worker cooperatives** are companies that are owned by the workers themselves. By giving workers a greater stake in the business, such cooperatives can lead to greater productivity and job satisfaction. Worker cooperatives also tend to have relatively egalitarian pay structures that distribute wages and profits more equitably compared to the pay structures of conventional corporations (Curl 2009; Hill 2010; Kelly and Massena 2009).

The Mondragón Cooperative Corporation in the Basque region of Spain is the world's largest consortium of worker-owned businesses, employing more than 100,000 worker-owners in an integrated network of more than 120 companies that generate about $24 billion annually. "[W]hile most businesses determine voting power based on how many company shares a person owns, [Mondragón] cooperatives allocate each worker one vote . . . [and] top management is rarely paid more than six times the lowest-paid worker" (Kelly and Massena 2009:1; see also Alperovitz, Williamson, and Howard 2010; Chapter 3).

In the United States, the Evergreen Cooperative Laundry is a worker-owned industrial-size laundry that began operating in fall 2009 in one of the poorest neighborhoods in Cleveland. "After a six-month initial 'probationary' period, employees . . . [are expected] to buy into the company through payroll deductions of 50 cents an hour over three years (for a total of $3,000), . . . building up a $65,000 equity stake in the business over eight to nine years" (Alperovitz, Williamson, and Howard 2010:2). The cooperative laundry is part of a larger consortium modeled after Mondragón that includes the Ohio Cooperative Solar company, which installs solar panels and weatherization products. Two other cooperatives, a hydroponic food production greenhouse and a community-based newspaper, are in development. "The only way this business will take off," says work supervisor Medrick Addison, "is if people are fully vested in the ideas of the company. If you're not interested in giving it everything you have, then this isn't the place for you" (quoted in Alperovitz, Williamson, and Howard 2010:1).

Short of complete worker ownership, another form of workplace democracy takes the form of companies that have a co-determined decisionmaking structure that is shared between conventional manager-owners and elected worker-owners who represent workers on the corporate board of directors. According to Steven Hill, "In Germany, the world's second largest exporter and fourth-largest national economy, fully half of the boards of directors of the largest corporations . . . are elected by

continues

Box 7.1 continued

workers. In Sweden, one-third of the company's directors are worker-elected" (2010:2).

Hill notes that elected **work councils** are another element of co-determination that gives employees significant input into the workplace:

> Work councils, which are separate from labor unions but often populated by trade unionists, have real clout. They enjoy veto power of certain management decisions pertaining to treatment of employees, such as redeployment or dismissal. They also have "co-decision" rights to meet with management to discuss the firm's finances, work and holiday schedules, work organization and other procedures. In addition, they benefit from "consultation rights" in planning the introduction of new technologies and in mergers and layoffs, as well as in obtaining useful information in contract negotiations, such as profit and wage data. . . . [W]ork councils contribute to efficiency by improving communication, which in turn improves the quality of decisions and legitimizes the decisions in the eyes of workers. . . . Studies . . . [show] that work councils are associated with lower absenteeism, more worker training, better handling of grievances and smoother implementation of health and safety standards. (p. 3)

While critics charge that co-determination hurts competitiveness, "the World Economic Forum in 2008–09 ranked Denmark, Sweden, Finland, Germany and the Netherlands—all of which employ some degree of co-determination—among the top ten most competitive economies in the world." And these economies also rank "at or near the top . . . for quality of life, healthcare and social benefits" (p. 4). Hill asks us to imagine what it would be like if Wal-Mart (see Box 3.1) were at least partly worker-controlled. How might this "change Wal-Mart's behavior toward its workers and supply chain"—indeed, how might worker control change American society as a whole?

Ellsberg spoke to various colleagues . . . about the advisability of releasing the classified documents, but received no encouragement. They felt obligated to keep the report secret since access to classified documents had been provided . . . on the understanding that the findings would not be published. While Ellsberg understood the desire to keep such commitments, he became increasingly exasperated that the newly installed Nixon administration seemed intent on pursuing the war. . . . Once he decided to release the papers, Ellsberg first approached Senator William Fulbright of Arkansas, chairman of the Senate Foreign Relations Committee and an opponent of the war . . . [who] told Ellsberg that the revelations . . . would not justify the risk of being [criminally] charged with releasing secret government documents. Respecting Fulbright's decision, Ellsberg waited two more years before deciding to take the materials to the *New York Times*. By 1971 he felt compelled to act. (1989:33–34)

The *New York Times* published key portions of the Pentagon Papers, and the Nixon Justice Department forthrightly obtained a court injunction against further publication. During a two-week legal battle that was prominently featured in the press, Ellsberg leaked additional documents to other newspapers.[13] Then, in a six-to-three vote, the US Supreme Court overturned the injunction, ruling that the public had the right to know what the government had been doing. Justice Hugo Black, who voted with the majority, summarized the decision in his concurring opinion:

Only a free and unrestrained press can effectively expose deception in government. And paramount among the responsibilities of a free press is the duty to prevent any part of the Government from deceiving the people and sending them off to distant lands to die of foreign fevers and foreign shot and shell. In my view, far from deserving condemnation for their courageous reporting, . . . [the media] should be commended for serving the purpose that the Founding Fathers saw so clearly. In revealing the workings of government that led to the Vietnam war, the newspapers nobly did precisely that which the founders hoped and trusted they would do. (cited in Glazer and Glazer 1989:34)

Ellsberg was and remains a controversial figure in US history. It is not a leap of logic, however, to speculate that the majority of justices on today's US Supreme Court would not have ruled in favor of the public's right to know (see Alter 2005). Chief Justice John Roberts and Justice Samuel Alito, for example, both appointed during the administration of George W. Bush, are known to be very deferential to presidential authority. Alito in particular has been a proponent of the controversial **unitary executive doctrine**, the view that the president alone, as commander in chief and head of the executive branch, has indivisible powers that are "beyond the reach . . . of legislative or judicial review," hence nullifying the checks and balances that the framers of the Constitution hoped to establish (Gelman 2008:96; see also Dean 2007; Gore 2007).[14] This was the essence of the legal counsel given by White House lawyers Jay Bybee and John Yoo regarding the Bush administration's torture policy (see Chapter 6). It is as if Richard Nixon was right after all: "When the president does it, that means that it is not illegal" (see Chapter 5).

It is not speculation to note, however, that the 2010 US Supreme Court decision in *Citizens United v. Federal Election Commission* has, as many knowledgeable observers believe, undermined US democracy in a fundamental way. In what is arguably the Court's most controversial decision since *Bush v. Gore* (see Chapter 5), the five-judge majority—all of whom were appointed by Republican presidents Ronald Reagan, George H. W. Bush, or George W. Bush—overturned a century of national policy by ruling that the First Amendment of the US Constitution grants corporations an unlimited right of free speech that allows them to spend unlimited sums of money in federal, state, and local elections.[15]

It was a Republican president, Theodore Roosevelt, who supported public financing of elections, who once told Congress: "All contributions by corporations to any political committee or for any political purpose should be forbidden by law" (quoted in *The Nation* 2010:4). But the current Republican-aligned majority decided to grant corporations a blank check to influence elections. According to the majority justices who concurred in the five-to-four decision:

> [A] corporation [is] an "association of citizens" that deserves the same free-speech rights as an individual. Because speech and debate are good for democracy, they said, the public should welcome more corporate-funded campaign ads. "To exclude or impede corporate speech is to muzzle the principal agents of the modern economy," Justice Antonin Scalia said. "We should celebrate rather than condemn the addition of this speech to the public debate." (Savage 2010:1)

Law professor Patricia Williams reminds us that the 1976 US Supreme Court decision of *Buckley v. Valeo*, as controversial as it was, only "allowed *individuals* unlimited spending in pursuit of political ends" (2010:9, emphasis added).[16] The *Citizens United* case, on the other hand,

> begs the question: for whom is our Bill of Rights? . . . The notion of "corporate citizenship" that the majority . . . touted so blithely is a very different beast from citizenship founded on a constitution of enfranchised individuals. . . . It takes the most simple-minded or the most cynical state of mind to conclude . . . that corporations are entitled to the same panoply of civil and dignitary rights as actual, fully endowed people. (Williams 2010:9)

Erwin Chemerinsky, a leading constitutional scholar, adds:

> [C]orporations have accumulations of wealth unmatched in our society . . . [and] can simply outspend all other interests and drown out all

other voices in the political process. There are many different interests in our society, but . . . corporations have zero interests other than maximizing the wealth of their shareholders. (quoted in Hoffman 2010:3)

And journalist Jonathan Alter notes:

> If Exxon wants to spend $1 million (a bar tab for big Oil) defeating an environmentalist running for city council, it can do so now. If Goldman Sachs wants to pay the entire cost of every congressional campaign in the U.S., the law of the land now allows it. The decision frees unions, too, but they already spend about as much as they can on politics. Fortune 100 firms currently spend only a fraction of 1 percent of their $605 billion annual profits on buying politicians. (2010:15)

Arguably, the *Citizens United* case poses a significant barrier to future efforts to prevent and control white-collar crime, aggravating the already corrosive impact of lobbying and campaign contributions on the US political system (see Chapter 5). All this is made more disconcerting by the consolidation of major mass media in the United States, where a relatively small number of "media giants . . . own or control virtually all" of the nation's television stations, radio stations, and newspapers and magazines (Kennedy 2004:178). To remedy this situation, Robert Kennedy Jr. calls for the reinstitution of the **Fairness Doctrine**. The roots of the Fairness Doctrine go back to the **Federal Radio Act** of 1927, which required "broadcasters, as a condition of their licenses, [to] operate in the 'public interest' by covering important policy issues and providing equal time to both sides of public questions"; and this requirement was established as an administrative rule by the Federal Communications Commission (FCC) in 1949 (Kennedy 2004:176; Rendall 2005). In the 1960s, for instance, the FCC ruled that public health and environmental advocates be given rebuttal time to respond to advertisements for cigarettes and gas-guzzling automobiles. "The clear intent," as Bill Moyers notes, "was to prevent a monopoly of commercial values from overwhelming democratic values—to assure that the official view of reality—corporate or government—was not the only view of reality that reached the people" (quoted in Kennedy 2004:176–177).

In 1988, however, the Reagan administration abolished the Fairness Doctrine, effectively ending the right of media access to "any but moneyed interests" (Kennedy 2004:177). The occasion for the abolition "was a case involving a Syracuse, New York, television station that had broadcast nine paid editorials advocating the construction of a nuclear power plant. When the station refused to air opposing viewpoints, an antinuke group complained. The three Reagan appointees who ran the FCC sided with the TV station, applying the same laissez-faire philosophy to the airwaves" that Reagan had advanced in other areas of commerce (Kennedy 2004:177; see also Gore 2007; McChesney and Nichols 2002; Rendall 2005).[17]

In politics as well, abolition of the Fairness Doctrine has increased the likelihood that moneyed interests will dominate US democracy, that the public will not be exposed, in John Stuart Mill's words, to "the fullest and freest comparison of opposition opinions" (quoted in Gore 2007:11).[18] But more than the media is at issue here, for as we have also seen, problems with the electoral system jeopardize US democracy, too, with computerized voting raising serious questions about the legitimacy of important elections in recent years (see Box 5.3). Clearly it is imperative that all electronic voting be supplemented with corroborative paper ballots in case of a dispute. Secretaries of state who administer elections should also be prohibited from cochairing political campaigns, as was the case in the presidential elections in Florida in 2000 and Ohio in 2004. Americans need to "[e]nsure that enough accessible voting machines and poll workers are available at all precincts so that waiting times are reasonable," and they should give consideration to the creation of a National Election Day holiday so that people will not have to take time off from work to vote (A. Miller 2005:104). These are some of the measures that would enhance US democracy in ways that could increase the public's leverage over white-collar crime and other important issues facing American society (Miller 2008).

Nowadays, as noted in the first chapter of this book, few would deny that the ties that once bound US citizens to their government have been "broken." What Americans face here is an erosion of **political legitimacy**. A legitimate political system is one that is generally accepted by the citizenry as representing its values and interests (Gerth and Mills 1946). A government forfeits this legitimacy when its leaders no longer enjoy that acceptance. But, we must ask, from where does this erosion of legitimacy spring? In part, the erosion comes from the very political corruption and state crimes we have reviewed in this book. But it is also an inconvenient truth that the delegitimation of government, at least at the federal level, has been a central theme of the Republican Party and the conservative movement since at least the presidency of Ronald Reagan (Dean 2007).[19]

In his inaugural address in January 1981, President Reagan asserted: "[G]overnment is not the solution to our problem; government is the problem. . . . From time to time we've been tempted to believe that society has become too complex to be managed by self-rule, that government by an elite group is superior to government for, by, and of the people." Reagan went on to ask: "who among us has the capacity to govern someone else?" The answer, according to Reagan, was not the federal government: "It is my intention to curb the size of influence of the federal establishment and to demand recognition of the distinction between the powers granted to the federal government and those reserved to the states or the people" (quoted in Dean 2007:18).[20]

Political observer Alan Wolfe (2006) notes astutely that contemporary conservatives seem to have little use for the federal government other than to provide for the common defense. They seek political power to cut taxes and create a regulatory-free climate for the pursuit of private profit-making. Liberals, on the other hand, want to use the government to try to solve the pressing problems of the day, and they see the essence of democracy in harnessing the resources of government to do so.[21] This does not in itself make one point of view right and the other view wrong. What it does do is place the problem of white-collar crime, broadly construed, in the midst of an ideological divide that marks not only debates over crime and criminal justice policy (Miller 1973), but also debates over nearly every social issue facing the United States today.

Summary

In this concluding chapter of the book, we reviewed various strategies aimed at the prevention and control of white-collar crime. We considered ways to promote ethical conduct through the creation of public awareness, the teaching of business ethics, the development of organizational codes of ethics, and the practice of whistle-blowing. We also examined issues related to regulatory compliance versus deterrence, criminal versus civil sanctions, individual versus organizational liability, and the need for political and media reform to make corporations and government more responsive to the broader public good.

But what that public good should entail is precisely what divides many Americans today. They are divided over the role of government in society and the value of using government to control white-collar crime, especially insofar as government itself is often the site of law violation. They have come to take for granted their dependency on large corporations for the fulfillment of basic needs—from employment to consumption—and they are fearful of change or have difficulty imagining that things could ever be different. As such, it seems naive to assume that the problem of white-collar crime can ever really be "solved." There are powerful interests at stake, interests that are able to generate considerable public support, that are willing to spend prodigious sums of money to preserve the status quo. Nonetheless, it is important for conscientious citizens to do what they can to support and align themselves with those who are working to mitigate the abuse of corporate and government power in contemporary society. Failure to do that may only prove the adage: we have met the enemy, and the enemy is us.

Notes

1. Glazer and Glazer (1989) call them "ethical resisters." For a review of some of the notable whistle-blowers of the past few decades, see also Johnson 2003.

2. According to Ossias, the companies' transgressions included

> inadequate and even cursory inspection of homes for damages; ridiculously low settlement offers insufficient to pay for needed repairs; unreasonable delays during which policyholders were forced to wrangle for benefits they were entitled to; long periods in which policyholders were out of their homes while repairs were being performed; delayed discovery of the full extent of damage; and unrepaired damages exacerbated by aftershocks, resulting in policyholders living in unsafe structures and their supplemental claims being denied because of a purportedly expired statue of limitations. (quoted in Johnson 2003:43)

3. Kaufman had previously come forward with complaints about the Carter administration's hazardous waste policy (Johnson 2003).

4. When attorneys work on the basis of a "win only" contingency fee, they typically take as much as a third of the compensatory payments (plus expenses).

5. For discussions of product liability law pertaining to criminal and civil cases involving harmful corporate products, see Cullen et al. 2006 and Laufer 2006.

6. One of the main reasons Consentino decided to pursue a criminal case was that Indiana civil law at the time did not provide for punitive damages. For a full explanation of the nuances of Consentino's position, see Cullen et al. 2006.

7. For an account of Boisjoly as a whistle-blower, see Johnson 2003.

8. For a review of the complexities of this debate, see Friedrichs 2007 and articles in Geis, Meier, and Salinger 1995.

9. Recall that Ford Motor Company was acquitted in the criminal case (see Chapter 4).

10. In contrast to individual civil lawsuits, "class action" lawsuits involve a group of injured parties who join together in a collective action to recover

large sums of money to be divided among them. High-powered attorneys working on a contingency basis are often willing to devote considerable time and energy "to a case in which they may ultimately recover millions of dollars in fees" (Friedrichs 2007:303–304). At the same time, "since the mid-1980s, legislation in various states has imposed caps on awards (especially for punitive damages), time limits for filing cases, and in some cases, restrictions on contingency fees" (p. 302).

11. The public exhibits the strongest support for white-collar prosecutions of consumer fraud and environmental offenses (Benson and Cullen 1998).

12. Ellsberg worked for the RAND Corporation, a private nonprofit think tank that does research and analysis for the US Defense Department.

13. Ellsberg also surrendered himself to the US Attorney's Office and was subsequently indicted on multiple charges. At trial, the Nixon White House's burglary of Ellsberg's psychiatrist's office and other illegal surveillance of him were revealed, and the judge summarily dismissed the case (Ehrlich and Goldsmith 2009; Ellsberg 2002).

14. In her testimony before the Senate Judiciary Committee during the Alito confirmation hearings, former Clinton White House councel Beth Nolan explained that the unitary executive doctrine "embodies the concept of presidential control over all executive functions, including those that have traditionally been exercised by 'independent' agencies and other actors not subject to the president's direct control . . . [and it embraces] strong limits on the legislative and judicial branches" (quoted in Dean 2007:103). She noted that Alito had been working in the Office of Legal Counsel during the Reagan administration when this office took the position that "the President is largely impervious to statutory law in the areas of foreign affairs, national security, and war, and Congress is effectively powerless to act as a constraint against presidential aggrandizement in these areas" (quoted in Dean 2007:104). Dick Cheney and his legal adviser David Addington have also been strong proponents of this dubious legal theory (Gelman 2008).

15. The five judges were Chief Justice John Roberts and Justices Samuel Alito, Anthony Kennedy, Antonin Scalia, and Clarence Thomas. Jonathan Alter notes the elective nature of the Court's decision: "This didn't have to happen. The court had been asked to rule on whether the Federal Election Commission had the right to regulate a corporate-backed outfit called Citizens United that made the conservative film *Hillary: The Movie*. But instead of ruling narrowly, . . . [it] struck down the laws of 22 states and the federal government" (2010:15). Alter also notes the irony, or rather hypocrisy, of conservative judges who for years have been bashing "liberal judges for 'legislating from the bench' and disrespecting precedent . . . [who] are now exposed as unprincipled poseurs." Justice Ruth Ginsberg, who dissented in the case, "asked if foreign companies should have the same free-speech rights as domestic ones, since foreign individuals are allowed to make a speech here. The majority had no answer, and opened the door to a Chinese bank or Russian oligarch buying Congress" (Alter 2010:15).

16. To be sure, there is precedent for treating a corporation as a "person" for the purpose of criminal and civil liability, with all the rights available to persons under the Fourteenth and Fifteenth Amendments (Cullen et al. 2006; Laufer 2006).

17. Congress responded by passing legislation that would have codified the Fairness Doctrine, but Reagan vetoed the bill (Kennedy 2004; Rendall 2005).

18. The Internet, to be sure, offers a powerful medium for the airing of diverse points of view. But like any other technology devised by humankind, it can be used for negative as well as positive purposes. Former vice president Al Gore encourages Americans to remain diligent in ensuring "that the Internet remains open and accessible to all citizens without any limitation on the ability of individuals to choose the content they wish regardless of the Internet service provider they use to connect to the World Wide Web" (2007:261). A key issue here is the maintenance of "net neutrality," as service providers have proposed charging differential fees to Web companies and other content providers, which would create a "tiered Internet" that would make some sites easier to access than others. Net neutrality is necessary to prevent commercial interests from dominating the Internet even more than they already do.

19. For further discussion of the public's mistrust of government, see Nye, Zelikow, and King 1997.

20. President Bill Clinton seemed supportive of this view when he declared in his 1996 State of the Union address: "The era of big government is over." But in saying this he did not mean to endorse the views of someone like antitax activist Grover Norquist, who, as noted earlier, once called for shrinking the federal government to so small a size that it could be drowned in a bathtub (see Chapter 5). According to Norquist, "The sole legitimate function of government is to create and protect liberty. That is why we have courts, police, and a national army. To keep out, stop, or punish those who would infringe on our liberty" (quoted in Dean 2007:19). On the basis of this principle, Norquist claims to speak for property owners who "do not want their property rights interfered with" and business owners who "do not want their businesses taxed and regulated."

21. Conservatives, of course, also seek power to prevent liberals from accomplishing their governmental agenda (Dean 2007; Wolfe 2006).

References

Abadinsky, Howard. 2007. *Organized Crime*. Belmont, CA: Wadsworth.

Ackerman, Spencer. 2004. "AWOL." *New Republic,* Feb. 9: 10–11.

Adler, Freda, Gerhard O. W. Mueller, and William S. Laufer. 2007. *Criminology and the Criminal Justice System*. New York: McGraw-Hill.

Ahmed, Nafeez Mosaddeq. 2005. *The War on Truth: 9/11, Disinformation, and the Anatomy of Terrorism*. Northampton, MA: Olive Branch.

Akers, Ronald J., and Christine S. Sellers. 2009. *Criminological Theories: Introduction, Evaluation, and Application*. New York: Oxford University Press.

Albrecht, W. Steven, Keith R. Howe, and Marshall Romney. 1984. *Deterring Fraud: The Internal Auditor's Perspective*. Altamonte Springs, FL: Institute of Internal Auditors Research.

Alexandrovna, Larisa. 2008. "The Ordeal of Don Siegelman." In Mark Crispin Miller (ed.), *Loser Take All: Election Fraud and the Subversion of Democracy, 2000–2008*. Brooklyn, NY: Ig.

Alonzo-Zaldivar, Ricardo. 2006. "FDA Pledges Conflict Reforms." *Los Angeles Times,* July 25: A12.

Alpern, David M. 1984. "A CIA Bombshell." *Newsweek,* Oct. 29: 30.

Alperovitz, Gar. 1996. *The Decision to Use the Atomic Bomb*. New York: Vintage.

Alperovitz, Gar, Thad Williamson, and Ted Howard. 2010. "The Cleveland Model." *The Nation,* Feb. 11. Retrieved from www.thenation.com.

Alter, Jonathan. 2005. "If Watergate Happened Now." *Newsweek,* June 13: 33.

———. 2010. "High-Court Hypocrisy." *Newsweek,* Feb. 1: 15.

Altheide, David L., and Jennifer N. Grimes. 2005. "War Programming: The Propaganda Project and the Iraq War." *Sociological Quarterly* 46: 617–643.

Anderson, Curt. 2003. "Feds Release Patriot Act Information." *Wisconsin State Journal,* May 21: A3.

Anderson, Curt, and Danny Robbins. 2010. "In Toyota Cases, Evasion Becomes Tactic." *Associated Press,* Apr. 11. Retrieved from www.yahoo.com.

Ardizzone, Simon, Russell Michaels, and Robert Carrillo Cohen. 2006. *Hacking Democracy*. HBO documentary.

225

Armstrong, David. 2002. "Dick Cheney's Song of America: Drafting a Plan for Global Dominance." *Harper's Magazine,* Oct.: 76–83.

Arvedlund, Erin. 2010. "Faces of Greed: Meet the Madoff Minions." *Mother Jones,* Jan./Feb.: 44–45.

Aulette, Judy, and Raymond J. Michalowski. 2006. "The Fire in Hamlet." In Raymond Michalowski and Ronald C. Kramer (eds.), *State-Corporate Crime: Wrongdoing at the Intersection of Business and Government.* New Brunswick, NJ: Rutgers University Press.

Ayres, Ian, and John Braithwaite. 1992. *Responsive Regulation: Transcending the Deregulation Debate.* New York: Oxford University Press.

Babwin, Don. 2010. "Holdout Juror Breaks Silence." *Wisconsin State Journal,* Aug. 28: A11.

Bamford, James. 2005. "The Man Who Sold the War." *Rolling Stone,* Nov. 18. Retrieved from www.commondreams.org.

———. 2008. *The Shadow Factory: The Ultra-Secret NSA from 9/11 to the Eavesdropping on America.* New York: Doubleday.

Barak, Greg (ed.). 1991. *Crimes by the Capitalist State: An Introduction to State Criminality.* Albany: State University of New York Press.

Barkan, Steven E. 2006. *Criminology.* Upper Saddle River, NJ: Prentice-Hall.

Barker, Thomas, and David L. Carter (eds.). 1999. *Police Deviance.* Cincinnati: Pilgrimage.

Barlow, Hugh. 1996. *Introduction to Criminology.* New York: HarperCollins.

Barlow, Hugh, and David Kauzlarich. 2002. *Introduction to Criminology.* Upper Saddle River, NJ: Prentice-Hall.

Barrett, Wayne, and Dan Collins. 2006. *Grand Illusion: The Untold Story of Rudy Giuliani and 9/11.* New York: Harper.

Barstow, David, and Lowell Bergman. 2003. "At a Texas Foundry, an Indifference to Life." *New York Times,* Jan. 8. Retrieved from www.nytimes.com.

Beck, Melinda. 1982. "Where Are They Now?" *Newsweek,* June 14: 42, 45.

Becker, Howard S. 1963. *Outsiders: Studies in the Sociology of Deviance.* New York: Free Press.

Begley, Sharon, and Andrew Murr. 2007. "Which of These Is Not Causing Global Warming Today?" *Newsweek,* July 2: 48–50.

Behan, R. W. 2006. "The Surreal Politics of Premeditated War." *Common Dreams News Center,* Dec. 3. Retrieved from www.commondreams.org.

Beirne, Piers, and James W. Messerschmidt. 1995. *Criminology.* Fort Worth, TX: Harcourt Brace.

Benson, Michael L. 1985. "Denying the Guilty Mind: Accounting for Involvement in White-Collar Crime." *Criminology* 23: 583–608.

Benson, Michael L., and Francis T. Cullen. 1998. *Combating Corporate Crime: Local Prosecutors at Work.* Boston: Northeastern University Press.

Benson, Michael L., and Sally S. Simpson. 2009. *White-Collar Crime: An Opportunity Perspective.* New York: Routledge.

Bergen, Peter. 2007. "War of Error: How Osama bin Laden Beat George W. Bush." *New Republic,* Oct. 22: 23–27.

Berger, Ronald J. 2002. *Fathoming the Holocaust: A Social Problems Approach.* New York: Aldine de Gruyter.

Berger, Ronald J., Marvin D. Free, and Patricia Searles. 2009. *Crime, Justice, and Society: An Introduction to Criminology.* Boulder, CO: Lynne Rienner.

Bergin, Tom. 2010. "Cost of Oil Spill Could Exceed $14 Billion." *Reuters,* May 2. Retrieved from www.reuters.com.

Bergman, Jake, and Julia Reynolds. 2002. "The Guns of Opa-Locka: How U.S. Dealers Arm the World." *The Nation,* Dec. 2: 19–22.

Berman, Ari. 2007. "Rudy's Dirty Money." *The Nation,* Oct. 29: 12–16.

———. 2008. "Swiftboat Blues." *The Nation,* Nov. 10: 4–5.

Bernstein, Carl, and Bob Woodward. 1974. *All the President's Men.* New York: Simon and Schuster.

Bernstein, Marvin H. 1955. *Regulating Business by Independent Commission.* Princeton, NJ: Princeton University Press.

Best, Joel. 2004. *Deviance: Career of a Concept.* Belmont, CA: Wadsworth.

Birsch, Douglas, and John H. Fielder (eds.). 1994. *The Ford Pinto Case: A Study in Applied Ethics, Business, and Technology.* Albany: State University of New York Press.

Black, Edwin. 2009. *Nazi Nexus: America's Corporate Connections to Hitler's Holocaust.* Washington, DC: Dialog.

Blakey, G. Robert, and Richard Billing. 1981. *The Plot to Kill the President: Organized Crime Assassinated JFK.* New York: New York Times Books.

Blitstein, Ryan. 2007. "Internet Crooks Steal Billions." *Wisconsin State Journal,* Nov. 25: A1, A9.

Bloch, Herbert A., and Gilbert Geis. 1962. *Man, Crime, and Society.* New York: Random House.

Block, Fred. 1977. "Beyond Corporate Liberalism." *Social Problems* 24: 352–361.

Bloomberg News. 2007. "Sale of KBR Bolsters Profit at Halliburton." *New York Times,* July 24. Retrieved from www.nytimes.com.

Blumberg, Paul. 1989. *The Predatory Society: Deception in the American Marketplace.* New York: Oxford University Press.

Blumenthal, Sidney. 2005a. "Katrina Comes Home to Roost." *The Guardian,* Sept. 2. Retrieved from www.guardian.co.uk.

———. 2005b. "What Didn't Go Right?" Salon.com, Sept. 8.

Boehlert, Eric. 2000. "Fox Guarding the Henhouse." Salon.com, Nov. 15.

———. 2005. "The Politics of Hurricane Relief." Salon.com, Sept. 5.

Boisjoly, Russell, Ellen Foster Curtis, and Eugene Mellican. [1989] 1992. "Ethical Dimensions of the *Challenger* Disaster." In M. David Ermann and Richard L. Lundman (eds.), *Corporate and Governmental Deviance: Problems of Organizational Behavior in Contemporary Society.* 4th ed. New York: Oxford University Press.

Booth, David. 2010. "Toyota Discovers Silence Is Golden." *Vancouver Sun,* May 3. Retrieved from www.vancouversun.com.

Braithwaite, John. 1982. "Enforced Self-Regulation: A New Strategy for Corporate Crime Control." *Michigan Law Review* 80: 1466–1507.

Braithwaite, John, and Brent Fisse. 1995. "On the Plausibility of Corporate Crime Control." In Gilbert Geis, Robert F. Meier, and Lawrence M. Salinger (eds.), *White-Collar Crime: Classic and Contemporary Views.* New York: Free Press.

Braithwaite, John, and Gilbert Geis. 1982. "On Theory and Action for Corporate Crime Control." *Crime and Delinquency* 28: 292–314.

Braithwaite, John, Peter Grabosky, and John J. Walker. 1987. "An Enforcement Taxonomy of Regulatory Agencies." *Law and Policy* 9: 315–343.

Brickey, Kathleen. [2008] 2009. "Major Corporate Crime Prosecutions: March 2002–July 2007." Cited in Michael L. Benson and Sally S. Simpson, *White-Collar Crime: An Opportunity Perspective.* New York: Routledge.

Brightman, Hank J. 2009. *Today's White Collar Crime: Legal, Investigative, and Theoretical Perspectives.* New York: Routledge.

Brinkley, Joel, and Stephen Engelberg (eds.). 1988. *Report of the Congressional Committees Investigating the Iran-Contra Affair.* New York: Random House.

Brisard, Jean-Charles, and Guillanme Dasquié. 2002. *Forbidden Truth: U.S.-Taliban Secret Oil Diplomacy and the Failed Hunt for Bin Laden.* New York: Thunder's Mouth and Nation Books.

Brownstein, Ronald, and Nina Easton. 1982. *Reagan's Ruling Class: Portraits of the President's Top One Hundred Officials.* New York: Pantheon.

Bugliosi, Vincent. 2007. *Reclaiming History: The Assassination of President John F. Kennedy.* New York: Norton.

Bullard, Robert, D., and Beverly Wright. 1989–1990. "Toxic Waste and the African American Community." *Urban League Review* 13: 67–75.

Bussey, John. 2002. "Cheney, Halliburton Accused of Fraud." *Wisconsin State Journal,* July 11: A3.

Calavita, Kitty. 1983. "The Demise of the Occupational Safety and Health Administration: A Case Study in Symbolic Action." *Social Problems* 30: 464–477.

Calavita, Kitty, and Henry N. Pontell. 1990. "Heads I Win, Tails You Lose: Deregulation, Crime, and Crisis in the Savings and Loan Industry." *Crime and Delinquency* 36: 309–341.

———. 1993. "Savings and Loan Fraud as Organized Crime: Towards a Conceptual Typology of Corporate Illegality." *Criminology* 31: 519–548.

Caldwell, Robert G. 1958. "A Reexamination of the Concept of White-Collar Crime." *Federal Probation* 22: 30–36.

Calhoun, Craig, and Henryk Hiller. 1988. "Coping with Insidious Injuries: The Case of Johns-Manville Corporation and Asbestos Exposure." *Social Problems* 35: 162–181.

Carey, James. 1978. *Introduction to Criminology.* Englewood Cliffs, NJ: Prentice-Hall.

Carlson, Peter. 2003. "The Relatively Charmed Life of Neil Bush." *Washington Post,* Dec. 28: D1.

Carson, Rachel. 1962. *Silent Spring.* New York: Houghton Mifflin.

Carter, David L, and Andra J. Bannister. 2002. "Computer-Related Crime." In David Shichor, Larry Gaines, and Richard Ball (eds.), *Readings in White-Collar Crime.* Prospect Heights, IL: Waveland.

Center for Auto Safety. 2010a. "The C/K Pickup with Unsafe Side Saddle Tanks." Retrieved from www.autosafety.org.

———. 2010b. "Ford Transmissions Failure to Hold in Park." Retrieved from www.autosafety.org.

Center for Responsible Lending. 2008. "Common Abuses: Seven Signs of Predatory Lending." Retrieved from www.responsiblelending.org.

Chambliss, William J. 1988. *On the Take: From Petty Crooks to Presidents.* Bloomington: Indiana University Press.

Chambliss, William J., and Robert Seidman. 1971. *Law, Order, and Power.* Reading, MA: Addison-Wesley.

Charns, Alexander. 1992. *Cloak and Gavel: FBI Wiretaps, Bugs, Informers, and the Supreme Court.* Urbana: University of Illinois Press.

Clarke, Richard, A. 2004. *Against All Enemies: Inside America's War on Terror.* New York: Free Press.

Clarke, Richard A., and Robert K. Knake. 2010. *Cyber War: The Next Threat to National Security and What to Do About It.* New York: Ecco Press.

Clifford, Mary. 1998. *Environmental Crime: Enforcement, Policy, and Social Responsibility.* Gaithersburg, MD: Aspen.

Clinard, Marshall B. 1983. *Corporate Ethics and Crime: The Role of Middle Management.* Beverly Hills, CA: Sage.

Clinard, Marshall B., and Richard Quinney. 1967. *Criminal Behavior Systems: A Typology.* New York: Holt, Rinehart, and Winston.

Clinard, Marshall B., and Peter C. Yeager. 1980. *Corporate Crime.* New York: Free Press.

Cloward, Richard, and Lloyd Ohlin. 1960. *Delinquency and Opportunity: A Theory of Delinquent Gangs.* New York: Free Press.

CNN.com. 2001. "Florida Recount Study: Bush Still Wins." Nov. 11.

———. 2003. "Commander in Chief Lands on USS *Lincoln.*" May 2.

———. 2006. "Report: Katrina Response a 'Failure of Leadership.'" Feb. 13.

———. 2009. "Mayors, Rabbis Arrested in Corruption Probe." July 23.

CNNMoney.com. 2008. "FBI Probing Bailout Firms." Sept. 23.

Cohan, William D. 2009. *House of Cards: A Tale of Hubris and Wretched Excess on Wall Street.* New York: Doubleday.

Cohen, Jeff, and Norman Solomon. 1994. "30-Year Anniversary: Tonkin Gulf Lie Launched Vietnam War." *Fairness and Accuracy in Reporting,* July 27. Retrieved from www.fair.org.

Cohen, Lawrence E., and Marcus Felson. 1979. "Social Change and Crime Rate Trends: A Routine Activity Approach." *American Sociological Review* 44: 588–608.

Cohen, Mark A. 1989. "Corporate Crime and Punishment: A Study of Social Harm and Sentencing Practices in the Federal Courts, 1984–1987." *American Criminal Law Review* 26: 605–662.

Cohen, Sharon. 2006. "Meatpacking Work Dangerous." *Wisconsin State Journal,* Apr. 23: A8.

Cole, David, and Jules Lobel. 2007. *Less Safe, Less Free: Why America Is Losing the War on Terror.* New York: New Press.

Cole, Luke W., and Sheila R. Foster. 2001. *From the Ground Up: Environmental Racism and the Rise of the Environmental Justice Movement.* New York: New York University Press.

Coleman, James W. 2006. *The Criminal Elite: Understanding White-Collar Crime.* New York: Worth.

Commission on CIA Activities Within the United States. 1975. *Report to the President.* Washington, DC: US Government Printing Office.

Conason, Joe, and Gene Lyons. 2000. *The Hunting of the President: The Ten-Year Campaign to Destroy Bill and Hillary Clinton.* New York: Thomas Dunne.

Conklin, John E. 1977. *Illegal but Not Criminal: Business Crime in America.* Englewood Cliffs, NJ: Prentice-Hall.

Continetti, Matthew. 2006. *The K Street Gang: The Rise and Fall of the Republican Machine.* New York: Doubleday.

Cooper, Michael. 2010. "Mine Agency's Powers Limited, Often Unused." *Wisconsin State Journal,* Apr. 11: A4.

Corn, David. 2001. "Bush and Butterflies." *The Nation,* Dec. 3: 5–6.

———. 2003. *The Lies of George W. Bush: Mastering the Politics of Deception.* New York: Crown.

———. 2007. "Cheney on Trial." *The Nation,* Mar. 26: 11–13.

Corporate Crime Reporter. 2007. "Louisiana Most Corrupt State in the Nation, Mississippi Second, Illinois Sixth, New Jersey Ninth." Oct. 8. Retrieved from www.corporatecrimereporter.com.

Courson, Paul. 2009. "Ex-Rep. Jefferson Convicted of Corruption." CNN.com, Aug. 6.

Court, Jamie. 2003. "Identity Thieves." *The Nation,* Nov. 3: 8, 22.

Cressey, Donald R. 1953. *Other People's Money.* Glencoe, IL: Free Press.

Crotty, William (ed.). 2004. *The Politics of Terror: The U.S. Response to 9/11.* Boston: Northeastern University Press.

Cruciotti, Tricia, and Rick A. Matthews. 2006. "The *Exxon Valdez* Oil Spill." In Raymond Michalowski and Ronald C. Kramer (eds.), *State-Corporate Crime: Wrongdoing at the Intersection of Business and Government.* New Brunswick, NJ: Rutgers University Press.

Crum, Rex. 2010. "BP Blames Failed Equipment on Rig." *Wisconsin State Journal,* May 3: A12.

Cruz, Humberto. 2003. "In Scandal's Wake: Tips for Picking a Fund." *Wisconsin State Journal,* Nov. 23: C1, C4.

Cullen, Francis T., Gray Cavender, William J. Maakestad, and Michael L. Benson. 2006. *Corporate Crime Under Attack: The Fight to Criminalize Business Violence.* Albany, NY: Anderson.

Curl, John. 2009. *For All the People: Uncovering the Hidden History of Cooperation, Cooperative Movements, and Communalism in America.* Oakland, CA: PM Press.

Currie, Elliott, and Jerome K. Skolnick. 1988. *Crisis in American Institutions.* Boston: Allyn and Bacon.

Daly, Kathleen. 1989. "Gender and Varieties of White-Collar Crime." *Criminology* 27: 769–793.

Davidson, Samuel. 2010. "Black Lung on the Rise Among U.S. Coal Miners." Jan. 11. Retrieved from www.wsws.org.

de Vogue, Ariane. 2008. "Voter Group Admits Mistakes, Defends Work." *ABC News,* Oct. 14. Retrieved from www.abcnews.go.com.

Dean, John W. 1976. *Blind Ambition.* New York: Pocket.

———. 2006. *Conservatives Without Conscience.* New York: Viking.

———. 2007. *Broken Government: How Republican Rule Destroyed the Legislative, Executive, and Judicial Branches.* New York: Viking.

deHaven-Smith, Lance. 2010. "Beyond Conspiracy Theory: Patterns of High Crime in American Government." *American Behavioral Scientist* 53: 795–825.

DeKeseredy, Walter S., and Martin D. Schwartz. 1996. *Contemporary Criminology*. Belmont, CA: Wadsworth.

Dershowitz, Alan M. 2001. *Supreme Injustice: How the High Court Hijacked Election 2000*. New York: Oxford University Press.

Dickenson, James R. 1977. "How the Scandals of History Left Mud on the White House Steps." In Jack D. Douglas and John M. Johnson (eds.), *Official Deviance: Readings in Malfeasance, Misfeasance, and Other Forms of Corruption*. Philadelphia: Lippincott.

Dickey, Christopher, and Rod Nordland. 2000. "Big Tobacco's Next Legal War." *Newsweek*, July 31: 36–39.

Dodge, Mary. 2009. *Women and White-Collar Crime*. Upper Saddle River, NJ: Prentice-Hall.

Dodge, Mary, and Gilbert Geis. 2003. *Stealing Dreams: A Fertility Clinic Scandal*. Lebanon, NH: Northeastern University Press of New England.

Domhoff, William G. 1990. *The Power Elite and the State: How Policy Is Made in America*. New York: Aldine de Gruyter.

Donn, Jeff, and Mitch Weiss. 2010. "Capped Wells Pose Unknown Risk." *Wisconsin State Journal*, July 7: A1, A9.

Douglas, Jack D. 1977. "Major John Lindsay and the Revenge of Boss Tweed." In Jack D. Douglas and John M. Johnson (eds.), *Official Deviance: Readings in Malfeasance, Misfeasance, and Other Forms of Corruption*. Philadelphia: Lippincott.

Douglas, Jack D., and John M. Johnson (eds.). 1977. *Official Deviance: Readings in Malfeasance, Misfeasance, and Other Forms of Corruption*. Philadelphia: Lippincott.

Douglass, James W. 2008. *JFK and the Unspeakable: Why He Died and Why It Matters*. Maryknoll, NY: Orbis.

Dowie, Mark. 1977. "Pinto Madness." *Mother Jones* 2: 18–24, 28–32.

Dowie, Mark, and Carolyn Marshall. 1980. "The Bendectin Cover-Up." *Mother Jones* 5: 43–56.

Dreier, Peter. 2006. "Why Mine Deaths Are Up." *The Nation*, June 12: 5–6.

Dreyfuss, Robert. 2005. *Devil's Game: How the United States Helped Unleash Fundamentalist Islam*. New York: Owl.

Drogin, Bob. 2003. "Friendly Fire." *New Republic*, Oct. 27: 23–27.

Drum, Kevin. 2010. "Capital City." *Mother Jones*, Jan./Feb.: 37–43, 78–79.

Durkheim, Émile. [1893] 1964. *The Division of Labor in Society*. New York: Free Press.

———. [1897] 1952. *Suicide*. New York: Free Press.

Edelhertz, Herbert. 1970. *The Nature, Impact, and Prosecution of White-Collar Crime*. Washington, DC: US Department of Justice.

Eggen, Dan. 2007. "Fired U.S. Attorney Says Lawmakers Pressured Him." *Washington Post*, Mar. 1. Retrieved from www.washingtonpost.com.

Ehrenreich, Barbara, Mark Dowie, and Stephen Minkin. 1979. "The Charge: Genocide; The Accused: The U.S. Government." *Mother Jones* 4: 26–37.

Ehrlich, Judith, and Rick Goldsmith. 2009. *The Most Dangerous Man in America: Daniel Ellsberg and the Pentagon Papers*. Documentary film.

Eichenwald, Kurt. 1999. "Three Sentenced in Archer Daniels Midland Case." *New York Times*, July 10. www.nytimes.com.

Eisenhower, Dwight D. 1963. *Mandate for Change, 1953–1956: The White House Years.* Garden City, NY: Doubleday.

Ellsberg, Daniel. 2002. *Secrets: A Memoir of Vietnam and the Pentagon Papers.* New York: Viking.

Environment News Service. 2010. "Salazar Splits Minerals Management Service in Three." May 19. Retrieved from www.ens-newswire.com.

Ermann, M. David, and William H. Clements. 1984. "The Interfaith Center on Corporate Responsibility and Its Campaign Against Marketing Infant Formula in the Third World." *Social Problems* 32: 185–196.

Ermann, M. David, and Richard J. Lundman (eds.). [1978] 2002. *Corporate and Governmental Deviance: Problems of Organizational Behavior in Contemporary Society.* New York: Oxford University Press.

Faber, Daniel. 2008. *Capitalizing on Environmental Injustice: The Polluter-Industrial Complex in the Age of Globalization.* Lanham, MD: Rowman and Littlefield.

Farberman, Harvey. 1975. "A Criminogenic Market Structure: The Automobile Industry." *Sociological Quarterly* 16: 438–457.

Farmer, John. 2009. *The Ground Truth: The Untold Story of America Under Attack on 9/11.* New York: Riverhead.

Featherstone, Lisa. 2005. "Down and Out in Discount America." *The Nation,* Jan. 3: 11, 13–14, 19.

Federal Trade Commission. 2004. "FTC Releases Consumer Fraud Survey." Feb. 5. Retrieved from www.ftc.gov.

Fessenden, Ford, and John M. Broder. 2001. "Ballot Study Finds Court Didn't Give Bush Win." *Wisconsin State Journal,* Nov. 12: A1, A8.

Fineman, Howard. 2005. "Money, Money, Everywhere." *Newsweek,* Sept. 26: 24–31.

Fisse, Brent, and John Braithwaite. 1983. *The Impact of Publicity on Corporate Offenders.* Albany: State University of New York Press.

Fitrakis, Bob. 2008. "As Ohio Goes . . ." In Mark Crispin Miller (ed.), *Loser Take All: Election Fraud and the Subversion of Democracy, 2000–2008.* Brooklyn, NY: Ig.

Fitzgerald, A. Ernest. 1972. *The High Priests of Waste.* New York: Norton.

Foley, Ryan J. 2010. "Man at Center of Salmonella Recall Has a Questionable Past." *Wisconsin State Journal,* Aug. 28: A1, A6.

Foley, Stephen. 2009. "Madoff: The $18bn Hunt for Justice Continues." *The Independent,* Sept. 29. Retrieved from www.independent.co.uk.

Follman, Mark, and Tracy Clark-Flory. 2006. "Prosecutions and Convictions." Salon.com, Mar. 14.

Fradkin, Philip L. 1989. *Fallout: An American Nuclear Tragedy.* Tucson: University of Arizona Press.

Frank, Nancy K., and Michael J. Lynch. 1992. *Corporate Crime, Corporate Violence: A Primer.* New York: Harrow and Heston.

Frank, Robert, Amir Efrati, Aaron Lucchetti, and Chad Bray. 2009. "Madoff Jailed After Epic Scam." *Wall Street Journal,* Mar. 13. Retrieved from www.online.wsj.com.

Frank, Thomas. 2007. "Coal Mine Deaths Spike Upward." *USA Today,* Jan. 1. Retrieved from www.usatoday.com.

Franklin, Alice. 1979. "Criminality in the Work Place: A Comparison of Male and Female Offenders." In Freda Adler and Rita James Simon (eds.), *The Criminality of Deviant Women*. Boston: Houghton Mifflin.

Friedman, Alan. 1993. *Spider's Web: The Secret History of How the White House Illegally Armed Iraq*. New York: Bantam.

Friedrichs, David O. 2007. *Trusted Criminals: White Collar Crime in Contemporary Society*. Belmont, CA: Wadsworth.

Fritz, Sara. 1994. "Clinton Ties to Tyson Scion Still Drawing Critics' Fire." *Los Angeles Times*, June 12. Retrieved from www.latimes.com.

Froomkin, Dan. 2000. "Untangling Whitewater." *Washington Post*, special report. Retrieved from www.washington.post.com.

Garrow, David J. 1981. *The FBI and Martin Luther King Jr.* New York: Penguin.

Gearty, Robert, and Larry McShane. 2008. "Ex-NYPD Cop Bernard Kerik Sentenced to Four Years in Federal Prison." *Daily News*, Feb. 18. Retrieved from www.nydailynews.com.

Geis, Gilbert. 1967. "White Collar Crime: The Heavy Electrical Equipment Antitrust Cases of 1961." In Marshall B. Clinard and Richard Quinney, *Criminal Behavior Systems: A Typology*. New York: Holt, Rinehart, and Winston.

Geis, Gilbert, and Colin Goff. 1983. Introduction to Edwin H. Sutherland, *White-Collar Crime: The Uncut Version*. New Haven, CT: Yale University Press.

Geis, Gilbert, and Robert F. Meier (eds.). 1977. *White-Collar Crime: Offenses in Business, Politics, and the Professions*. New York: Free Press.

Geis, Gilbert, Robert F. Meier, and Lawrence M. Salinger (eds.). 1995. *White-Collar Crime: Classic and Contemporary Views*. New York: Free Press.

Gelman, Barton. 2008. *Angler: The Cheney Vice Presidency*. New York: Penguin.

Gerber, Jurg, and James F. Short. 1986. "Publicity and Control of Corporate Behavior: The Case of Infant Formula." *Deviant Behavior* 7: 195–216.

Gerth, Hans H., and C. Wright Mills. 1946. *From Max Weber: Essays in Sociology*. New York: Oxford University Press.

Gibb, Gordon. 2010. "Toyota Sudden Acceleration Litigation: 320 Lawsuits Filed." LawyersandSettlements.com, May 3.

Gibbs, Carole, Edmund F. McGarrell, and Mark Axelrod. 2010. "Transnational White-Collar Crime and Risk: Lessons from the Global Trade in Electronic Waste." *Criminology and Public Policy* 9: 543–560.

Gilgoff, Dan. 2005. "Understanding Katrina." *U.S. News and World Report*, Sept. 12: 27–32.

Gioia, Dennis. [1992] 1996. "Why I Didn't Recognize Pinto Fire Hazards: How Organizational Scripts Channel Managers' Thoughts and Actions." In M. David Ermann and Richard J. Lundman (eds.), *Corporate and Governmental Deviance: Problems of Organizational Behavior in Contemporary Society*. 5th ed. New York: Oxford University Press.

Giraldi, Philip. 2005. "Forging the Case for War." *American Conservative*, Nov. 21. Retrieved from www.amconmag.com.

Glanz, James. 2010. "New Fraud Cases Point to Lapses in Iraq Rebuilding." *Wisconsin State Journal*, Mar. 14: A3.

Glazer, Myron Peretz, and Penina Migdal Glazer. 1989. *The Whistle-Blowers: Exposing Corruption in Government and Industry.* New York: Basic.

Goldbaum, Ellen. 2000. "Students Tackle Hickory Woods Issue." *University of Buffalo Reporter,* Mar. 30. Retrieved from www.buffalo.edu.

Goldhagen, Daniel. 2009. *Worse than War: Genocide, Elimination, and the Ongoing Assault on Humanity.* New York: PublicAffairs.

Goldsmith, Jack. 2010. "The New Vulnerability." *New Republic,* June 24: 21–28.

Goldstein, David. 2007. "Poison for Profit." *The Nation,* July 30/Aug. 6: 5–6.

Gordon, Marcy. 2002. "Investigator: Big Banks Helped Enron Hide True Financial State." *Wisconsin State Journal,* July 24: A4.

———. 2010. "Goldman Charged with Fraud." *Wisconsin State Journal,* Apr. 17: B1, B5.

Gore, Al. 2007. *The Assault on Reason.* New York: Penguin.

Graham, Bob. 2004. *Intelligence Matters: The CIA, the FBI, Saudi Arabia, and the Failure of America's War on Terror.* New York: Random House.

Gray, L. Patrick. 2008. *In Nixon's Web: A Year in the Crosshairs of Watergate.* New York: Holt, Rinehart, and Winston.

Gray, Mike, and Ira Rosen. 2003. *The Warning: Accident at Three Mile Island.* New York: Norton.

Gray, Wayne B., and John T. Scholz. 1993. "Does Regulatory Enforcement Work? A Panel Analysis of OSHA Enforcement." *Law and Society Review* 27: 177–213.

Green, Gary S. 1990. *Occupational Crime.* Belmont, CA: Wadsworth.

Green, Penny, and Tony Ward. 2004. *State Crime: Governments, Violence, and Corruption.* London: Pluto.

Greenberg, David. 2000. "Was Nixon Robbed?" Slate.com, Oct. 16.

Greenberger, Michael. 2010. "Out of the Black Hole." *American Prospect,* June: A8–A10.

Greenhouse, Steven. 2009. "Work-Related Injuries Underreported." *New York Times,* Nov. 17. Retrieved from www.nytimes.com.

Greider, William. 2009. "Memo to Investigators: Dig Deep." *The Nation,* Oct. 26: 16–20.

Griffin, David Ray. 2004. *The New Pearl Harbor: Disturbing Questions About the Bush Administration and 9/11.* Northampton, MA: Olive Branch.

———. 2008. *9/11 Contradictions: An Open Letter to Congress and the Press.* Northampton, MA: Olive Branch.

Griffin, Malanie L. 1988. "The Legacy of Love Canal." *Sierra* 73: 26–30.

Gross, Daniel. 2009. "Membership Has Its Penalties." *Newsweek,* Jan. 12: 18.

Gross, Edward. 1978. "Organizational Crime: A Theoretical Perspective." In Norman K. Denzin (ed.), *Studies in Symbolic Interaction.* Greenwood, CT: JAI.

Guilloton, Sheila. 2009. "Pfizer Fined $2.3 Billion to Settle Medicare and Medicaid Fraud Case." Examiner.com, Sept. 2.

Gumbel, Andrew. 2005. *Steal This Vote: Dirty Elections and the Rotten History of Democracy in America.* New York: Nation Books.

Gundlach, James H. 2008. "A Statistical Analysis of the Gubernatorial Vote in Baldwin County, Alabama in 2002." In Mark Crispin Miller (ed.), *Loser*

Take All: Election Fraud and the Subversion of Democracy, 2000–2008. Brooklyn, NY: Ig.

Guyon, Janet. 2005. "Jack Grubman Is Back: Just Ask Him." *Fortune*, May 16. Retrieved from www.money.cnn.com.

Haddington, Michael. 1996. "Susan McDougal Gets 2 Years for Fraud Tied to Whitewater." *Washington Post*, Aug. 21: A14.

Hagan, Frank E. 1997. *Political Crime: Ideology and Criminality.* Boston: Allyn and Bacon.

Hagan, John. 1992. "The Poverty of a Classless Criminology." *Criminology* 30: 1–20.

Halbfinger, David M. 2009. "44 Charged by U.S. in New Jersey Corruption Sweep." *New York Times*, July 24. Retrieved from www.nytimes.com.

Halperin, Morton H., Jerry J. Berman, Robert L. Borosage, and Christine M. Marwick. 1977. *The Lawless State: The Crimes of the U.S. Intelligence Agencies.* New York: Penguin.

Hamlin, John E. 1988. "The Misplaced Role of Rational Choice in Neutralization Theory." *Criminology* 26: 425–438.

Harr, Jonathan. 1995. *A Civil Action.* New York: Vintage.

Harris, Richard. 1977. "Reflections: Crime in the F.B.I." *New Yorker*, Aug. 8: 30–42.

Hartjen, Clayton. 1974. *Crime and Criminalization.* New York: Praeger.

Hayes, Christopher. 2010. "System Failure." *The Nation*, Feb. 1: 22–24.

Hebert, H. Josef. 2010. "Execs Get Oil-Spill Grilling." *Wisconsin State Journal*, May 12: A12.

Heilprin, John. 2006. "Global Warming in Policy Gridlock." *Wisconsin State Journal*, Oct. 7: A1–A9.

Henderson, Charles R. 1901. *Introduction to the Study of Dependent, Defective, and Delinquent Classes.* Boston: Heath.

Hersh, Seymour M. 2004. *Chain of Command: The Road from 9/11 to Abu Ghraib.* New York: HarperCollins.

Hickman, Kennedy. 2010. "Vietnam War; Gulf of Tonkin Incident." Retrieved from www.militaryhistory.about.com.

Higham, Charles. 1983. *Trading with the Enemy: The Nazi-American Money Plot, 1933–1949.* New York: Barnes and Noble.

Hill, Steven. 2010. "Europe's Answer to Wall Street." *The Nation*, Apr. 21. Retrieved from www.thenation.com.

Hirschi, Travis. 1969. *Causes of Delinquency.* Berkeley: University of California Press.

Hitchens, Christopher. 1999. *No One Left to Lie To: The Values of the Worst Family.* New York: Verso.

Hoffman, Damien. 2009. "Exclusive Interview: Top Constitutional Law Authority Erwin Chemerinsky Talks Corporate Speech." *Wall St. Cheat Sheet*, Sept. 30. Retrieved from www.wallstcheatsheet.com.

Holtfreter, Kristy. 2005. "Is Occupational Fraud 'Typical' White-Collar Crime? A Comparison of Individual and Organizational Characteristics." *Journal of Criminal Justice* 33: 353–365.

Horton, Scott. 2007. "We Do Not Torture." *Harper's Magazine*, Oct. 8. Retrieved from www.harpers.org.

Huber, Tim. 2007. "Mining Reforms Not in Effect." *Wisconsin State Journal,* Aug. 8: A3.

Huffington Post. 2010. "West Virginia Mine Explosion: Massey Energy Mine Had Scores of Safety Violations." Apr. 6. Retrieved from www .huffingtonpost.com.

Hull, Elizabeth. 2006. *The Disenfranchisement of Ex-Felons.* Philadelphia: Temple University Press.

Hutcheson, Ron. 2007. "Bush Keeps Libby Out of Prison." *Wisconsin State Journal,* July 3: A1, A5.

Iglesias, David. 2009. *In Justice: An Insider's Account of the War on Law and Truth in the Executive Branch.* New York: Wiley.

Inverarity, James M., Pat Lauderdale, and Barry C. Feld. 1983. *Law and Society: Sociological Perspectives on Criminal Law.* Boston: Little, Brown.

Isikoff, Michael, and David Corn. 2006. *Hubris: The Inside Story of Spin, Scandal, and the Selling of the Iraq War.* New York: Crown.

Ivins, Molly, and Lou Dubose. 2003. *Bushwhacked: Life in George W. Bush's America.* New York: Random.

Jackson, Brooks. 1988. *Honest Graft: Big Money and the American Political Process.* New York: Knopf.

———. 1990. *The Savings and Loan Crisis.* CNN documentary.

Janis, Irving L. 1972. *Victims of Groupthink.* Boston: Houghton Mifflin.

Jaspin, Elliot, and Scott Montgomery. 1998. "Review Uncovers Thousands of Unsafe Meat Shipments." *Wisconsin State Journal,* Jan. 18: A7.

Jessop, Bob. 2002. *The Future of the Capitalist State.* Cambridge: Polity.

Johnson, Bob. 2009. "Siegelman Appeal: Court Upholds Most Charges." *Huffington Post,* Mar. 6. Retrieved from www.huffingtonpost.com.

Johnson, John M., and Jack D. Douglas (eds.). 1978. *Crime at the Top: Deviance in Business and the Professions.* Philadelphia: Lippincott.

Johnson, Roberta Ann. 2003. *Whistle-Blowing: When It Works—and Why.* Boulder, CO: Lynne Rienner.

Johnson, Simon, and James Kwak. 2010. "Too Big for Us to Fail." *American Prospect,* June: A4–A6.

Judis, John. 2002. "Strategic Disinformation." *American Prospect,* Sept.: 12–13.

Kanter, Donald L., and Philip H. Mirvis. 1989. *The Cynical Americans: Living and Working in an Age of Discontent and Disillusion.* San Francisco: Jossey-Bass.

Kappeler, Victor E., and Gary W. Potter. 2005. *The Mythology of Crime and Criminal Justice.* Long Grove, IL: Waveland.

Katz, Jack. 1979. "Concerted Ignorance: The Social Construction of Cover-Up." *Urban Life* 8: 295–316.

———. 1980. "The Social Movement Against White-Collar Crime." In Egon Bittner and Sheldon L. Messinger (eds.), *Criminology Review Yearbook.* Beverly Hills, CA: Sage.

Kaufman, Leslie, and Joseph Berger. 2010. "Officials Weigh Options." *Wisconsin State Journal,* May 3: A1, A12.

Kauzlarich, David, and Ronald C. Kramer. 2006. "Nuclear Weapons Production." In Raymond Michalowski and Ronald C. Kramer (eds.), *State-*

Corporate Crime: Wrongdoing at the Intersection of Business and Government. New Brunswick, NJ: Rutgers University Press.

Kelly, Georgia, and Shaula Massena. 2009. "Mondragón Worker-Cooperatives Decide How to Ride Out a Downturn." *Yes Magazine,* June 5. Retrieved from www.yesmagazine.org.

Kennedy, Robert F., Jr. 2004. *Crimes Against Nature: How George W. Bush and His Corporate Pals Are Plundering the Country and Hijacking Our Democracy.* New York: HarperCollins.

———. 2008. "Diebold and Max Cleland's Loss in Georgia." In Mark Crispin Miller (ed.), *Loser Take All: Election Fraud and the Subversion of Democracy, 2000–2008.* Brooklyn, NY: Ig.

Kerr, Jennifer C. 2003. "Envoy: Bush Manipulated Findings." *Wisconsin State Journal,* July 7: A9.

Kinser, Stephen. 2006. *Overthrow: America's Century of Regime Change from Hawaii to Iraq.* New York: Times Books.

Kirk, Michael. 2009. *The Warning.* PBS documentary.

Klein, Naomi. 2007. *The Shock Doctrine: The Rise of Disaster Capitalism.* New York: Metropolitan.

Koenig, David. 2010. "Airline Faces Record Penalty." *Wisconsin State Journal,* Aug. 27: B8.

Kolbert, Elizabeth. 2002. "Fellowship of the Ring." *New Yorker,* May 6. Retrieved from www.newyorker.com.

Komisar, Lisa. 2001. "After Dirty Air, Dirty Money." *The Nation,* June 18: 16–19.

Kouba, Jeff. 2008. "April Glaspie and Saddam Hussein." *Truth vs. The Machine,* Mar. 26. Retrieved from www.truthvmachine.com.

Kramer, Ronald. 2006. "The Space Shuttle *Challenger* Explosion." In Raymond J. Michalowski and Ronald C. Kramer (eds.), *State-Corporate Crime: Wrongdoing at the Intersection of Business and Government.* New Brunswick, NJ: Rutgers University Press.

Kramer, Ronald, and Raymond J. Michalowski. 2005. "War, Aggression, and State Crime: A Criminological Analysis of the Invasion and Occupation of Iraq." *British Journal of Criminology* 45: 446–469.

Krugman, Paul. 2007. *The Conscience of a Liberal.* New York: Norton.

Kuhnhenn, Jim. 2009. "Plan Would Make Companies Pay for Size." *Wisconsin State Journal,* July 6: A11.

Kunzelman, Michael, Mike Baker, and Jeff Donn. 2010. "Witness: BP Pushed on Well." *Wisconsin State Journal,* May 27: A1, A11.

Kurlantzick, Joshua. 2006. "What Lies Beneath?" *American Prospect,* Nov.: 26–31.

Kuttner, Robert. 2003. "The Great Crash, Part II." *American Prospect,* June: 47–49.

Lantigua, John. 2001. "How the GOP Gamed the System in Florida." *The Nation,* Apr. 30: 11–17.

Lardner, James. 2010. "Watching the Watchers." *American Prospect,* June: A10–A11.

Lasley, James R. 1988. "Toward a Control Theory of White-Collar Offending." *Journal of Quantitative Criminology* 4: 347–362.

Laufer, William S. 2006. *Corporate Bodies and Guilty Minds: The Failure of Corporate Criminal Liability.* Chicago: University of Chicago Press.

Lee, Matthew T., and M. David Ermann. 1999. "Pinto 'Madness' as a Flawed Landmark Narrative: An Organizational and Network Analysis." *Social Problems* 46: 30–47.

Leonard, William N., and Marvin Glenn Weber. 1970. "Automakers and Dealers: A Study of Criminogenic Market Forces." *Law and Society Review* 4: 407–424.

Leopold, Les. 2009a. *The Looting of America: How Wall Street's Game of Fantasy Finance Destroyed Our Jobs, Pensions, and Prosperity.* White River Junction, VT: Chelsea Green.

———. 2009b. "Wall Street's Gall." *Progressive Magazine,* Sept.: 26–28.

Leslie, Jacques. 2010. "What's Killing the Babies of Kettleman City?" *Mother Jones,* July/Aug.: 45–54.

LeVine, Mark. 2005. "Waist Deep in Big Oil." *The Nation,* Dec. 12: 5–6.

Liazos, Alexander. 1972. "The Poverty of the Sociology of Deviance: Nuts, Sluts, and Preverts." *Social Problems* 20: 103–120.

Lichtblau, Eric. 2003. "Some Fear FBI Is Back to Hooverism." *Wisconsin State Journal,* Nov. 23: A3.

———. 2005. "9/11 Report Cites Many Warnings About Hijackings." *New York Times,* Feb. 10. Retrieved from www.nytimes.com.

———. 2008. "Report Sees Illegal Hiring Practices at Justice Dept." *New York Times,* June 25. Retrieved from www.nytimes.com.

Lichtenstein, Nelson. 2009. *The Retail Revolution: How Wal-Mart Created a Brave New World of Business.* New York: Metropolitan.

Lin, Rong-Gong II, and Bettina Boxall. 2010. "Technician: Key Safety Systems Disabled." *Wisconsin State Journal,* July 24: A10.

Lipton, Eric. 2004. "Security Post Would Put Kerik Atop Field That Enriched Him." *New York Times,* Dec. 10: A1, A26.

Lithwick, Dahlia. 2008. "Getting Away with Torture." *Newsweek,* May 5: 17.

Lobe, Jim. 2005. "Powell Aide Blasts Rice, Cheney-Rumsfeld 'Cabal.'" *Inter Press Service,* Oct. 20. Retrieved from www.commondreams.org.

Lowi, Theodore J. 1979. *The End of Liberalism.* New York: Norton.

Lumpkin, John T. 2003. "Official Weapons Assertions Doubtful." *Wisconsin State Journal,* Oct. 5: A3.

Lynn, Barry C. 2009. "How Detroit Went Bottom-Up." *American Prospect,* Oct.: 21–24.

Maher, Kris. 2009. "Black Lung on Rise in Mines, Reversing Trend." *Wall Street Journal,* Dec. 15. Retrieved from www.wsj.com.

Manza, Jeff, and Christopher Uggen. 2005. *Locked Out: Felon Disenfranchisement and American Democracy.* New York: Oxford University Press.

Marek, Angie C. 2006. "The Toxic Politics of Chemicals." *U.S. News and World Report,* Jan. 23: 32.

Marolda, Edward J. 2010. "Tonkin Gulf Crisis, August 1964." Retrieved from www.history.navy.mil.

Martin, Gus. 2003. *Understanding Terrorism: Challenges, Perspectives, and Issues.* Thousand Oaks, CA: Sage.

Martz, Larry. 1986. "True Greed." *Newsweek,* Dec. 1: 48–50.

Marx, Gary T. 1981. "Ironies of Social Control: Authorities as Contributors to Deviance Through Escalation, Non-Enforcement, and Covert Facilitation." *Social Problems* 28: 221–246.

Matthews, Rick A. 2006. "Ordinary Business in Nazi Germany." In Raymond Michalowski and Ronald C. Kramer (eds.), *State-Corporate Crime: Wrongdoing at the Intersection of Business and Government*. New Brunswick, NJ: Rutgers University Press.

Matthews, Rick A., and David Kauzlarich. 2006. "The Crash of ValuJet Flight 592." In Raymond Michalowski and Ronald C. Kramer (eds.), *State-Corporate Crime: Wrongdoing at the Intersection of Business and Government*. New Brunswick, NJ: Rutgers University Press.

Mayer, Jane. 2009. *The Dark Side: The Inside Story of How the War on Terror Turned Into a War on American Ideals*. New York: Anchor.

McCaffrey, Shannon. 2003. "Detainees Faced Abuse." *Wisconsin State Journal,* June 3: A3.

McCaghy, Charles H., Timothy A. Capron, and J. D. Jamison. 2003. *Deviant Behavior: Crime, Conflict, and Interest Groups*. Boston: Allyn and Bacon.

McChesney, Robert W., and John Nichols. 2002. *Our Media, Not Theirs: The Democratic Struggle Against Corporate Media*. New York: Seven Stories.

McClam, Erin. 2003. "Judge Sets Date for Martha Stewart." *Wisconsin State Journal,* June 20: D10.

McClellan, Scott. 2008. *What Happened: Inside the Bush White House and Washington's Culture of Deception*. New York: PublicAffairs.

McClelland, Edward. 2008. "How Close Were Barack Obama and Tony Rezko?" Salon.com, Feb. 1.

McCormack, Win. 2001. "Deconstructing the Election: Foucault, Derrida, and GOP Strategy." *The Nation,* Mar. 26: 25–34.

McCormick, Albert E. 1977. "Rule Enforcement and Moral Indignation: Some Observations on the Effects of Criminal Antitrust Convictions upon Societal Reaction Processes." *Social Problems* 25: 30–39.

McCoy, Alfred M. 2003. *The Politics of Heroin: CIA Complicity in the Global Drug Trade*. Chicago: Lawrence Hill.

———. 2006. *A Question of Torture: CIA Interrogation, from the Cold War to the War on Terror*. New York: Metropolitan.

McLean, Bethany, and Peter Elkind. 2004. *The Smartest Guys in the Room: The Amazing Rise and Scandalous Fall of Enron*. New York: Portfolio.

Media Matters for America. 2007. "Myths and Falsehoods in the U.S. Attorney Scandal." Mar. 16. Retrieved from www.mediamatters.org.

Medvedev, Zhores A. 1990. *The Legacy of Chernobyl*. New York: Norton.

Merton, Robert K. 1938. "Social Structure and Anomie." *American Sociological Review* 3: 672–682.

———. 1968. *Social Theory and Social Structure*. New York: Free Press.

Messerschmidt, James W. 1993. *Masculinities and Crime: Critique and Reconceptualization of Theory*. Lanham, MD: Rowman and Littlefield.

———. 1997. *Crime as Structured Action: Gender, Race, Class, and Crime in the Making*. Thousand Oaks, CA: Sage.

Micci-Barreca, Daniele. 2004. "With Criminal Intent." *Fraud International,* May/June: 30–34.

Michalowski, Raymond. 1985. *Order, Law, and Crime*. New York: Random House.

Michalowski, Raymond, and Ronald C. Kramer. 1987. "The Space Between Laws: The Problem of Corporate Crime in a Transnational Context." *Social Problems* 34: 34–53.

——— (eds.). 2006. *State-Corporate Crime: Wrongdoing at the Intersection of Business and Government.* New Brunswick, NJ: Rutgers University Press.

Miller, Anita (ed.). 2005. *What Went Wrong in Ohio: The Conyers Report on the 2004 Presidential Election.* Chicago: Academy Chicago.

Miller, Mark Crispin. 2005. *Fooled Again: How the Right Stole the 2004 Election and Why They'll Steal the Next One Too (Unless We Stop Them).* New York: Basic.

——— (ed.). 2008. *Loser Take All: Election Fraud and the Subversion of Democracy, 2000–2008.* Brooklyn, NY: Ig.

Miller, Marvin. 1974. *The Breaking of a President.* Vol. 4. City of Industry, CA: Therapy Productions.

Miller, Walter B. 1973. "Ideology and Criminal Justice Policy: Some Current Issues." *Journal of Criminal Law and Criminology* 64: 141–162.

Mills, C. Wright. 1957. *The Power Elite.* New York: Oxford University Press.

———. 1959. *The Sociological Imagination.* New York: Oxford University Press.

Minor, W. William. 1984. "Neutralization as a Hardening Process: Considerations in the Modeling of Change." *Social Forces* 62: 995–1019.

Mintz, Morton. 1985. *At Any Cost: Corporate Greed, Women, and the Dalkon Shield.* New York: Pantheon.

Mohai, Paul, and Robin Saha. 2007. "Racial Inequality in the Distribution of Hazardous Waste: A National-Level Reassessment." *Social Problems* 54: 343–370.

Mokhiber, Russell. 1988. *Corporate Crime and Violence: Big Business and the Abuse of Public Trust.* San Francisco: Sierra Club.

Mooney, Chris. 2005. "Some Like It Hot." *Mother Jones,* May/June: 36–49.

Moore, David W. 2008. "Because Jeb Said So: What Really Happened on Election Night in Florida." In Mark Crispin Miller (ed.), *Loser Take All: Election Fraud and the Subversion of Democracy, 2000–2008.* Brooklyn, NY: Ig.

Morgenson, Gretchen. 2004. "Suit Accuses Halliburton of Fraud in Accounting." *New York Times,* Aug. 6. Retrieved from www.nytimes.com.

Morris, Albert. 1935. *Criminology.* New York: Longmans, Green.

Morris, Errol. 2004. *The Fog of War.* Documentary film.

Morrison, Chris. 2010. "Gulf Oil Spill: Who's to Blame? BP, Halliburton, and the Feds Are All Implicated." BNET.com, May 3. Retrieved from www.industry.bnet.com.

Moss, Michael. 2009. "E. Coli Path Shows Flaws in Beef Inspection." *New York Times,* Oct. 4. Retrieved from www.nytimes.com.

Moyers, Bill. 1988. *The Secret Government: The Constitution in Crisis.* Cabin John, MD: Seven Locks.

———. 1990. *High Crimes and Misdemeanors.* PBS documentary.

———. 2006. *Capitol Crimes.* PBS documentary.

Mullins, Christopher W. 2006. "Bridgestone-Firestone, Ford, and the NHTSA." In Raymond Michalowski and Ronald C. Kramer (eds.), *State-Corporate Crime: Wrongdoing at the Intersection of Business and Government.* New Brunswick, NJ: Rutgers University Press.

Nader, Ralph. [1965] 1972. *Unsafe at Any Speed: The Designed-In Dangers of the American Automobile.* New York: Grossman.

The Nation. 2010. "Democracy Inc." Editorial. Feb. 15: 3–6.

Naughton, Keith. 2000. "Spinning Out of Control." *Newsweek,* Sept. 11: 58.

Neuman, W. Lawrence. 1998. "Negotiated Meanings and State Transformation: The Trust Issue in the Progressive Era." *Social Problems* 45: 315–335.

———. 2003. *Social Research Methods: Qualitative and Quantitative.* Boston: Allyn and Bacon.

———. 2005. *Power, State, and Society: An Introduction to Political Sociology.* New York: McGraw-Hill.

New Republic. 2003. "Sixteen Words." Editorial. July 28/Aug. 4: 8–9.

———. 2006. "Lost City." Editorial. Aug. 14/Aug. 21: 7.

Newman, Donald J. 1958. "Public Attitudes Toward a Form of White-Collar Crime." *Social Problems* 4: 228–332.

NewsInferno.com. 2007. "Vioxx Lawsuit Settlement Could Rank Among the Largest Defective Drug Settlements." Nov 12. Retrieved from www .newsinferno.com.

Nguyen, Tomson, and Henry N. Pontell. 2010. "Mortgage Origination Fraud and the Global Economic Crisis." *Criminology and Public Policy* 9: 591– 612.

Noggle, Burl. 1965. *Teapot Dome: Oil and Politics in the 1920s.* New York: Norton.

Nye, Joseph S., Philip Zelikow, and David King (eds.). 1997. *Why People Don't Trust Government.* Cambridge: Harvard University Press.

O'Conner, James. 1973. *The Fiscal Crisis of the State.* New York: St. Martin's.

O'Huallachain, D. L., and J. Forrest Sharpe (eds.). 2005. *Neo-Conned! Again: Hypocrisy, Lawlessness, and the Rape of Iraq.* Vienna, VA: Light in the Darkness.

Oliphant, James. 2008. "Court Slices *Exxon Valdez* Damage Award." *The Swamp,* June 28. Retrieved from www.swamppolitics.com.

Oliver, Melvin L., and Thomas M. Shapiro. 2008. "Sub-Prime as Black Catastrophe." *American Prospect,* Oct.: A9–A11.

Palast, Greg. 2003. *The Best Democracy Money Can Buy: The Truth About Corporate Cons, Globalization, and High-Finance Fraudsters.* New York: Plume.

———. 2007. *Armed Madhouse: From Baghdad to New Orleans—Sordid Secrets and Strange Tales of a White House Gone Wild.* New York: Plume.

Parenti, Christian. 2009. "Zombie Nuke Plants." *The Nation,* Dec. 7: 26–31.

Pareto, Vilfredo. [1901] 1991. *The Rise and Fall of Elites: An Application of Theoretical Sociology.* Introduction by Hans L. Zetterberg. New Brunswick, NJ: Transaction.

Parks, Brad. 2009. "Poison Ivy in the Garden State." *Wall Street Journal,* July 25. Retrieved from www.online.wsj.com.

Pasha, Shaheen. 2006. "Skilling Gets 24 Years." CNNMoney.com, Oct. 24.

Passas, Nikos. 1990. "Anomie and Corporate Deviance." *Contemporary Crises* 14: 157–178.

———. 1995. "The Mirror of Global Evils: A Review Essay on the BCCI Affair." *Justice Quarterly* 12: 377–405.

Pelley, Scott. 2000. "Convicted Exec Says R.J. Reynolds Made $100 Million by

Smuggling Cigarettes from U.S. into Canada." *CBS News, 60 Minutes II* interview, Jan. 18. Retrieved from www.cbsnews.com.

Perkins, John. 2004. *Confessions of an Economic Hit Man.* New York: Plume.

Perry, Susan, and Jim Dawson. 1985. *Nightmare: Women and the Dalkon Shield.* New York: Macmillan.

Phillips, Kevin. 2004. *American Dynasty: Aristocracy, Fortune, and the Politics of Deceit in the House of Bush.* New York: Viking.

———. 2006. *American Theocracy: The Peril and Politics of Radical Religion, Oil, and Borrowed Money in the 21st Century.* New York: Viking.

Pincus, Walter. 2005. "British Intelligence Warned of Iraq War." *Washington Post,* May 13: A18. Retrieved from www.washingtonpost.com.

Pizzo, Stephen., Mary Fricker, and Paul Muolo. 1989. *Inside Job: The Looting of America's Savings and Loans.* New York: McGraw-Hill.

Plumer, Bradford. 2010. "Morning-After Drill." *New Republic,* July 22: 8–10.

Plungis, Jeff. 2010. "BP Agrees to Record $50.6 Million Fine for Texas City Blast." Bloomberg.com, Aug. 12.

Polgreen, Lydia, and Hari Kumar. 2010. "8 Former Executives Guilty in '84 Bhopal Chemical Leak." *New York Times,* June 7. Retrieved from www.nytimes.com.

Poole, James. 1997. *Who Financed Hitler: The Secret Funding of Hitler's Rise to Power, 1919–1933.* New York: Pocket.

Posner, Eric. 2010. "The Limits of Limits." *New Republic,* May 27: 36–40.

Posner, Gerald. 1994. *Case Closed: Lee Harvey Oswald and the Assassination of JFK.* New York: Anchor.

Possley, Maurice. 2007. "Three Children Die, Leading to Massive Recall." *Wisconsin State Journal,* Sept. 22: A3.

Poveda, Tony. 1990. *Lawlessness and Reform: The FBI in Transition.* Belmont, CA: Brooks and Cole.

———. 1994. *Rethinking White-Collar Crime.* Westport, CT: Praeger.

Power, Stephen, Neil King Jr., and Siobhan Hughes. 2010. "U.S. to Break Up Oil-Rig Regulator." *Wall Street Journal,* May 12. Retrieved from www.online.wsj.com.

Prechel, Harland, and Theresa Morris. 2010. "The Effects of Organizational and Political Embeddedness on Financial Malfeasance in the Largest U.S. Corporations: Dependence, Incentives, and Opportunities." *American Sociological Review* 75: 331–354.

Prentice, Robert. 2002. "An Ethics Lesson for Business Scandals." *New York Times,* Aug. 20: A19.

Presidential Commission on the Space Shuttle *Challenger* Accident. 1986. *Report of the Presidential Commission on the Space Shuttle* Challenger *Accident.* Vols. 1–4. Washington, DC: US Government Printing Office.

Priest, Dana, and Walter Pincus. 2004. "U.S. 'Almost All Wrong' on Weapons: Report on Iraq Contradicts Bush Administration Claims." *Washington Post,* Oct. 7: A1.

Prins, Nomi. 2004. *Other People's Money: The Corporate Mugging of America.* New York: New Press.

Pulido, Laura, Steve Sidawi, and Robert O. Vos. 1996. "An Archaeology of Environmental Racism in Los Angeles." *Urban Geography* 17: 419–439.

Pulliam, Susan, Deborah Solomon, and Carrick Mollenkamp. 2002. "Former WorldCom CEO Built an Empire on Mountain of Debt." *Wall Street Journal*, Dec. 31. Retrieved from www.wsj.com.

Puzzanghera, Jim. 2010. "Senators Grapple with Derivatives Rules in Financial Overhaul." *Los Angeles Times*, May 19. Retrieved from www.latimes.com.

Quaid, Libby. 2007. "Giuliani's Judgment on the Line with Kerik." *Wisconsin State Journal*, Nov. 10: A4.

Quinney, Richard. 1963. "Occupational Structure and Criminal Behavior: Prescription Violations by Retail Pharmacists." *Social Problems* 11: 179–185.

———. 1970. *The Social Reality of Crime*. Boston: Little, Brown.

———. 1974. *Critique of Legal Order: Crime Control in Capitalist Society*. Boston: Little, Brown.

———. 1977. *Class, State, and Crime: On the Theory and Practice of Criminal Justice*. New York: David McKay.

Rashke, Richard. 1981. *The Killing of Karen Silkwood*. New York: Penguin.

Reiman, Jeffrey. 2007. *The Rich Get Richer and the Poor Get Prison: Ideology, Class, and Criminal Justice*. Boston: Allyn and Bacon.

Reiss, Albert J., and Michael Tonry. 2001. "Organizational Crime." In Neal Shover and John Paul Wright (eds.), *Crimes of Privilege: Readings in White-Collar Crime*. New York: Oxford University Press.

Rendall, Steve. 2005. "The Fairness Doctrine." *Fairness and Accuracy in Reporting*, Feb. 12. Retrieved from www.commondreams.org.

Revkin, Andrew. 2009. "Hacked E-Mail Is New Fodder for Climate Dispute." *New York Times*, Nov. 21. Retrieved from www.nytimes.com.

Rich, Frank. 2006. *The Greatest Story Ever Sold: The Decline and Fall of Truth, from 9/11 to Katrina*. New York: Penguin.

Richards, James R. 1999. *Transnational Criminal Organizations, Cybercrime, and Money Laundering: A Handbook for Law Enforcement Officers, Auditors, and Financial Managers*. Boca Raton, FL: CRC.

Ricks, Thomas E. 2006. *Fiasco: The American Military Adventure in Iraq*. New York: Penguin.

Ridgeway, James. 2005. *The Five Unanswered Questions About 9/11: What the 9/11 Commission Report Failed to Tell Us*. New York: Seven Stories.

Roberts, Joel. 2002. "Plans for Iraq Attack Began on 9/11." *CBS News*, Sept. 4. Retrieved from www.cbsnews.com.

Roche, Walter F., Jr., and Ken Silverstein. 2004. "War Boosters Do Related Business." *Los Angeles Times*, July 14: A7–A9.

Roebuck, Julian, and Stanley C. Weeber. 1978. *Political Crime in the United States: Analyzing Crime by and Against Government*. New York: Praeger.

Rolling Stone. 2006. "A Call for Investigation: Electronic Voting Machines Pose a Grave Threat to Democracy." Editorial. June 15: 54.

Rosenberg, Debra. 2003. "Love Canal's Long Shadow." *Newsweek*, Aug. 4: 50–51.

Rosoff, Stephen, Henry Pontell, and Robert Tillman. 2007. *Profit Without Honor: White-Collar Crime and the Looting of America*. Upper Saddle River, NJ: Prentice-Hall.

Ross, Edward Alsworth. [1907] 1977. "The Criminaloid." In Gilbert Geis and

Robert F. Meier (eds.), *White-Collar Crime: Offenses in Business, Politics, and the Professions.* New York: Free Press.

Rothe, Dawn. 2006. "Iraq and Halliburton." In Raymond Michalowski and Ronald C. Kramer (eds.), *State-Corporate Crime: Wrongdoing at the Intersection of Business and Government.* New Brunswick, NJ: Rutgers University Press.

———. 2009. *State Criminality: The Crime of All Crimes.* Chicago: Lexington Books.

SafetyForum.com. 2003. "Chrysler Minivan Latch Failure Is a Safety Defect That Involves Children."

Safire, William. 1992a. "Democrats Slow to See Potential in Bush Cover-Up of Lavoro Scandal." *Milwaukee Journal,* April 4: A9.

———. 1992b. "Iraq Diverted Grain, Bush Admits." *Milwaukee Journal,* Oct. 9: A9.

———. 1993. "Iraqgate Giveaway." *New York Times,* May 20: A13.

Saltonstall, David. 2008. "Illinois Gov. Rod Blagojevich Arrested in Conspiracy to Benefit from Obama's Replacement." *Daily News,* Dec. 10. Retrieved from www.nydailynews.com.

Savage, Charlie. 2008. "Sex, Drug Use, and Graft Cited in Interior Department." *New York Times,* Sept. 11. Retrieved from www.nytimes.com.

Savage, David. 2010. "Corporate Free-Speech Ruling Speaks of Shift in Supreme Court." *Los Angeles Times,* Feb. 10. Retrieved from www.latimes.com.

Scahill, Jeremy. 2007. *Blackwater: The Rise of the World's Most Powerful Military Army.* New York: Nation Books.

———. 2009a. "The Acorn Standard." *The Nation,* Nov. 2: 4–5.

———. 2009b. "U.S. War Privatization Results in Billions Lost in Fraud, Waste, and Abuse—Report." *Halliburton Watch,* June 10. Retrieved from www.commondreams.com.

———. 2010. "WikiLeaks and War Crimes." *The Nation,* Aug. 30/Sept. 6: 6–8.

Schapiro, Mark. 2002. "Big Tobacco: Uncovering the Industry's Multibillion-Dollar Global Smuggling Network." *The Nation,* May 6: 11–20.

Schell, Jonathan. 2008. "When the Gloves Come Off." *The Nation,* Nov. 3: 18–24.

Scherer, Michael. 2003. "K Street on the Tigris." *Mother Jones,* Nov./Dec. Retrieved from www.motherjones.com.

———. 2008. "Governor Gone Wild: The Blagojevich Scandal." *Time,* Dec. 11. Retrieved from www.time.com.

Schmidt, Susan, and James V. Grimaldi. 2007. "Ney Sentenced to 30 Months in Prison for Abramoff Deals." *Washington Post,* Jan. 20. Retrieved from www.washingtonpost.com.

Schrager, Laura Shill, and James F. Short. 1978. "Toward a Sociology of Organizational Crime." *Social Problems* 25: 407–419.

Schur, Edwin M. 1979. *Interpreting Deviance: A Sociological Introduction.* New York: Harper and Row.

Schuyten, Peter J. 1979. "Computers and Criminals." *New York Times,* Sept. 27: D2.

Schwendinger, Herman, and Julia Siegel Schwendinger. 1970. "Defenders of Order or Guardians of Human Rights?" *Issues in Criminology* 5: 123–157.

———. 1985. *Adolescent Subcultures and Delinquency.* New York: Praeger.

Scott, Peter Dale, and Jonathan Marshall. 1991. *Cocaine Politics: Drugs, Armies, and the CIA in Central America.* Berkeley: University of California Press.

Seely, Ron. 2010. "Big Dairies, Little Oversight." *Wisconsin State Journal,* Feb. 28: A1, A9–A10.

Senate Select Committee on Intelligence. [1976] 1978. "Report of the Senate Select Committee on Intelligence." In M. David Ermann and Richard L. Lundman (eds.), *Corporate and Governmental Deviance: Problems of Organizational Behavior in Contemporary Society.* 1st ed. New York: Oxford University Press.

Sethi, S. Prakash. 1982. "The Santa Barbara Oil Spill." In M. David Ermann and Richard L. Lundman (eds.), *Corporate and Governmental Deviance: Problems of Organizational Behavior in Contemporary Society.* 2nd ed. New York: Oxford University Press.

Setterberg, Fred, and Lonny Shavelson. 1993. *Toxic Nation: The Fight to Save Our Communities from Chemical Contamination.* New York: Wiley.

Shane, Scott, and Ron Nixon. 2007. "In Washington, Contractors Take on Biggest Role Ever." *New York Times,* Feb. 4. Retrieved from www.nytimes.com.

Shapley, Dan. 2010. "So How Big Was the B.P. Oil Spill?" *Daily Green,* July 16. Retrieved from www.thedailygreen.com.

Shenon, Philip. 2008. *The Commission: The Uncensored History of the 9/11 Investigation.* New York: Twelve.

Shorrock, Tim. 2003. "Big Bucks in Iraq." *The Nation,* Nov. 10: 5–6.

———. 2008. *Spies for Hire: The Secret World of Intelligence Outsourcing.* New York: Simon and Schuster.

Shover, Neal, and Andy Hochstetler. 2006. *Choosing White-Collar Crime.* New York: Cambridge University Press.

Sick, Gary. 1991. *October Surprise: America's Hostages in Iran and the Election of Ronald Reagan.* New York: Times Books.

Siegel, R. P. 2010. "Lawsuits Against MMS Weigh in for the Public." *Triple Pundit,* May 19. Retrieved from www.triplepundit.com.

Silk, Leonard Solomon, and David Vogel. 1976. *Ethics and Profits: The Crisis of Confidence in American Business.* New York: Simon and Schuster.

Silverman, Fred. 2002. *Who Counts? Election Reform in America.* PBS documentary.

Simmons, Christine. 2007. "More Toys, Necklaces with Lead Are Recalled." *Wisconsin State Journal,* Sept. 27: A3.

Simon, David R. [1982] 2002, 2006. *Elite Deviance.* Boston: Allyn and Bacon.

Sinclair, Upton. 1906. *The Jungle.* New York: New American Library.

Singer, Merrill, and Hans Baer (eds.). 2009. *Killer Commodities: Public Health and the Corporate Production of Harm.* Lanham, MD: Rowman and Littlefield.

Sloan, Allan. 2006. "Wall Street Weaselwords." *Newsweek,* Oct. 2: E28.

Slocum, Tyson. 2010. "The Oil Spill . . . BP's $485 Million in Fines." *Public Citizen,* Apr. 29. Retrieved from www.publiccitizenenergy.org.

Smith, Hedrick. 2002. *Bigger Than Enron.* PBS documentary.

———. 2003. *The Wall Street Fix.* PBS documentary.

Smith, Yves. 2010. *ECONned: How Unenlightened Self Interest Undermined Democracy and Corrupted Capitalism.* New York: Palgrave Macmillan.

Smyth, Julie Carr. 2003. "Voting Machine Controversy." *Cleveland Plain Dealer*, Aug. 28. Retrieved from www.commondreams.org.

Snider, Laurren. 2010. "Frame E-Waste Regulation: The Obfuscating Role of Power." *Criminology and Public Policy* 9: 569–577.

SourceWatch.org. 2010a. "Abscam Bribery Scandal."

———. 2010b. "Massey Energy."

South, Nigel, and Piers Beirne (eds.). 2006. *Green Criminology*. Burlington, VT: Ashgate.

Spake, Amanda. 2007. "Dying for a Home." *The Nation*, Feb. 26: 16–22.

Sperry, Paul. 2003. *Crude Politics: How Bush's Oil Cronies Hijacked the War on Terrorism*. Nashville: WND.

Spitzer, Steven. 1975. "Toward a Marxian Theory of Deviance." *Social Problems* 22: 638–651.

Stewart, James B. 1991. *Den of Thieves*. New York: Simon and Schuster.

———. 1996. *Blood Sport: The President and His Adversaries*. New York: Simon and Schuster.

Stiglitz, Joseph E. 2010. *Freefall: America, Free Markets, and the Sinking of the World Economy*. New York: Norton.

Stiglitz, Joseph E., and Linda J. Bilmes. 2008. *The Three Trillion Dollar War*. New York: Norton.

Stone, Christopher D. 1975. *Where the Law Ends: The Social Control of Corporate Behavior*. Prospect Heights, IL: Waveland.

Stotland, Ezra. 1977. "White-Collar Criminals." *Journal of Social Issues* 33: 179–196.

Stretesky, Paul B., and Michael Lynch. 1999. "Corporate Environmental Violence and Racism." *Crime, Law, and Social Change* 30: 163–184.

Suddath, Claire. 2008. "Illinois Corruption." *Time*, Dec. 11. Retrieved from www.time.com.

Summers, Anthony. 2000. *The Arrogance of Power: The Secret World of Richard Nixon*. New York: Viking.

Suskind, Ron. 2004. "Faith, Certainty, and the Presidency of George W. Bush." *New York Times Magazine*, Oct. 17. Retrieved from www.nytimes.com.

———. 2006. *The One Percent Doctrine: Deep Inside America's Pursuit of Its Enemies Since 9/11*. New York: Simon and Schuster.

Sutherland, Edwin H. [1940] 1977. "White-Collar Criminality." In Gilbert Geis and Robert F. Meier (eds.), *White-Collar Crime: Offenses in Business, Politics, and the Professions*. New York: Free Press.

———. 1947. *Principles of Criminology*. Philadelphia: Lippincott.

———. [1949] 1983. *White Collar Crime: The Uncut Version*. New Haven: Yale University Press.

Swasy, Alecia. 1993. *Soap Opera: The Inside Story of Procter & Gamble*. New York: Times Books.

Swigert, Victoria, and Ronald Farrell. 1980–1981. "Corporate Homicide: Definitional Processes in the Creation of Deviance." *Law and Society Review* 15: 161–182.

Sykes, Gresham M., and David Matza. 1957. "Techniques of Neutralization: A Theory of Delinquency." *American Sociological Review* 22: 664–670.

Szasz, Andrew. 1986a. "Corporations, Organized Crime, and the Disposal of

Hazardous Waste: An Examination of the Making of a Criminogenic Regulatory Structure." *Criminology* 24: 1–27.

———. 1986b. "The Process and Significance of Political Scandals: A Comparison of Watergate and the 'Sewergate' Episode at the Environmental Protection Agency." *Social Problems* 33: 202–217.

Talbot, David. 2007. *Brothers: The Hidden History of the Kennedy Years.* New York: Free Press.

Talking Points Memo. 2007a. "TPM Canned U.S. Attorney Scandal Timeline." Retrieved from www.talkingpointsmemo.com.

———. 2007b. "TPM Grande Ole Docket." Retrieved from www.talkingpointsmemo.com.

Tankersley, Jim, and Josh Meyer. 2009. "Former Interior Secretary Gale Norton Is Focus of Corruption Probe." *Los Angeles Times,* Sept. 17. Retrieved from www.latimes.com.

Tankersley, Jim, and Maurice Possley. 2008. "Product Watchdog to Get Overhaul." *Wisconsin State Journal,* Jan. 1: A5.

Tansey, Bernadette. 2004. "Huge Penalty in Drug Fraud." *San Francisco Chronicle,* May 14. Retrieved from www.sfgate.com.

Tappan, Paul W. 1947. "Who Is the Criminal?" *American Sociological Review* 12: 96–102.

Tawney, R. W. 1920. *The Acquisitive Society.* New York: Harcourt, Brace.

Tett, Gillian. 2009. *Fool's Gold: The Inside Story of J.P. Morgan and How Wall St. Greed Corrupted Its Bold Dream and Created a Financial Catastrophe.* New York: Free Press.

Thio, Alex. 1973. "Class Bias in the Sociology of Deviance." *American Sociologist* 8: 1–12.

Thomas, Andrew R. 2003. *Aviation Insecurity: The New Challenges of Air Travel.* Amherst, NY: Prometheus.

Thomas, Evan. 2005. "Understanding Deep Throat: Why a Source Took on a President Then, and How Nixon's Fall Shapes Us Even Now." *Newsweek,* June 13: 22–32.

Thorne, Kym, and Alexander Kouzmin. 2010. "The USA PATRIOT Acts (et al.): Convergent Legislation and Oligarchic Isomorphism in the 'Politics of Fear' and State Crime(s) Against Democracy (SCADs)." *American Behavioral Scientist* 53: 885–920.

Toffler, Barbara Ley. 2003. *Final Accounting: Ambition, Greed, and the Fall of Arthur Andersen.* New York: Broadway Books.

Urbina, Ian, and Andrew W. Lehren. 2006. "U.S. Is Reducing Safety Penalties for Mine Flaws." *New York Times,* Mar. 2. Retrieved from www.nytimes.com.

US House of Representatives. 1986. *Committee on Science and Technology Investigation of the* Challenger *Accident.* Washington, DC: US Government Printing Office.

Van de Bun, Henk. 2010. "Walls of Secrecy and Silence: The Madoff Case and Cartels in the Construction Industry." *Criminology and Public Policy* 9: 435–453.

Vaughan, Diane. 1982. "Toward Understanding Organizational Behavior." *Michigan Law Review* 80: 1377–1402.

———. 1983. *Controlling Unlawful Organizational Behavior.* Chicago: University of Chicago Press.

———. 2005. "The Normalization of Deviance: Signals of Danger, Situated Action, and Risk." In Henry Montgomery, Raanan Lipshitz, and Berndt Brehmer (eds.), *How Professionals Make Decisions.* Mahwah, NJ: Lawrence Erlbaum.

Venkatesan, V. 2003. "The Issue of Extradition." *Frontline,* Apr. 11. Retrieved from www.frontlineonnet.com.

Vioxx Heart Attack Lawsuit. 2006–2007. "Current News." Retrieved from www.yourlawyer.com.

Vold, George B., Thomas J. Bernard, and Jeffrey B. Snipes. 2002. *Theoretical Criminology.* New York: Oxford University Press.

Von App, Lisa. 2010. "Toyota to Pay Unprecedented $16.4 Million Fine." *Salt Lake City Page One Examiner,* Apr. 22. Retrieved from www.examiner.com.

Von Zielbauer, Paul. 2006. "Kurds Tell of Gas Attacks by Hussein's Military." *New York Times,* Aug. 23. Retrieved from www.nytimes.com.

Vosters, Helene. 2003. "Partial Chronology of Union Carbide's Bhopal Disaster." CorpWatch.com.

Waldron, Lamar, with Thom Hartmann. 2005. *Ultimate Sacrifice: John and Robert Kennedy, the Plan for a Coup in Cuba, and the Murder of JFK.* New York: Carroll and Graf.

———. 2008. *Legacy of Secrecy: The Long Shadow of the JFK Assassination.* Berkeley: Counterpoint.

Walker, J. Samuel. 2004. *Three Mile Island: A Nuclear Crisis in Historical Perspective.* Berkeley: University of California Press.

Warren, Elizabeth. 2010. "Consumer Protection as Systemic Safety." *American Prospect,* June: A6–A7.

Webster, Barbara, and Michael S. McCampbell. 1992. "International Money Laundering: Research and Investigation Join Forces." *NIJ Research in Brief,* Sept.: 1–8.

Weisberg, Jacob. 2008. "A Battle for the Basement." *Newsweek,* Dec. 13. Retrieved from www.newsweek.com.

Wheeler, Stanton, and Mitchell L. Rothman. 1982. "The Organization as Weapon in White Collar Crime." *Michigan Law Review* 80: 1403–1426.

White, Jonathan R. 2003. *Terrorism: An Introduction.* Belmont, CA: Wadsworth.

Wiener, Jon. 2010. "Big Tobacco and the Historians." *The Nation,* Mar. 15: 11–17.

Wilber, Del Quentin, and Carrie Johnson. 2008. "Abramoff Gets Reduced Sentence of Four Years." *Washington Post,* Sept. 5. Retrieved from www.washingtonpost.com.

Wilkes, Paul. 1989. "The Tough Job of Teaching Ethics." *New York Times,* Jan. 22: E1, E24.

Will, Susan, Henry N. Pontell, and Richard Cheung. 1998. "Risky Business Revisited: White-Collar Crime and the Orange County Bankruptcy." *Crime and Delinquency* 44: 367–387.

Williams, Mary E. (ed.). 2003. *The Terrorist Attack on America.* Farmington Hills, MI: Greenhaven.

Williams, Patricia J. 2010. "Corpus Ex Machina." *The Nation,* Feb. 15: 9.

Wilson, Glynn. 2007. "A Whistleblower's Tale." *The Nation,* Oct. 24. Retrieved from www.thenation.com.

Wilson, James Q. (ed.). 1980. *The Politics of Regulation.* New York: Basic.

Wilson, Joseph. 2005. *The Politics of Truth: Inside the Lies that Put the White House on Trial and Betrayed My Wife's CIA Identity.* New York: Carroll and Graf.

Wisconsin State Journal. 2002. "Ford Settles Claims over Rollover Risks." Dec. 24: C9–C10.

———. 2005. "Congressman Resigns After Bribery Plea." Nov. 29: A3.

———. 2006. "*Exxon Valdez* Oil Spill Award Cut in Half." Dec. 23: A3.

———. 2007a. "Drug Firm Officials Fined for Misleading Public." May 11: A3.

———. 2007b. "Kerik, Former Head of New York Police, Indicted." Nov. 10: A3.

———. 2007c. "Merck Agrees to Pay $4.85 Billion for Vioxx." Nov. 10: A3.

———. 2009a. "Court Upholds Tobacco Ruling." May 23: A10.

———. 2009b. "Freezer Cash." Nov. 11: A9.

Wise, David. 1973. *The Politics of Lying: Government Deception, Secrecy, and Power.* New York: Vintage.

Wolf, Brian. 2009. *Organized Environmental Crime: An Analysis of Corporate Noncompliance with the Law.* Lewiston, NY: Edwin Mellen.

Wolfe, Alan. 2006. "Why Conservatives Can't Govern." *Washington Monthly,* July/Aug. Retrieved from www.washingtonmonthly.com.

Woodward, Bob. 1999. *Shadow: Five Presidents and the Legacy of Watergate.* New York: Touchstone.

———. 2006. *State of Denial: Bush at War, Part III.* New York: Simon and Schuster.

World Nuclear Association. 2010. "Chernobyl Accident." Retrieved from www.world-nuclear.org.

Wright, Lawrence. 2006. *The Looming Tower: Al-Qaeda on the Road to 9/11.* New York: Knopf.

Yeager, Peter C. 1987. "Structural Bias in Regulatory Law Enforcement: The Case of the U.S. Environmental Protection Agency." *Social Problems* 34: 330–344.

Yen, Hope. 2007. "More Katrina Money Wasted." *Wisconsin State Journal,* Apr. 23: A3.

Yost, Pete. 2010. "Tobacco's Plea—No Big U.S. Payments." *Associated Press.* Retrieved from www.news.yahoo.com.

Zagorin, Adam. 2008. "More Allegations of Misconduct in Alabama Governor Case." *Time,* Nov. 14. Retrieved from www.time.com.

Zajac, Andrew, and Tom Hamburger. 2010. "Safety Survey May Point to 'Much Larger Problem.'" *Wisconsin State Journal,* Aug. 24: A9.

Zengerle, Jason. 2009. "Murthaville." *New Republic,* Sept. 9: 21–25.

Zietz, Dorothy. 1981. *Women Who Embezzle or Defraud: A Study of Convicted Felons.* New York: Praeger.

Zimbardo, Philip. 2007. *The Lucifer Effect: Understanding How Good People Turn Evil.* New York: Random House.

Index

About the Book

WHEN DOES CUTTING CORNERS IN PURSUIT OF CORPORATE profit become a crime? When should the misdeeds of government officials warrant a prison sentence? This lucid introduction to the notoriously complex problem of white-collar crime provides students with a set of tools for exploring the abuse of corporate and government power.

This student-friendly text:

- Covers the gamut of corporate crimes and government malfeasance.
- Accessibly introduces theoretical concepts.
- Includes both classic case studies and contemporary examples.
- Documents the devastating impact of white-collar crime.
- Discusses the dilemmas of regulatory reform and ways to prevent white-collar crime.

For students, the result is a critical approach to separating right from wrong and lawful from illegal in the gray areas of professional and civic life.

Ronald J. Berger is professor of sociology at the University of Wisconsin–Whitewater. His previous publications include *Crime, Justice, and Society,* 3rd edition (with Marvin D. Free, Jr. and Patricia Searles); *Juvenile Delinquency and Justice* (with Paul Gregory); and *Storytelling Sociology* (with Richard Quinney).